# Wealth after work

**FT** Prentice Hall
FINANCIAL TIMES

London • New York • San Francisco • Toronto • Sydney
Tokyo • Singapore • Hong Kong • Cape Town • Madrid
Paris • Milan • Munich • Amsterdam

In an increasingly competitive world, we believe it's quality of
thinking that will give you the edge – an idea that opens new
doors, a technique that solves a problem, or an insight that
simply makes sense of it all. The more you know, the smarter
and faster you can go.

That's why we work with the best minds in business and finance
to bring cutting-edge thinking and best learning practice to a
global market.

Under a range of leading imprints, including Financial Times
Prentice Hall, we create world-class print publications and
electronic products bringing our readers knowledge, skills and
understanding which can be applied whether studying or at work.

To find out more about our business publications, or tell us about
the books you'd like to find, you can visit us at
**www.business-minds.com**

For other Pearson Education publications, visit
**www.pearsoned-ema.com**

# Wealth after work

## PLANNING YOUR GREAT ESCAPE

Debbie Harrison

FINANCIAL TIMES

*An imprint of* **Pearson Education**

London / New York / Toronto / Sydney / Tokyo / Singapore / Hong Kong
Cape Town / New Delhi / Madrid / Paris / Amsterdam / Munich / Milan / Stockholm

PEARSON EDUCATION LIMITED

Head Office:
Edinburgh Gate
Harlow CM20 2JE
Tel: +44 (0)1279 623623
Fax: +44 (0)1279 431059

London Office:
128 Long Acre
London WC2E 9AN
Tel: +44 (0)20 7447 2000
Fax: +44 (0)20 7447 2170
Website: www.business-minds.com

First published in Great Britain in 2002

ISBN 0 273 65681 3

British Library Cataloguing in Publication Data
A CIP catalogue record for this book can be obtained from the British Library.

This publication is designed to provide accurate and authoritative information
in regard to the subject matter covered. It is sold with the understanding that
neither the author nor the publisher is engaged in rendering legal, investing,
or any other professional service. If legal advice or other expert assistance is
required, the service of a competent professional person should be sought.

The publisher and contributors make no representation, expressed or implied,
with regard to the accuracy of the information contained in this book and
cannot accept any responsibility or liability for any errors or omissions that it
may contain.

10 9 8 7 6 5 4 3 2 1

Designed by Sue Lamble
Typeset by Northern Phototypesetting Co. Ltd, Bolton
Printed and bound in Great Britain by Bell & Bain Ltd, Glasgow

*The Publishers' policy is to use paper manufactured from sustainable forests.*

# About the author

Debbie Harrison is an award-winning financial author and journalist. She writes regularly for the *Financial Times*, *Investment Week* and *Bloomberg Money*, and is the author of five *Financial Times* reports on retail and institutional investment. Her consumer books include *The First Time Investor*, *Personal Financial Planner*, *Pension Power* and *The Money Zone*, all published by Financial Times Prentice Hall, and *How to Make it in The City*, published by Virgin Publishing.

# Acknowledgements

Many people helped with this book. In particular I would like to thank the following organisations: the Association of Private Client Investment Managers (APCIMS), Barclays Capital, Chiswell Associates, the Ethical Investment Research Service, the Financial Services Authority, the Financial Ombudsman Service, the Recruitment and Employment Confederation, Forties People, The Institute of Financial Planning, the Life Coaching Academy, ProShare, the Stock Exchange, Watson Wyatt.

The film quotations used throughout this book were provided by The Internet Movie Database – a treasure trove for movie lovers. The web site is at **www.imdb.com**

# Contents

**SECTION 2** La dolce vita

## SECTION 6 The long goodbye

## 25 You pays your money and you makes your choice    283

## 26 Retiring in the sun    303

### APPENDICES

**I will not make any deals with you. I've resigned. I will not be pushed, filed, stamped, indexed, briefed, debriefed or numbered. My life is my own. I resign.**

Number 6, *The Prisoner* (1967)

# Preface

**Announcer** *And now for the stock market report by Exchange Telegraph.*
**Reporter** *Trading was crisp at the start of the day, with some brisk business on the floor. Rubber hardened and string remained confident. Little bits of tin consolidated, although biscuits sank after an early gain and stools remained anonymous. Armpits rallied well after a poor start. Nipples rose dramatically during the morning but had declined by mid-afternoon, while teeth clenched and buttocks remained firm. Small dark furry things increased severely on the floor, whilst rude jellies wobbled up and down and bounced against rising thighs, which had spread to all parts of the country by mid-afternoon. After lunch naughty things dipped sharply, forcing giblets upwards with the nicky nacky noo. Ting tang tong rankled dithely, little tipples pooped and poppy things went pong. Gibble gabble went the rickety rackety roo …*

*Monty Python's Flying Circus (1969)*

**THIS IS A BOOK ABOUT CHANGE.** It is also a book about money. It is about managing your money so you can transform your life, so you can pursue the activities you start to yearn for when you've been in the wrong job for the right reasons for too long. If that happy bunny feeling has gone and you have unwittingly become a fully paid-up member of the rat race, this book is for you.

You may have grown up during the 1960s with revolution in your heart. Then you got a career and everything was hunky dory for a couple of decades. If you've now turned 50, you may be looking around and wondering whatever happened to your generation.

Chances are you used to tell everyone you loved your job, but recently you've acknowledged that what you really liked was the money, the status and the feeling of being good at something. You don't love your job at all. In fact you don't even like it. If you can identify with this dilemma the chances are that the underlying dissatisfaction has gone unnoticed for years because your friends and family constantly tell you how successful and lucky you are.

So you want to move on, but you don't know how and you are surrounded by well-intentioned people who have a vested interest in you staying just the way you are.

In this book we have simplified the process of change. This doesn't mean to say it is going to be easy, but it does mean you will know how to get started. God, as they say, can move mountains, but you will have to bring a shovel. Here are the three things you need to kick-start your own great escape:

■ You need to discover or rediscover a genuine enthusiasm for an occupation, whether this is paid or voluntary.

■ You need a map that shows you how to get from where you are now to where you want to be.

■ You need the money to enable you to make the transition to the new occupation and to provide financial security for now and for later when you decide to opt for full retirement.

Let's look at these in turn. We say a 'paid or *voluntary* occupation' because with our increased longevity and good health even the wealthiest of entrepreneurs rarely wants to stop work in order to holiday full time. Experience indicates that the active mind is unlikely to find salvation through scenery. Instead men and women are leaving their careers as high fliers in finance and business in order to work for charitable organisations in Britain and overseas. If the 18-year-olds can take a gap year between school and college, there is no reason why you can't take a gap year or five between work and retirement.

Now for the map. Goal mapping is a simple exercise that reaps tremendous rewards and has been tried and tested by thousands here in Britain. If it sounds a bit hippy then bear in mind that as a child of the 1960s you may have been a hippy yourself and had a glorious time of it. Just because you became an accountant later on doesn't mean you can't rediscover your earlier open-mindedness and sense of fun, although for health reasons we do not recommend a return to psychedelic substances.

Goal mapping is no different from a business plan. You need to set out a personal profit and loss account, a list of personal assets and liabilities and a realistic assessment of what is required – for example, time, money, new skills, the support of your family – to enable you to achieve your target. A sensible time frame for each step is essential, especially for the many perfectionists among us. This helps you to view your new goal with realistic expectations and to congratulate yourself for progress made rather than beating yourself up for failing to achieve perfection by yesterday.

A lot of this book is about money. You need to manage your finances because you have to eat and pay the bills while you are changing your life. Money allows you to buy the things you require to reach your goal, whether this is a new computer or the freedom to work part time at your current job in order to train for the new occupation.

> **Sherif Ali** From here until we reach the other side, no water but what we carry with us. For the camels, no water at all. If the camels die, we die. And in twenty days they will start to die.
> **Lawrence** There's no time to waste then is there?
>
> *Lawrence of Arabia* (1962)

If you want to handle all of your finances yourself there is enough information in this book to get you started. If, on the other hand, you want someone to help you or even to do everything for you, we explain how to find a Mary Poppins of the financial world who is practically perfect in every way. Doing it all yourself can be very time consuming and may prevent you getting on with your life. So, if you want to run a speculative investment portfolio that's fine, but let an expert look after your pension fund.

Whatever your starting point on finance, now is the time to dump the adage that a little bit of knowledge is a bad thing. It isn't. You also need a sense of humour and the ability to question received wisdom.

So, read on and find out what you need to do to kick-start your great escape. The only failures are those who never try.

Debbie Harrison

# Metamorphosis

**Schultz** Colonel Hogan if you ever escape ...
**Hogan** Yeah?
**Schultz** Be a good fellow and take me with you.

*Hogan's Heroes* (1965)

**Anything can be great, I don't care, brick laying can be great, if a guy knows what he's doing and why and if he can make it come off.**

Fast Eddie, *The Hustler* (1961)

# 1

# Kick-start your great escape

After reading this chapter you will

*dust down your LPs and attempt to entertain your kids with some* real *music*

*set up a commune*

*remember why you always hated lentils*

**CHANGE IS EXHILARATING AND SCARY** in equal measure. Most people have an idea of what it is they really want to do but to explore those ideas and put them into action takes courage. For a while you are going to feel out on a limb – far removed from your friends, who are still stuck in their comfort zones – still complaining, but not doing anything about it.

This chapter suggests some ways to kick-start your career change and how to get the support you need to see you through. At the end are some useful contacts and a reading list. If you used to scoff at the idea of self-help books then now is the time to take a look. When you get used to the language you will find that the best of these books are written by people who have themselves taken a quantum leap in faith and moved out of their comfort zone into a dynamic new life. They 'walk the talk' as the Americans would say.

## What do you want to change?

If the answer to this question is 'everything' then you need to sit down with a sheet of paper or in front of your computer screen and break down your ideas into bite-sized chunks – otherwise you will feel overwhelmed and won't get started.

The important point at this stage is to find out what it is specifically you don't like about your work. For example, many people find on reflection that they enjoy the job but they don't like their employer or the people, the working environment, the hours, the commuting, and so on. In this case a career consultant that specialises in older employees will be able to help you find a new job to suit your experience and qualifications but where you will be working for a very different type of employer (see Chapter 2).

> **cool advice**   The best self-help books are written by people who have taken a quantum leap in faith and moved out of their comfort zone into a dynamic new life. They 'walk the talk' as the Americans would say.

If you would like to do something quite different your choice will be based on your personal interests and/or the skills you have built up through your first career. Use the SWOT test to see if your ideas are realistic for your type of personality and circumstances. If you feel happy with your choice of new career you may need an independent guide to help you achieve your goal. One source of help is to find a 'life coach'. This is discussed below.

## The SWOT test

SWOT stands for Strengths, Weaknesses, Opportunities and Threats. This exercise is similar to the techniques employed by a business that needs to assess its current position and future prospects. The recruitment consultant Reed, for example, uses this self-analytical exercise for new graduates, but it is equally applicable to you now and will help you identify your real talents and skills.

What you do is list the positive and negative aspects of your character, achievements and potential under the SWOT headings. This will get you to think along the right lines. Many people know what they don't like about their job, but few take the time to assess what they are good at and enjoy and to draw a profile of the ideal occupation.

> **99** Sometimes I wish you were just an ordinary businessman.
> **Agent 86, Maxwell Smart**
> Well 99, we are what we are. I'm a secret agent, trained to be cold, vicious, and savage. Not enough to be a businessman.
>
> *Get Smart* (1965)

Honesty is important if you want to paint an accurate picture of where your future lies. It is very helpful to get a close friend to work with you on this task – perhaps someone who is also trying to find a new direction. Make sure that this person genuinely wants to help you achieve your goals. It is counterproductive to attempt to change your life if the person with whom you share your ideas is convinced that you should be happy with your lot and that your project is doomed to failure.

## Strengths

On the positive side under strengths you might list qualities like dependability, loyalty and intelligence. OK, so you sound like a sheepdog, but add 'numerate' and 'good presentation skills' and you enter the primate zone.

It is vital to make a realistic assessment of your personality and all of your skills. 'Soft' skills can be quite difficult to define, but don't be bashful about listing as positive strengths such attributes as 'a good listener', 'intuitive' or 'get on well with young children/animals/drug addicts'.

## Weaknesses

Here you might list perceived flaws such as poor communication skills. Honesty about your shortcomings at this stage may prevent you from pursuing a new occupation that you can do in theory, but which in practice would make you unhappy. You probably have one of those already.

Consider these negative aspects and decide whether you want to change any of them. For example, if you are shy you might consider some presentation training, an evening class in public speaking or even a drama class. On the other hand, if you simply don't like working with people, then this suggests a more solitary pursuit is in order. If you have fantastic business skills but people say you don't listen to them, you may benefit from a life-coaching course (see below), which will explain how to listen properly, among other 'people' skills.

## Opportunities

These could be your contacts in the field in which you want to work – people who could give you some practical advice and perhaps put you in touch with someone who could offer you a job. Opportunities might also include access to further education – for example, the chance to do a higher degree, to study a practical skill that you have always wanted to learn or one which you need for your proposed new business. For example, many people over 45 do not have the IT skills that are essential these days, whether you plan to work for a company or set up your own business.

cool advice
Under 'strengths' you might list qualities like dependability, loyalty and intelligence. OK, so you sound like a sheepdog, but add 'numerate' and 'good presentation skills' and you enter the primate zone.

Further education may appear daunting, but don't be put off. Remember, times have changed and universities are much keener these days to attract mature students than they were when you may have done your first degree. In the good old days you needed a 2:1 to get on to a masters course, but you will find that universities are far more interested in what you have achieved to date than in the degree you took 30 years ago.

## Threats

We tend to assume that finance is the biggest single barrier to change, but in practice most of the threats are likely to be inside your own head. For the successful businessman or woman, one of the toughest obstacles to overcome is perfectionism. This is the little voice that says, 'If I'm going to do it I've got to get it absolutely right and since I can't be sure it will be right I had better not try.' Fear of failure is a characteristic of the perfectionist mentality.

Perfectionism is also behind the tendency to take on far too much and then feel overwhelmed and abandon everything. If you find yourself writing lists that are impossible to achieve, you are setting yourself up for a fall and need to consider how you can be more realistic.

Other 'threats' could include the negative responses from those around you. Members of your family may rubbish your efforts, for example, or former colleagues may tell you you've gone barking mad to consider giving up a successful career and big salary for a pipe dream. The most insidious comments are likely to be the ones that start, 'It's not that we don't want you to do … but we are very concerned about your health/well being/wife/husband/children'.

Top achievers recommend you keep the sort of company that reflects your aspirations. If you surround yourself with negative people it is hard to maintain a positive outlook, just as it is for someone who is trying to give up drink and cigarettes but who constantly hangs out with drinking and smoking friends in bars.

## Life coaching

A life coach is a personal adviser who is trained to help you discover within yourself the confidence and ability to move forward in a positive manner in the areas of your life where you want to change. This is not psychotherapy, which deals with the past and how it affects your current behaviour. Life coaching is about the here and now and the future. It helps you to set appropriate goals and shows you what you need to do to achieve those goals. You can find a life coach through the contact details provided at the end of this chapter.

> Well, uh, I guess I'd do it all different. First off, I wouldn't live in the same state where we pull our jobs. We'd live in another state. We'd stay clean there and then, when we'd take a bank, we'd go to the other state.
>
> Clyde Barrow, *Bonnie & Clyde* (1967)

Coaching can take place face to face but after an initial meeting you can do most of it on the phone. Phone coaching usually takes place once a week and is ideal for those who are still working full time.

At the first meeting you can discuss the things you want to change and explain where you might experience difficulties. One of the techniques used by life coaches is 'goal mapping', which is based on Tony Buzan's theory of mind mapping – a pictorial way of taking notes. Goal mapping, developed by Brian Mayne, is a way of using this technique to help you achieve your ambitions. Essentially it enables you to set down on paper as a series of images where you are now, where you want to get to and what you will need to do along the way to achieve your goal. The use of pictures rather than words helps you tap into the right side of your brain, which is the creative centre. Most people use left-brain analysis for assessing situations and this can be restrictive and lead to negative thinking.

Goal maps should be updated at regular intervals to take account of developments and to accommodate changes in your views.

## Positive change

Let's suppose you are the public relations officer of a financial institution. You chose the job initially because you have good communication skills, an academic mind that enables you to understand the services and products your employer offers, and you were attracted to life in the fast lane, working for a major company in the City.

Twenty years on and you no longer want a 90-minute commute twice a day, you have grown weary of the materialistic nature of the financial community and you feel intellectually unfulfilled.

In this situation you might decide that working in a similar role but for a prominent charity, for example, would be more satisfying. To make the change you may need to find out more about the sector and consider which type of charity or foundation appeals to you. Your life coach might suggest you make time to learn about how charities work, what drives them and how they are financed (usually rather precariously). You may even decide to spend some time working on a voluntary basis to find out how a charity that appeals to you works at grass-roots level.

Alternatively, let's suppose that after years in public relations you want to write novels and work from home. This is a much bigger change and will require careful planning. Assuming that you want to get something published before you give up work, your list of requirements might include setting aside a realistic amount of time to write, buying a new computer, going on a creative writing course, researching the market for the type of fiction you would like to write, finding a literary agent, securing the co-operation of your partner/family to allow you to devote time to this project without feeling guilty, and contact with other aspiring authors to gain confidence and swap tips.

If you got a book published but made only a modest amount out of the deal (this is quite typical for new authors), you would then write a new goal map to take you from new author to successful author. This second map might focus far more on the financing of your new career, given the long lead times between getting a book accepted and actually making enough money to live on. You may need to rely on your partner/spouse for financial support for several years or you might have to raise a loan to see you through. This map may also include a contingency plan that sets a time limit on working as a full-time author by setting a date at which you might start looking for part-time work which is interesting and allows you to continue with your creative writing.

## Morale booster

Going through this type of long-term change is very unsettling and it is rare for anyone to feel 100 per cent confident through the ups and downs. A life coach can provide a much-needed shot in the arm when your confidence is flagging and when everyone around you is talking doom and gloom. A good coach will be well versed in morale boosting and motivation techniques and will help you maintain a positive attitude through the tough times.

---

❄ **cool advice** Time was when you needed a 2:1 to get on to a masters course but you will find that universities are far more interested in what you have achieved to date than in the degree you took 30 years ago.

---

Do bear in mind though, that if you take on a life coach you should be prepared to put in a lot of work. As Fiona Harrold says in *Be Your Own Life Coach*, 'If you stick with the known and familiar you'll rule out the new and end up staying just where you are.' Instead you need to be prepared to develop:

- motivation
- self-belief
- self-discipline
- willingness to change.

## When change is forced upon you

Of course not everyone makes big changes out of choice. Make no mistake about it, if you are forced to change career through redundancy or early retirement, it can feel as though you are up against a life crisis of the same magnitude as divorce, serious illness and bereavement. Victims of the late redundancy/early retirement syndrome also make potentially easy targets for the less scrupulous financial services salesmen who often appear to know where the 'downsizing' is taking place before the employees do themselves. Chapter 4 explains how to find the right sort of adviser who can steer you safely through these troubled waters and give you time to think about where you want to go from here.

Late redundancy and early retirement are endemic in the UK, with an estimated 40 per cent of people over 55 out of full-time employment. If it happens to you, your first priority will be to sort out your finances. Seek the help of an expert and draw up a financial plan. In particular, if this is the end of your high earning years then you need to think very carefully about how you will supplement your income with your pensions and investments. Your investment portfolio will also need some adjustments. If it was geared up for growth you should look again at the asset allocation and consider a more defensive approach in the light of your new outlook on investment risk.

> When you live for a while of time, your past significant events catch up with you.
>
> Jade, *The Outer Limits* (1963)

If you receive cash as part of your severance settlement, avoid hasty investment decisions. Good financial planning for the long term can only be achieved where both the current situation and future financial goals are known. If early retirement was thrust upon you and you are still in shock, only the current position can be assessed and therefore long-term investment projects should be avoided.

An excellent rule to follow if your future plans are uncertain is to adopt a holding position for at least 12 months. Find the best deposit rates and, where appropriate, take advantage of annual tax and investment allowances. Some advisers also suggest you avoid splashing out on a world cruise, an expensive car and other 'feel good' spends until your future plans are known.

A life coach can provide a much-needed shot in the arm when your confidence is flagging and when everyone around you is talking doom and gloom.

## Further information

For information on goal mapping, contact Lift International (01983 856750; www.liftinternational.com).

To find out about life coaching, The Life Coaching Academy trains coaches and can put you in touch with a coach. It also runs seminars for those who want to find out more about being coached and becoming a coach. (e-mail info@lifecoachingacademy.com; website www.lifecoachingacademy.com).

### Recommended reading

Tony Buzan, *The Mind Map Book*, BBC Consumer Publishing.
Miles Downey, *Effective Coaching*, Orion Business Books.
Laura Berman Fortgang, *Take Yourself to the Top*, Thorsen.
Anthony Grant and Jayne Greene, *Coach Yourself*, Pearson Education.
Fiona Harrold, *Be Your Own Life Coach*, Hodder & Stoughton.
Susan Jeffers, *Feel the Fear and Do It Anyway*, Arrow Books.
Brian Mayne, *Goal Mapping Study Pack*, Lift International.
Eric Parsloe, *The Manager as Coach and Mentor*, The Institute of Personnel and Development.
Chery Richardson, *Take Time for Your Life*, Bantam.
John Whitmore, *Coaching for Performance*, Nicholas Brealey.
Laura Whitworth, Henry Kimsey-House and Phil Sandahl, *Co-Active Coaching*, Oxford Press.

**Well, here goes. I hope I get the job. Of course, with my spider-power I could get all the money I'd ever need, but that wouldn't be honest. I'm a crime fighter now.**

Peter Parker/Spiderman, *Spider-Man* (1967)

# Work is a four-letter word

After reading this chapter you will

*feel more sympathetic towards your aimless teenagers*

*bore for Europe on job satisfaction versus money*

*set up your own career consultancy to get the job done properly*

**AS YOU CARRY OUT YOUR RESEARCH** you will build up a list of useful contacts for your future career. Most professions and trades have an association for members who work in the given field, so find out about them and take a look at the websites. Use these in conjunction with any relevant websites for employer and specialist recruitment agencies, all of which can provide useful information.

Remember, if you believe that the people you work with are as important as the type of work you do, take the time to consider the business environment, culture and pay structure of any new field you want to explore. It may well be an interesting market, but if the people who work in it are largely remunerated through sales commission, for example, the environment will be very competitive and aggressive.

## Recruitment consultants

Employer websites are a valuable source of information about a company and its recruitment programme, but you should use them in conjunction with a recruitment agency that specialises in your area of knowledge. A good agency will be able to explain what it's like on the inside of competing organisations.

The Recruitment and Employment Confederation (REC, see below) is the professional association for this area and has 7750 individual members and 6000 corporate members. Its website provides useful information about CVs and job interviews and also lets you search for agencies by location and specialisation. If you are looking for agencies that specialise in a specific market, the REC website can direct you to agencies that cover:

- interim management
- childcare
- drivers
- education
- hotel and catering
- IT
- nurses and carers
- medical
- technical.

> **c o o l advice** Recruitment agencies can be extremely helpful if you know broadly what it is you are seeking or you are happy doing the same job but would like a very different working environment.

Agencies can be extremely helpful if you know broadly what it is you are seeking or if you are happy doing the same job but would like a very different working environment. What they are not going to do is discover the long lost skill you had at age 17 and develop it into a going concern. For this type of inspiration a life coach and your own research will be more fruitful (see Chapter 1).

The Recruitment and Employment Confederation has over 200 agencies on its register that specialise in finding work for older people. If you have been made redundant then this type of agency may prove to be more sympathetic to your aims. In addition they will tell you which new skills you need to learn. Typical gaps include IT skills, even if it is just a case of learning how to use e-mail and the internet, or becoming familiar with Microsoft Office programmes. You may also need to improve your presentation skills.

> I'd say the odds against a successful escape are about 100 to one. But may I add another word? The odds against survival in this camp are even worse.
>
> Major Shears, *The Bridge on the River Kwai* (1957)

## Change within your profession

Where career consultants really score is in helping you make big changes *within* your profession. This can transform your life without you having to abandon your training and experience. Ideas you might consider include:

- Moving from a large company where you are a small fish to a very small operation where you would have the opportunity to get involved in a wider range of jobs.

- Working for a charity or similar organisation where the ethos is the public good rather than corporate profit. For example, as an accountant your job could be to ensure that as much of the donations as possible are used to fund good works rather than to make the senior partners or shareholders (and yourself) even more wealthy.

- Working fewer hours so you can find time for your own interests – for example, to pursue academic ambitions that you abandoned at 21. This could be achieved by working locally instead of commuting or by opting for a less responsible position, possibly both.

Whatever choice you make will have consequences and you will need to consider these very carefully. The most obvious of these is a lower income – at least initially – but if the upside is much greater job satisfaction or a significant reduction in stress, then you may decide this is worthwhile.

# Temporary work

According to the REC, over 1 million temporary workers are on assignment through the country at any one time. It is important to remember that, unlike when we were in our twenties, temporary work is no longer a second-class substitute for the real thing but is used by many people of all ages as a way of life. Temping is flexible and can pay very well. It also helps you keep a healthy distance from the organisational politics.

Temporary work has many attractions. First and foremost, you don't have to commit yourself to a specific employer. If you want to travel you can fit in your plans around some lucrative temporary contracts and maybe take on some extra IT training as well to boost your credentials.

Temps do need to be mobile and flexible but this should be a two-way trade-off. If you can meet the employer's requirements you should be able to find the flexibility you need to fit your new lifestyle.

## Select the right agency

As a temporary worker you rely heavily on your recruitment consultancy to highlight job opportunities for you. For this reason you should treat the selection of your agency or agencies as though this were your full-time employer.

Look for a consultancy that is a member of the REC, which means it will work to a code of good recruitment practice. Apart from stringent membership criteria, the REC has a complaints and disciplinary procedure. Employers or job candidates who feel that they have not been treated properly have the right to ask the REC to investigate.

> ❄ cool advice    Temporary work is no longer a second-class substitute for the real thing but is used by many people of all ages as a way of life. Temping is flexible and can pay very well. It also helps you keep a healthy distance from the organisational politics.

Once you have identified consultancies you would like to work with, contact them to discuss the type of work you are looking for. They are likely to ask you to make an appointment to visit one of their staff. When you go for an interview, take a CV, details of referees and your national insurance (NI) number. Treat the interview just as you would any other.

## Registration and payment

Make sure you know how the agency will pay you and remember to hand over your P45 and bank details before your first assignment. Different agencies have different payment systems and you need to keep track of these if you register with more than one (and see 'Contract Employment' below). Most will credit your bank account directly one week in arrears.

Once you are registered, the recruitment consultancy will start to search for suitable vacancies. Ask them to explain how they will put you forward for jobs. For example, you might want the agency to contact you before it sends your CV to a prospective employer in case there are certain organisations you prefer to avoid.

The REC stresses the importance of keeping in touch with your recruitment consultancy: 'Those candidates who appear most keen to work are understandably contacted first,' it said.

> **Agent 86, Maxwell Smart**
> If you're trying to scare me Chief, you're wasting your time. I don't know the meaning of the word fear.
> **Chief** You'll parachute from 6 000 feet.
> **Agent 86** I think I just learned it.
>
> *Get Smart* (1965)

## First assignment

When the consultancy offers you an assignment, think about whether you can be available for its duration, for the hours required and whether you can actually get there comfortably. The agency will confirm the rate of pay with you at this point. It should also tell you the name of your boss and cover house rules such as dress code, smoking policy and meal breaks. You will need to fill in a timesheet at the end of the week and ask your supervisor at the company to sign it to verify your hours of work.

## Attitude is all!

Above all, temporary workers are required to fit in rapidly and easily. You will develop flexibility and adaptability as you gain more temping or contracting experience. Try and keep a low profile and be enthusiastic and professional.

As a temp you should run yourself like any other business. Get feedback from employers on how you performed and make changes where necessary. This is all part of business survival and development.

# Contract employment

This is a half way house between full-time and temporary work, although for some professions – IT and engineering, for example – it is a way of life. Contract employment is becoming more common across all sectors, however, as companies strive to reduce their overheads and cut the numbers of full-time employees on their books. It is important to check carefully what benefits the employer provides. This will vary considerably. Some companies provide a similar benefits package to that enjoyed by full-time employees. Others will use contract employment as a way to cut the employee benefits bill, in which case you are likely to get little more than the pay cheque so you will need to pay for your own pension plus death and disability insurances.

> **cool advice** Some companies recognise that contract employment is a way of life and may provide similar benefits to those enjoyed by full-time employees. Others will use contract employment as a way to cut the employee benefits bill, in which case you are likely to get little more than the pay cheque.

You may engage in contract work directly with employers if you are known in a specific field, but otherwise this is likely to be found through an agency. The distinction between a temporary job and a contract job is vague. One of the differences is that for contract appointments the employer is likely to pay you directly and deduct your tax and national insurance. If this is the arrangement the recruitment consultancy will tell you. Employers offering longer-term contracts may want to see you before confirming the job. If you work on a contract basis, the assignment is likely to be for three months or longer and you should be prepared to give your commitment for this period.

## Interim management

Skilled managers are hard to find and many employers are happy to take on interim managers – those with considerable experience who can step easily into the position – while they find the right full-time employee.

A division of the REC is the Interim Management Association – the trade body created to maintain standards in the field. Most major recruitment consultancies belong to the organisation (see below) and you can find one by going to the website directly or via the REC website.

> It's a dangerous thing, ambition. Ruined Mickey Mouse's whole career.
>
> Myron, *Myra Breckenridge* (1970)

If you are interested in this type of work the organisation runs a workshop to introduce new people to the demands and challenges of a career in this field. The workshop covers the market, moving from an employee to an interim manager, getting assignments and tips on how to manage your business. Details are on the website.

## Reading matters

To maintain a professional image it is important to keep up with current and financial events as well as news specific to the industry in which you wish to work. Check out the trade and professional bodies in your new field and find out if they publish members' journals and ask which other publications are relevant. Get sample copies and subscribe where necessary. It's a good idea to pay a visit once a week to a large public library to keep up with all the specialist press.

### Local sources

If you've had a couple of decades of commuting you may want to find work that is closer to home. In this case you need to check out the local recruitment agencies, the local press, radio and TV. If you have a skill to sell and want to build up a local client base, then advertising is important and again you should check press, TV and radio opportunities.

## Nationals

The national press provides access to a wide range of jobs but most of these are likely to be full-time positions. Keep an eye on the companies that are taking on staff in your area of expertise by checking their websites and contacting the personnel officer. Many employers are happy to take on interim skilled staff even if their long-term goal is to find a full-timer.

---

❄ c o o l
 advice    **Skilled managers are hard to find and many employers are happy to take on interim managers – those with considerable experience who can step easily into the position – while they find the right full-time employee.**

---

The nationals are also a good source of contacts for recruitment consultants. The large consultancies offer a range of specialisations and may well have an interim management and temporary employment section that can help you find your niche.

*The Financial Times*: www.ft.com
*Daily Mail*: www.mail.co.uk
*Daily Telegraph*: www.telegraph.co.uk
*Evening Standard*: www.standard.co.uk
*The Express*: www.expressnewspapers.co.uk
*Financial Mail on Sunday*: www.financialmail.co.uk
*Financial News*: www.financialnews.co.uk
*The Guardian*: www.guardian.co.uk
*The Independent*: www.independent.co.uk
*International Herald Tribune*: www.iht.com
*The Mirror*: www.mirror.co.uk
*Money Observer*: www.moneyobserver.com
*The Observer*: www.observer.co.uk
*The Scotsman (City)*: www.scotsman.com
*The Sunday Business*: www.sundaybusiness.co.uk
*The Sunday Express*: www.expressnewspapers.co.uk
*Sunday Mirror*: www.sundaymirror.co.uk
*Sunday Post (City)*: www.sundaypost.com
*The Sunday Telegraph*: www.telegraph.co.uk

*The Sunday Times*: www.sunday-times.co.uk
*The Times*: www.the-times.co.uk
*The Wall Street Journal*: www.wsj.com

## Further information

The REC is at www.rec.uk.com
The Interim Management Association is at wwew.interimmanagement.uk.com

**You don't go wheelin 'n dealin for money. You do it for fun. Money's just the way you keep score.**

Henry Tycoon, *The Wheeler Dealers* (1963)

# The company of wolves

After reading this chapter you will

*knit yourself a jumper like Richard Branson's*

*sell your soul to the devil for a business loan*

*decide there's a lot to be said for being a penpusher in the civil service*

**THINGS HAVE CHANGED SINCE** the mid-twentieth century. Steady jobs for life are history. These days five years shows an uncalled for commitment to one company unless you are shooting up the corporate ladder so fast you need oxygen.

If you've done your time as a small cog in a big wheel and you fancy doing your own thing either as a sole trader or going into business with friends, family or like-minded colleagues, there are some fantastic opportunities. There are also some unbelievably deep pitfalls.

About 320,000 people become self-employed and start up small businesses each year. Over two-thirds of these do not have any previous experience of running a small firm. A third of these need external funding, while others require additional funding to develop and expand an existing business. Whichever stage you are at, if you want to start your own business this chapter will point you in the right direction.

Banks are the main source of loans. However, there is a wide range of other sources of finance. One of the best guides to starting your own business is free from the Department of Trade and Industry (DTI): *Small Firms: Financing Your Business*. Contact details for this and other information sources are provided at the end of this chapter.

Prior to seeking funding, talk to your local Business Link, and your account-ant. The Business Link and Department for Education and Employment (DfEE) also cover a range of subjects including employment law and training.

# Why are you going into business?

Your reason for being in business in the first place is the single most important factor in determining what type of finance is suitable. You may be in business to provide for your family, to be your own boss, because you cannot find another job, to make lots of money, or because you are teeming with ideas and no one company can contain you.

Whatever your reason, it is important to recognise how it will affect your attitude to risk and to whether or not you feel comfortable handing over some of the control to investors.

## Are you an entrepreneur?

If your chief aim in business is to provide a low-risk way of looking after your family or to establish a steady source of income, which you cannot find else-where, then you had better stick to the traditional methods of raising finance such as a bank overdraft or loan.

> ❄️ cool advice
> Your reason for being in business in the first place is the single most important factor in determining what type of finance is suitable.

If, on the other hand, you recognise the following characteristics in your-self, you may have the key entrepreneurial attributes that make your business suitable for raising venture capital (and see 'Venture Capital' below). Do you have:

- drive and energy
- the ability to learn from others
- the ability to respond to what the market wants
- tenacity and courage
- hunger for success
- self-confidence
- willingness to assess opportunities and to take a calculated risk
- the ability to motivate other people to work productively for you
- the ability to set high achievable goals
- the belief in your ability to control your own destiny
- a long-term view of where your business in going
- readiness to learn from your mistakes and setbacks
- the ability to be competitive with good self-discipline.

    *Source:* DTI

## Structures for business

Businesses are either unincorporated – like sole traders and partnerships – or they are incorporated limited companies. The distinction affects the way you can raise money:

- **Unincorporated businesses:** sole traders and partnerships are only able to raise additional capital from their own resources or by allowing new partners to buy into the business.
- **Incorporated limited companies** are able to raise equity by issuing shares. However, there are many constraints on this type of company – for example, you have to submit accounts to the Registrar of Companies and recognise the rights of shareholders.

## Why do you need money?

This is not a daft question. In order to convince a lender that you are trust-worthy, you will need to demonstrate that you have thought very carefully about how much money you require, for how long and for which aspects of your business. For example, do you need it to buy equipment or to pay for project development costs?

## Funding facts

- The average cost of setting up in business is about £18,000. Typically one-third of this is funded externally.

- External funding is primarily used to finance business premises (29 per cent) and stock (21 per cent). It is rarely used for wages or recruitment.

- Banks are the main source of external finance for both start-up businesses (72 per cent) and established businesses (86 per cent). Friends and families are an important secondary source.

- Only one in five firms investigate whether they are eligible for government or EU grants.

*Source:* Barclays Bank

In general you can expect to borrow from £500 to £25,000. You are likely to be asked to repay in monthly instalments over a term of between one and ten years. If this is a start-up, you may be able to negotiate an interest and capital repayment holiday for up to six months to tide you over the crucial first months when cash flow can be a problem.

> **Let me tell you one thing son. Noooobody ever lends money to a man with a sense of humour.**
>
> Peter Tork, *Head* (1968)

The average time for a small business to raise finance varies considerably. This can be anything from a week to a month, but this is for fairly straightforward loans. If you are after venture capital, for example, you should allow four to seven months – longer if you do not yet have a business plan.

## Financing your business

The main sources of finance for businesses are banks and similar financial institutions, although the government does provide some help, particularly in areas where it is trying to increase employment and attract new business.

How you raise money will depend on your specific needs, the amount required and, frankly, sheer availability. Discuss this with your accountant before approaching any lenders.

## Equity capital

Raising equity capital involves selling a share of your company to a venture capital company or an informal investor (sometimes known as a business angel). Venture capital companies are the main providers of equity finance for new companies. However, their preference for larger investments makes them rather inaccessible for small start-ups, although it is still worth checking the British Venture Capital Association (BVCA) website.

## Business angels

Business angels are private individuals, usually with a business background, who are willing to invest in small businesses in return for an equity stake. Generally they are willing and usually very keen to offer the benefits of their own management experience.

> **cool advice** If this is a start-up business, you may be able to negotiate with your lender an interest and capital repayment holiday for up to six months to tide you over the crucial first months when cash flow can be a problem.

Several organisations have grouped together under the umbrella of the Business Angels network to match businesses seeking equity finance with potential investors. Further information is available from the BVCA and Business Links.

## Loans

Probably the best starting point is your local bank if you have a good track record. However, you should also check the market for top borrowing rates. An excellent source of information is *Business Moneyfacts*.

The figures mentioned above for availability of finance and the time it takes to secure a loan or investment are averages only. In general banks are much more willing to lend to older people with a business track record than to a young entrepreneur, so your experience and grey hair may stand you in good stead.

It may be tempting to approach your friends and family for finance but do be aware of the drawbacks. The bank will set its terms and conditions and stick to them. If you get into trouble you will know in advance at exactly which point the bank will start to pester you and what action you will be required to take. Friends and family may have a tendency to interfere and if things do go wrong your personal as well as your professional peace of mind is at risk. Having said that, family businesses are among

> We're about to do a job in Italy and the only way we're gonna do it is by working together and that means doing everything I say.
>
> Charlie C, *The Italian Job* (1969)

the robust in the economy.

Look at all available sources of finance and consider a combination of more than one source. Loan finance normally requires regular payments of capital and interest. Leasing and hire purchase may be another way of financing some of your business requirements.

## How to present your business proposal

Barclays Bank has put together a good formula for presentations, which it calls CAMPARI.

- **Character** Present yourself positively and demonstrate your commitment and enthusiasm for your business. Bank managers place a great deal of importance on these qualities when assessing proposals.

- **Ability** Demonstrate that you have the appropriate experience, training and drive to plan and run your business effectively. An up-to-date copy of your CV will help here.

- **Management** Show that you have the ability to produce up-to-date and accurate financial information to demonstrate your control over the business.

- **Purpose** Explain in detail your reason for seeking bank funding. This will enable the bank to identify the right loan package for your needs if it decides to help you. It will also enable the bank to calculate the level of risk it is taking in lending you money. This in turn will affect the rate of interest it offers and the terms and conditions it attaches to the loan.

- **Amount** Be precise and show how you calculated the size of loan you need. If you borrow too much this will add to your costs. Do however make an allowance for contingencies. If you ask for too little, you may have to return to the bank at a later date.

- **Repayment** Be clear about the sources of repayment. Develop cash flow and budget forecasts that show accurately how you expect the business to develop over the term of the loan. Outline the sources from which repayments will be met.

- **Insurance** Protect yourself and your business. The bank will want to know how you will meet repayments if your business experiences cash flow problems. You may need to offer some sort of security. You should also consider taking out appropriate insurance to protect the repayment of the loan in case you are unable to meet the cost from normal trade due to accident, illness or even death! Key personnel should be covered as well as yourself.

Barclays commented: 'Bank managers look first and foremost at the character, ability and experience of the business owner and the cash-generating capacity of the business itself. In this respect it is essential to stress the importance of proper planning and forecasting before any meeting with the bank manager.'

## Your business plan

Your business plan needs to present the key facts to the lender or investor in a clear and concise fashion. You need to set out where you are going and how you are going to get there. The plan, therefore, will combine your own objectives and the potential of your business. As an owner the DTI suggests you should set out:

- what you want out of the business
- when you want to realise your wealth (that is, sell up)
- your strengths and weaknesses.

Both lenders and equity investors will need to be convinced about the viability of the business. This depends initially on two factors – sales and management. So when you approach a source of funding or investment your priority is to prove that there is a market for the product or service and that the management team is sufficiently experienced and capable of identifying problems and devising solutions to steer a successful path.

## Business plan outline

- Executive summary.
- The business: history, current status.
- Products: description, regulatory requirements, research and development.
- Production process: techniques, location, supplier, capacity.
- Sales and marketing: market size, competition, sales analysis by product and customer, marketing techniques.
- Management and organisation: management team with full CVs, organisation chart, remuneration policies.
- Financial information: historical results (if relevant), profit and cash flow projections, sensitivity (e.g. to changing interest rates), financing requirements.
- The future: future prospects, exit routes for the investor.

# The finance providers' aims

The providers of loans and equity will have different priorities and motives in assessing a business plan. Providers of equity are looking for a significant capital gain to justify their risk. They will also need a built-in exit route.

> ❄ cool advice    Look at all available sources of finance. Loan finance normally requires regular payments of capital and interest. Leasing and hire purchase may be another way of financing some of your business requirements.

Lenders are not seeking to make such large returns, nor will they accept such a high level of risk as an equity investor. What they want from you is an assurance that you can pay the interest and, at the end of the loan period, that you will be able to repay the capital. However, since their aim is to minimise losses, they may ask you to provide adequate security for the loan.

## How to sell your plan

Restrict circulation to just a few potential sources of finance. With each rejection (and there may be many of these!) revise your plan to reflect what you have learned.

The four key steps suggested by the DTI are:

1 Sell the idea on paper. Convey what it is that makes the project exciting in the minimum number of words and ensure your presentation is eye catching.

2 Consult professional advisers with knowledge of financiers.

3 Follow up with a telephone call and arrange a meeting at which you, the management, can sell the idea and prove your ability.

4 After the meeting consider amending the plan to take account of the financier's comments.

## Business support services

Your first port of call for most business enquiries is your nearest Business Links service. These are local partnerships, which bring together the business support services of the Department of Trade and Industry (DTI), training and enterprise councils, chambers of commerce, enterprise agencies, local authorities and other local bodies. There are 85 partnerships nationwide with some 240 outlets and 650 advisers.

These centres can help with a wide range of issues including advice for start-up businesses, training, finance packaging, design, export, marketing and access to other specialist businesses. For details of the Business Links Signpost Line, the Scottish Business Shops, the Northern Ireland Local Enterprise Development Unit (LEDU) and the Business Connect service in Wales, see the end of this chapter. You can also visit the Business Links website for information on the following:

- business and market research
- sources of grants and finance
- company and product sourcing
- Companies House and credit information.

# Government development areas

The government provides discretionary grants if you are brave enough to set up business in what are euphemistically called 'assisted areas'. Projects must either create new jobs or safeguard existing ones to qualify. Check out Regional Selective Assistance (RSA), Regional Enterprise Grants and Regional Innovation Grants.

# Other sources of help

- **The Enterprise Zone:** provides an internet-based information service to business.

- **Trade associations:** represent the interests of specialist industries or groups of traders and can be a valuable source of information. Good reference libraries should stock the *Directory of British Associations*, which lists all the trade associations.

- **Professional help:** local accountants are well geared towards helping the small business (try yellow pages), while many solicitors participate in the 'Lawyers for your Business' scheme, which offers a free legal consultation or a legal health check if you are about to set up your own business.

- **Franchising:** one option for budding entrepreneurs is to buy a franchise or turn an existing business into a franchise operation. There is a dedicated organisation for help with franchising – the British Franchise Association. It is also worth getting copies of two DTI small firms publications – *Buying a Franchise* and *Franchising your Business*.

## Patent Office

It is important to protect a new business idea, invention or logo through the Patent Office. Contact the office for advice on patents, designs, trademarks and copyright.

## Information technology

The Information Society Initiative (ISI) Programme for Business has established a network of local support centres, which offer advice and guidance on the benefits and use of information and communications technology by business. Some centres offer access to facilities like video conferencing and may provide training or point you in the right direction for local expertise. The ISI produces a range of helpful brochures.

---

 **cool advice** | The government provides discretionary grants if you are brave enough to set up business in what are euphemistically called 'assisted areas'. Projects must either create new jobs or safeguard existing ones to qualify.

---

The Software Business Network is an internet-based information service for young software companies. It provides support in marketing, management and access to capital, among other services. A good starting point for internet sites for business is the Enterprise Zone Internet Service.

## Employment law

This is a minefield, but a good place to start is the Employers' Helpline which gives advice on tax, national insurance contributions, statutory sick pay and value added tax registration.

# Further information

Many of the figures in this chapter were provided by Barclays Bank Small Business Team. The Barclays website is at **www.smallbusiness.barclays.co.uk**
  The DTI publishes a range of useful booklets for people thinking of setting up or developing a small business. A good starter pack would be:

- *Small Firms – Financing Your Business* (URN 98/805)
- *Guide to Help for Small Business (URN 98/942)*
- *Small Firms Publication List* (URN 99/1058)

To order, telephone 0870 1502 500 or e-mail **dtipubs@echristian.co.uk**. You should also check out the DTI publications website on **www.dti.gov.uk/publications/sme**

## Business Link

Business Link: www.businesslink.co.uk
Business Link Connect Wales: 08457 969798 (www.bc.wales.org.uk)
Business Link Signpost Line: 08457 567765
LEDU Northern Ireland: 01232 491031

## Business support services

British Franchise Association: 01491 578049/50 (www.british-
franchise.org.uk)
Companies House: 0870 333 3636 (www.companieshouse.gov.uk)
Employment Zones: 020 7925 5958 (www.dfee.gov.uk)
English Tourist Board: 020 8846 9000 (www.visitbritain.com)
Enterprise Zone: www.enterprisezone.org.uk
Federation of Small Businesses: 01253 33600 (www.fsb.co.uk)
Lawyers for your Business: 020 7405 9075 (www.lfyb.lawsociety.org.uk)
Livewire (start-up awards): 0191 261 5584
Livewire Hotline for information and advice: 0345 573252 (local rate)
(www.shell-livewire.org)
Northern Ireland Tourist Board: 020 7766 9920
Patent Office: 08459 500 505 (www.patent.gov.uk)
Scottish Business Shops-Lowlands freephone: 0800 78 78 78
Scottish Enterprise: 0141 248 2700 (www.scottish-enterprise.com)
Wales Tourist Board: 02920 499909 (www.visitwales.com)

## Finance

British Venture Capital Association (BVCA): 020 7240 3846
(www.brainstorm.co.uk/BVCA)
Regional Selective Assistance England: contact Business Link
RSA in Scotland: 0141 242 5675/5676
RSA in Wales: 01222 823216
Small Firms Loan Guarantee Scheme: 0114 259 7308/9
Small Firms Training Loans: freephone 0800 132660

## Information technology

Enterprise Zone Internet Service: **www.enterprisezone.org.uk**
Information Society Initiative: **www.isi.gov.uk**
Software Business Network: 020 7395 6700 – part of Computer Software
Services Association (**www.cssa.com**)

## Employment

Employers' helpline: 0345 143143

## Insolvency

The DTI's insolvency service is at **www.open.gov.uk/insolv_s/insolvhm.htm**

## Business Moneyfacts

01603 476102 (**www.moneyfacts.co.uk**)

**Advice is cheap Ms Malloy. It's the things that come gift wrapped that count.**

Horace, *Hello Dolly* (1969)

# 4

# Your financial minder

After reading this chapter you will

stash all your money under the mattress

look upon your old insurance and investment policies with dismay

become a rich financial adviser

**IF YOU WANT TO ENJOY** robust financial health, you need a good adviser who will come to know you like a trusted friend, anticipate your every requirement and keep all your investments and insurances shipshape.

But in a market beset by serial misselling and financial muggings, where do you find a Mary Poppins of the adviser world who is practically perfect in every way? There is no single answer but the following guide may help.

## What is a financial adviser?

The term financial adviser is as broad and misleading as the terms consultant and engineer. It can mean anything from the one-man band who sells everything from motor insurance to mortgages to the well-resourced professional firms of stockbrokers, chartered accountants and solicitors.

There are more than 27,000 independent financial advisers (IFAs) in the UK, several thousand more professional advisers (accountants and solicitors who give investment advice, for example) and a further 70,000 company representatives who work for financial institutions. Your starting point is to consider carefully what you want, not what they sell.

> **Leo** Let's assume, just for the moment, that you are a dishonest man.
> **Max** Assume away.
>
> *The Producers* (1968)

Under the Financial Services Act (FSA) 1986 it is a criminal offence to give investment advice without being authorised. The regulatory system has been criticised for being too slow. Several mainstream investments – personal pensions, endowments and home income plans, for example – have been the subject of major misselling scandals. Caveat emptor – buyer beware – is as important today as it ever was.

The FSA covers every firm or company providing investment advice or an investment service. If someone gives you advice on products covered by the Act and is not authorised, he or she is breaking the law. You can check authorisation by making a quick phone call to the FSA, which runs a comprehensive database. Details are provided at the end of this chapter. Appendix 3 deals with complaints.

## The Act doesn't cover everything

Not everything sold as an investment has to be authorised. Most regulated investments are non-tangible assets like shares, gilts, bonds and collective funds. When you buy physical or tangible assets directly rather than through a collective fund – gold coins, rare stamps, antiques, vintage cars and wines, for example – you are not covered by the Act. This means the FSA regulators cannot investigate your case and you are not entitled to compensation if things go wrong.

## Types of adviser

Under the FSA, advisers are split into two broad categories. Representatives of a company are authorised to sell only that company's products and this will be stated on the letterhead and terms of business agreement. Representatives are not permitted to recommend other products, even if they are better.

IFAs are not tied to one company. Their job is to examine your needs and to search the market for products that offer the best value in terms of performance, charges and contract flexibility, among other factors. In theory at least, you stand a better chance of coming away with the right insurances and investments than if you go to a company representative. In practice many commission-based IFAs focus on selling products rather than providing overall advice. Moreover, the term independent is not synonymous with expert. Some firms are excellent, others are less knowledgeable, while a minority are less than scrupulous.

 **cool advice**    Not everything sold as an investment has to be authorised.

# Financial planners

The general practitioners of the financial world, and among the best-qualified advisers, are the certified financial planners (CFPs). CFPs can be found in many different disciplines including accountancy, banking, investment and the law. A good planner will take a holistic or integrated approach to your financial affairs. He or she will identify your objectives, review the strengths and weaknesses of your current arrangements and then make appropriate recommendations that will be updated regularly. This will cover:

- investments
- risk management
- insurance
- retirement and estate planning, including wills and trusts
- school fee planning
- taxation
- cashflow planning
- special needs including long-term healthcare.

The planner co-ordinates your financial requirements and will work alongside your other professionals – for example your stockbroker, solicitor and accountant, making sure that everyone is working towards the same overall objectives. If you don't have a planner you still need someone to co-ordinate your financial affairs. Tax is a key issue for wealthy families and you might decide a chartered accountant with investment expertise would make a good co-ordinator. Over 1000 chartered accountants are authorised to offer investment advice and sell collective funds. You can find them through the Institute of Chartered Accountants' website. However, these firms do not offer stockbroker services so you or the accountant will need to appoint a firm to buy individual equities and bonds.

A growing number of solicitors offer a full portfolio management service and these can be found on the website for the Association of Solicitor Investment Managers (ASIM). If you are on the receiving end of an inheritance or planning to hand on your wealth, for example, or if you need to set up a trust for charitable purposes or perhaps to look after an incapacitated relative, then a solicitor-stockbroker might be an ideal wealth manager.

## Stockbroker services

If investment management is your primary requirement, you should consider a stock exchange firm. The Association of Private Client Investment Managers (APCIMS) represents more than 90 per cent of private client stockbrokers, as well as an increasing number of other investment managers. Members have direct access to the stockmarket for buying and selling shares. The APCIMS directory of members provides a brief guide to the services offered by its member firms and gives an indication of the minimum size of portfolio accepted by the firm.

In theory there are three types of stockbroker service, although in practice the boundaries between advisory and discretionary are blurred and many investors require a combination of the two. The following definitions, therefore, are intended only as a guide:

### Dealing or 'execution only' service

This service is designed for investors who do not require advice but who need a stockbroker to buy and sell shares for them. Some stockbrokers specialise in this low-cost, no-frills service and offer competitive rates and a rapid service – particularly via the internet.

Do remember though, with an execution only service you will get information on prices of shares but no comment or opinion on the merits of your choice. So don't expect a phone call even if your broker has a hot tip.

## Advisory service

With an advisory service, usually you would make the buying and selling decisions based on a combination of your own ideas and the advice of your manager. In practice there are different types of advisory service. You may want a stockbroker to advise on the sale and purchase of your shares. Alternatively, you may want a more comprehensive service to include advice on capital gains tax and to provide regular valuations of your portfolio.

> Some people will pay a lot of money for that information, but then your daughter would lose a father, instead of gaining a husband.
>
> Michael Corleone, *The Godfather* (1972)

The main point to remember is that an advisory manager will not take any investment decisions without your authority, although he will give you an opinion. Whether you contact your broker at regular intervals or he phones you with tips is a matter of preference. A mixture of both is probably pragmatic.

## Discretionary service

If you want your stockbroker to make all the decisions for you, then you need a discretionary or portfolio management service. This does not mean you lose control entirely. You and your manager will have meetings to discuss your current financial circumstances, your investment aims and any ethical views you may have. Your discretionary manager will work with this plan and keep you up to date with changes in your portfolio.

In addition to investment management, many stockbrokers offer a broader financial planning service. This can cover tax, pensions, mortgages, life assurance, school fees, inheritance tax, cash and deposits.

# Paying for advice

Professional advisers – stockbrokers, accountants and solicitors, for example – are fee based and any sales commission would be offset against fees or reinvested in your plan. The broader band of IFAs may operate on a fee basis, accept commission or do both. This can be convenient or confusing depending on your point of view.

As a rough guide, for good independent advice you can expect to pay at least £80 to £130 per hour. If you think this is expensive remember that in most cases you will pay far more through commission for a long-term invest-ment plan. Like the proverbial lunch, there is no such thing as free advice.

---

❄ c o o l
❄ advice
A good financial planner will take a holistic or integrated approach to your financial affairs, identify your objectives and review the strengths and weaknesses of your current arrangements and then make recommendations.

---

Some adviser websites offer a discount on initial (upfront) commission but the company will usually take what is known as a 'trailer' commission worth 0.5 per cent of your fund after the first year. On a long-term investment this can still be more costly than an upfront fee with all the commission reinvested.

## Sales commission reduces flexibility

Investment companies are required by law to disclose all their charges, includ-ing sales commission, in a pre-sale 'key features' document. You get at least 14 days after receiving this, during which time you can cancel if you change your mind.

Just because a company gives you this document it doesn't mean it has to make it easy for you to understand it. It's worth wading through the key fea-tures mountain of papers to find the reduction in yield. This figure tells you by how much the total charges will reduce your annual return.

Commission rates vary depending on the size of premium and the term of the contract. As a rough guide you can assume that on a 'single premium' or one-off payment to a pension or life assurance investment plan the sales com-mission will be 4–6 per cent of your investment. For a 25-year 'regular pre-mium' plan, where you agree to pay a certain amount each month or each year, the commission could be worth about 70 per cent of the value of your first year's contributions.

Now, over the long term there is very little difference between the total commission cost for a regular premium plan and a plan where you pay in the same amount but your contributions are classed as a series of single premi-ums. However, regular premium plans can be inflexible. This is because many life and pension companies, particularly the direct sales operations, pay advisers upfront all of the commission that would otherwise have been paid over the entire investment period. This means that if you pull out in the early years you will have very little to show for your money.

If you do buy commission-based products, your best bet is to ask for single premium or 'recurring' single premium terms. Under this system each contribution is treated as a one-off and only the commission related to that amount is paid to the adviser. However, to encourage regular savers some companies have low charges on regular premium contracts, so do ask before signing up.

> **Julie** Is that a proposition?
> **John Steed** More of a sly suggestion.
>
> *The Avengers* (1961)

Charges are very important but should not be the sole selection criterion. If your investment company turns out to be one of the worst performers in its category, it is little comfort to know that the charges are modest.

# The client agreement

If you plan to use your adviser on a regular basis you should have a written agreement that sets out the firm's terms and what services it will provide. A clearly worded client agreement gives you a benchmark against which you can judge the adviser's performance, particularly where the firm has direct responsibility for investing your money. The following checklist includes the main points in a client agreement. You should add any further points that apply to your particular circumstances.

## Client agreement checklist

- The regulation of the adviser under the Financial Services Act 1986
- Which services this entitles the adviser to carry out and the services it is not authorised to undertake. For example, is the adviser authorised to hold client money?
- Permission (required by the Consumer Credit Act 1974) for the adviser to act on your behalf to negotiate mortgages, loans and overdrafts.
- The period of agreement and period of notice on both sides (usually a minimum of 30 days).
- Your responsibility to provide the information the adviser needs. (For example, to give appropriate advice your adviser needs a clear idea of your existing investments and your attitude to risk).

▶

- Details of access to your other advisers, for example, your bank manager, accountant and pension provider.

- Your right to veto any recommendations.

- A confidentiality clause.

- Details of how your documents will be stored.

- Fee rates per hour for different level of advisers within the firm and details of any due dates for regular fees.

- Details of VAT likely to be charged.

- Treatment of commissions if the adviser acts on a fee basis – for example, does the firm reinvest this money or offset it against fees.

- Treatment of complaints and disputes.

## Changing your adviser

By the time you realise you need a new and better adviser you are likely to have collected a lot of financial baggage and be the proud owner of an un-co-ordinated assortment of investments and insurance plans sold by an even less co-ordinated range of financial institutions.

> **cool advice** Charges are very important but should not be the sole selection criterion. If your investment company turns out to be one of the worst performers in its category, it is little comfort to know that the charges are modest.

Your new adviser cannot plan for your future goals if he or she doesn't know where you are now. So, one of the adviser's first jobs is to evaluate what you have already got so that the firm can prepare a full fact find. To do this it will need to contact all of your existing providers and notify them that it has taken over as your adviser. At the same time it will send a pro-forma to providers to get an up-to-date picture of the terms and conditions of your insurance policies and investment plans. Many people accumulate duplicate pension plans and insurance policies. Overall you might be paying the right amount in pension contributions for your age and earnings but the cost in policy fees and commissions is likely to be excessive.

When you transfer the agency agreement to the new firm you need to discuss how your adviser is to be remunerated. With most insurance policies and regular premium investments the provider is likely to pay a commission to your existing adviser. The simplest way to deal with this is to transfer the commission payments to your new adviser who will accept this as part of the overall remuneration, if the firm works on a commission basis, or offset it against fees.

In the case of an investment plan, what you can't do is arrange to reinvest the commission in your fund once it is established on a commission-paying basis. This is not the fault of the adviser. Insurance companies in particular have notoriously archaic systems designed to deduct commissions for advisers from your premiums. Once a plan or policy is set up on this basis, it is virtually impossible to change it.

For the same reasons, if you dismiss an adviser and deal with an insurance company directly, in most cases you will not benefit from reduced costs. Instead the insurance company will pocket the commission it would otherwise have paid to your adviser.

> **Colonel Harry Brightman** Look, sir, we can't just do nothing.
> **General Allenby** Why not? It's usually best.
> *Lawrence of Arabia* (1962)

If you plan to use your adviser on a regular basis you should have a written agreement that sets out the firm's terms and what services it will provide.

In the terms of business client agreement (see above) your new adviser should explain its services clearly and set out the level and method of charging. Don't entrust the adviser with anything until you have signed this agreement. This is your assurance that the firm will act within the guidelines and boundaries agreed and if it fails to do so the agreement provides you with access to redress and eligibility to the Financial Ombudsman's Service (see Appendix 3).

# Further information

Association of Solicitor Investment Managers: 01892 870065 (www.asim.org.uk)
Association of Private Client Investment Managers and Stockbrokers: (www.apcims.co.uk)
Financial Services Authority: 0845 606 1234 (www.fsa.gov.uk)

IFA Promotion: 0117 971 1177 (www.unbiased.co.uk)
Institute of Chartered Accountants: 020 7920 8100 (www.icaew.co.uk)
Institute of Financial Planning (IFP): 0117 606 4434
(www.financialplanning.org.uk)
Money Management Register of Fee Based Advisers: 0870 013 1925
Look for firms authorised to give investment advice or phone the investment
business enquiry line on 01908 546 319.
Society of Financial Advisers: 020 7417 4419 (www.sofa.org)
Solicitors for Independent Financial Advice: 01372 721172
(www.solicitor-ifa.co.uk)

# La dolce vita

**I honestly think you should calm down, take a stress pill and think things over.**

Hal, *2001: A Space Odyssey* (1968)

**Chamlee**  They say he isn't fit to be buried here.
**Robert**  What? In Boot Hill?
**Henry**  Why there's nothing up there but murderous cut throats and derelict old barflies, and if they ever felt exclusive brother, they're past it now.

*The Magnificent Seven* (1960)

5

# Life assurance:
# Your money and your life

After reading this chapter you will

*take out membership of the gym*

*get new glasses so you can read the small print*

*feel like you have a price tag on your head – and be right*

**IF YOU HAVE ANY DEPENDANTS** who would suffer financially as a result of your death then you need life assurance. If you die your family gets very little from the state. The sum assured – that is the amount of cover you take out – should do two things:

- ■ It should repay any outstanding loans including the mortgage.
- ■ It should allow your family to maintain its standard of living by replacing your income in full or by topping up any other benefits you may receive.

## How much cover do you need?

The amount of cover you buy must be geared to your liabilities. As a rough guide you could multiply your salary by 10 to provide a lump sum for your dependants which, when invested, will generate a reasonable replacement annual income. A more precise method is to calculate the income you actually need to meet expenditure, including the cost of outstanding loans.

Consider carefully the period you need to insure. One way of looking at this is to cover the period during which any borrowing remains outstanding and until the children have ceased to be dependent – up to age 23 if you expect them to go to university. Wealthy individuals who plan to retire early should provide cover until they expect their earnings to stop. Don't forget that if you still have young children, the partner responsible for childcare must also be insured. The cost of a full-time nanny could easily run to £10,000 a year.

The basic calculation then is 'income requirement plus debt minus any existing cover'. Existing cover may be provided by your company pension scheme or other private insurances. Pension schemes can provide up to four times the level of your annual salary as a tax-free cash lump sum if you die. They should also provide a spouse's pension and possibly a pension for your children if they are under 18.

 **Most life assurance policies work on the 'you drop dead, we pay up' principle.**

The main drawback with life assurance linked to your company pension scheme is that it only applies while you are working and contributing. If you are in this position, make the most of it while it lasts, but be prepared to top up with private insurance if your employment circumstances change. In particular, make sure the cover provided by your old and new jobs overlaps. A common mistake is to go off for a holiday between jobs and to forget to arrange stop-gap insurance.

Personal pension plans provide life cover. However, in this case the value will not be linked to your salary but instead will depend on how much is in your fund. If you have only recently started a pension plan this could be very little so you will need to pay for extra life assurance while your fund is building up. You can also use up to 5 per cent of your personal pension contribution allowance to pay for life assurance. However, you may need to pay maximum contributions to your pension so think carefully before you use this option.

# Which type of policy?

Once you identify the shortfall in your provision you can use one of the methods listed below to fill the gap. The two simplest products are level term assurance and family income benefit. The term assurance lump sum can be invested to provide an annual income and/or used to pay off debt, while family income benefit can directly replace the shortfall in annual income.

> I got the motive, which is money, and the body, which is dead.
>
> Chief Gillespie, *In the Heat of the Night* (1967)

Most life assurance policies work on the 'you drop dead, we pay up' principle. However, some companies offer whole of life plans which combine insurance and investment by deducting the cost of life cover from your savings plan. The following descriptions explain your basic options.

## Level term assurance

This provides a tax-free cash lump sum if you die within the period insured. However, if you die the day after the term expires you get nothing. Unless the policy is assigned to cover a specific liability – for example, your mortgage debt – it is sensible to write it under trust so that the lump sum does not form part of your estate if you die. In this way the policy proceeds could be passed on to your children, for example, without having to wait for probate to be granted to your executors.

 **cool advice** As a general rule it is better to avoid products that combine insurance and investment.

Life assurance can be written on a single or joint life basis. A joint life policy covers more than one person – typically a husband and wife. It may be written to pay out if just one of the spouses dies ('joint life first death') or only when both have died ('joint life second death'). Experts reckon that in most cases it is better – and only slightly more expensive – to arrange individual policies. However, joint policies can be useful in inheritance planning so that the sum covers the bill for inheritance tax that your children might otherwise have to pay when the second parent dies. Term assurance comes in other forms.

- **Convertible renewable** term assurance gives you the right to extend the insurance period without further medical underwriting or, in some cases, to convert to an investment linked plan. The former can be useful if you need to increase your life cover when you are older. Generally you would be asked to undergo a medical and could pay much higher premiums if you are not in good health.

- **Decreasing** term assurance reduces at regular intervals and can be used to protect a debt which reduces in a similar way – for example, where the outstanding debt decreases over the loan period at regular intervals. However, repayment mortgage protection insurance is structured in a slightly different way to accommodate the specific pattern of the capital debt reduction.

  Decreasing term assurance can also be used as a means of covering an inheritance tax (IHT) liability where you have transferred assets to someone other than your spouse (known as a 'potentially exempt transfer') and there would be a reducing IHT liability if you died during the seven years following the transfer. Remember, the insurance need only cover the potential tax liability – that is, a maximum of 40 per cent of the asset value in excess of £250,000 (in 2002–2003) – not the whole of the gift.

> ❄ c o o l
> **advice**
> If you are considerably overweight or you smoke, your premiums may be 'loaded' – in other words you pay more because there is a greater chance of an early death.

- **Increasing** term assurance automatically increases the level of cover, usually in line with retail price inflation or a fixed amount – say, 5 per cent – without further medical underwriting. If you opt for this type of insurance your annual premiums will also increase.

- **Personal pension** term assurance is available to the self-employed and employees not in company schemes. Premiums attract full tax relief provided they fall within your overall annual contribution limits. As mentioned above, although you can use up to 5 per cent of your annual pension contribution allowance to pay for life assurance, you may not want to do so if you need to pay the maximum amount to your pension plan.

## Family income benefit

Family income benefit (FIB) provides a regular income from the date of death until the end of the insurance period. Tax treatment is favourable because although the proceeds are paid in the form of a regular monthly income, technically they are classed as capital so there is no income tax to pay. You can arrange for the income to remain the same ('level') or to increase each year.

## Whole of life plans

As the name suggests, whole of life plans pay a benefit whenever you die: there is no specific term. Given the certainty that the policy must pay out at some point, naturally the premiums tend to be higher than for term assurance. Whole of life policies combine insurance and investment. Your monthly premiums are invested and from this fund the insurance company deducts the amounts necessary to provide the life cover. When you die you get the fund value or the sum assured, whichever is greater. Some policies require you to pay premiums up to the time of your death, while others make them 'paid up' at a certain age, after which you no longer need to pay premiums. One common use for this type of policy is to provide a lump sum to cover your inheritance tax liability when you die.

## Tips on buying your insurance

As a general rule it is better to avoid products that combine insurance and investment. If what you need is a sensible amount of life cover, then simple term assurance is likely to offer best value. If you want to build up some capital for your dependants you could, for example, invest in funds held in a tax-efficient individual savings account (ISA) and take out a decreasing term assurance plan to provide a lump sum if you die early before your fund has had a chance to build up.

> My Lord, whatever I done, don't strike me blind for another couple of minutes.
>
> Dragline, *Cool Hand Luke* (1967)

The premium you pay for your insurance will depend on your age, sex and state of health, among other factors. You have a duty to complete the proposal form honestly and accurately. If you are considerably overweight or you smoke, your premiums may be 'loaded' – in other words you pay more because there is a greater chance of an early death. Certain dangerous sports will also raise eyebrows in the underwriting department and in turn may raise your premiums. In some cases your policy may not cover you while you indulge in these activities.

The proposal form will also ask if you have ever been tested for HIV (AIDS). If you are a single man and want a substantial amount of cover, you will probably be requested to complete a 'lifestyle' questionnaire which is designed to discover whether your private life exposes you to a higher than average risk of AIDS or other sexual diseases.

## The medical

Both men and women who want to take out a large amount of cover should expect to be asked to undergo a medical examination. Despite the aversion most people have to this, it does actually work in your favour. Where policies are not fully medically underwritten (this is usually the case with policies sold by direct mail or through off-the-page advertising), the underwriters assume there will be a much greater incidence of claims so the premiums may be much higher than a medically underwritten contract.

> Well, your blood pressure is off the scale, if you call that green stuff in your veins blood.
>
> Dr McCoy, *Startrek* (1966)

The premium will also depend on the company. Life assurance is a very competitive market, which is why independent advice is essential. These days a good adviser will have access to a comprehensive database that will enable him or her to select the right features and the best rates available at any given time.

Your adviser should also make sure your premium rate is guaranteed. The cheapest rates are often offered by companies that reserve the right to 'review' premiums at any time. With reviewable premiums, effectively you are writing the insurance company a blank cheque.

## How to pay

You may be offered a choice of payment options – for example, you could pay annually by cheque or monthly by direct debit. Direct debit is probably the safest method because the payments are guaranteed. If by mistake you over-look a reminder for your annual cheque your cover may lapse and if you have to reapply you may find that rates have increased due to your increased age or a change in your state of health.

## Further information

The best way to buy protection insurances is through an independent adviser. See Chapter 4.

**Mrs Banks** She seemed so solemn and cross.

**George Banks** Never confuse efficiency with a liver complaint.

*Mary Poppins* (1964)

# 6

# Disability insurance: What's up doc?

After reading this chapter you will

*take 20 supplements a day*

*be glad your new employer pays for this insurance*

*treat your body with respect – repairs are costly*

**LIFE ASSURANCE PROTECTS YOUR FAMILY** if you die, but it is equally important to insure against loss of income if you become disabled or too ill to work.

Despite the plethora of product names, there are essentially two types of insurance policy – one that pays a replacement income (also known as permanent health insurance or PHI) and a second that pays a lump sum (critical illness). If you bear in mind that everything else is just a variation on these two themes you will avoid overinsuring through multiple policies or underinsuring by purchasing a policy that is very restrictive.

> It's the story of my life. I always get the fuzzy end of the lollipop.
>
> Sugar Kane, *Some Like It Hot* (1959)

Buying income protection ought to be an easy exercise – but it isn't. Some protection products are very complicated and riddled with small print. Others may not be regulated by the Financial Services Act. When disaster strikes you could find out too late that the exclusions render the policy worthless. Ideally you should buy through an independent financial adviser who should search the market for the best terms as well as the best price.

## State benefits

Employees have very little statutory protection when it comes to long-term sickness. The only requirement for an employer is to pay statutory sick pay from day four of your illness to week 28. Statutory sick pay is less than £65 per week, while the state long-term incapacity benefit is about £71, although there are various supplements for dependants and age. You can claim the state incapacity benefit while you are in receipt of your income replacement benefits.

---

**cool advice**   Some employers provide good disability insurance through group schemes at work, so if you leave make sure you buy private insurance.

---

The chances of qualifying for the state incapacity benefit are slim. In April 1995 the government changed the definition of qualifying disability from 'can't do *own* job' to 'can't do *any* job'. This means that even though your medical condition prevents you from continuing your profession, if you can sweep the streets you will be classed as fit for work and you will not qualify for the state long-term incapacity benefit.

## Your employer's scheme

Some employers provide good disability insurance through group schemes at work, so while you are with your current employer it is important to check your existing levels of cover. This is an important point to consider if you change jobs. The company's policy should be set out in your contract of employment. For example, the contract might say that if you are ill the company will pay your full salary for a specified period, after which your pay will depend on the terms and conditions of the group disability scheme. If your employer does not cover you or you are self-employed, then you need a private policy.

Under a group PHI scheme the insurer pays the benefit to your employer who then deducts PAYE, national insurance and pension contributions in the usual way before paying you. This means that you are able to remain an active member of your company pension scheme and maintain eligibility to state benefits.

 The best definition of disability is 'unable to follow *own* occupation'.

PHI only replaces your income during the years you would actually have been at work. Once you reach your employer's normal retirement age the PHI benefit stops and your employer's pension scheme starts to pay you a retirement income.

Of course in most cases you would expect to return to work after a full recovery. At this point the benefit stops and your normal salary resumes. But what if you only partially recover from an accident or your recovery is not complete and you are unable to resume your former occupation? In these very common circumstances, assistance with rehabilitation forms an integral feature of top of the range group PHI schemes.

An increasing number of employers offer PHI at a cheap rate even though they do not make a contribution towards your premiums. This type of 'voluntary' benefit can offer excellent value, but employers are under no obligation to arrange good terms. So caveat emptor – buyer beware – applies just as much if you buy through your employer as if you buy elsewhere.

## Private 'income protection' insurance

Income protection or PHI is the most comprehensive insurance product. It pays you an income worth up to two-thirds of your salary (depending on how much you are prepared to pay in premiums) and will maintain payments until you are well enough to return to work or, if necessary, right up until retirement.

This type of insurance typically costs £500 a year for a man in his early fifties. Women pay much higher premiums due to the higher incidence of gynaecology claims (sorry ladies). You can cut premiums if you opt for a waiting period between the date you fall ill or become disabled and the date you claim benefit. The minimum waiting period is four weeks but premiums reduce if you sign up for a three, six or twelve-month 'deferment' period. If you do opt for a long deferment, then make sure you have enough savings to cover your outgoings during this period. Policies with a 'reviewable' premium may be cheaper, but before you buy one you should understand the risks. 'Reviewable' means you have no control over future rate increases, so frankly it's a gamble.

> No 9000 computer has ever made a mistake or distorted information. We are all, by any practical definition of the words, foolproof and incapable of error.
>
> Hal 9000, *2001: A Space Odyssey* (1968)

Advisers stress that it is essential to link the insured income to retail price inflation – both during the insurance period and during the payment period. This will cost extra but without it the purchasing power of your income would quickly be eroded.

## The definition of disability

This is the deciding factor when the company considers whether you are too ill to work and therefore eligible to claim benefit. The best definition is 'unable to follow *own* occupation', with the possible addition of the phrase 'or an occupation suitable by training, education, experience and status'. The worst definition – and one to avoid at all costs – is 'unable to follow *any* occupation'. This type of policy will be cheaper but you must be totally incapacitated in order to claim – as is the case with the state scheme.

# Critical illness

Critical illness insurance is quite different from PHI and if you can afford it you should have both. Critical illness insurance pays the owner of the policy – which could be you, your spouse or even your business partner – a tax-free lump sum on the diagnosis of a range of illnesses or accidents. Most policies use six standard definitions – for example cancer, heart attack, stroke, coronary artery bypass surgery, kidney failure and major organ transplant. The lump sum is extremely useful if you become disabled or frail and you either need to move to special accommodation or to alter your present home.

> Oh, Marilyn ... the circles under your eyes. How lovely you look today.
>
> Lily Munster, *The Munsters* (1964)

However, if your illness or disability is not on the list of qualifying conditions you won't get a penny, even though you are unable to work. Some policies include 'permanent total disability' on the payment list and this is a valuable addition.

Probably less important, but a consideration nevertheless, is that critical illness insurance may create a potential inheritance tax bill. If you have a major illness before you die, your insurance lump sum will boost the value of your estate and in the 2002–2003 tax year anything above £250,000 will be subject to IHT at 40 per cent.

## Waiver of premium for pension plans

This is another restricted version of PHI. Waiver of premium insurance guarantees your pension premiums are credited until you are well enough to return to work or, if necessary, up to your retirement date. If you cannot afford an adequate level of PHI then do try to get waiver of premium, as this will at least keep your pension planning on target.

 **c o o l advice** You can cut premiums if you opt for a waiting period between the date you fall ill or become disabled and the date you claim benefit.

## Further information

The best way to buy protection insurance is through an independent adviser. See Chapter 4.

**Lycus**  Is it contagious?
**Psuedolus**  Have you ever seen a plague
that wasn't?

*A Funny Thing Happened on the Way to the Forum* (1966)

# 7

# Medical insurance:
# Carry on nurse

After reading this chapter you will

*treat your GP with greater respect*

*get that facelift on the company's medical insurance while you can*

*marry a medical consultant*

**THE WAITING LIST FOR MANY OPERATIONS** under the National Health Service (NHS) is still over a year for 1 in 20 patients and over six months for one in four. This does not include the often lengthy period between GP referral and seeing a specialist. Regional variations in the provision of care can also make a huge difference to how quickly your particular condition will be treated.

If you want to jump the queue you have to pay. While the more wealthy may decide to draw on cash reserves, for most people the only realistic option is to take out private medical insurance (PMI). About 11 per cent of the population has some form of private cover at a cost of over £1.5 billion in annual premiums.

## What the state provides

The NHS aims to provide a full range of medical services for all residents, regardless of their income. These services are financed mainly out of general taxation. Most forms of treatment, including hospital care, are provided free of charge 'at the point of delivery', to use the jargon, but you may have to wait a considerable time before being treated. This waiting period varies from area to area.

## What your employer provides

Some employers offer group PMI as part of an employee benefits package but the level of cover varies considerably. Many employers have increased the number of exclusions – for example, stress-related conditions are likely to be excluded since these can be very complicated and expensive. Your employer may also ask you to pay an excess or he may agree to pay your premiums but will not cover the rest of your family. Premiums paid by your employer are treated as a benefit in kind and are therefore taxable.

> Come with us quietly Rosemary. Don't argue or make a scene.
>
> R. Abe Sapirstein, *Rosemary's Baby* (1968)

If you are in a group scheme, find out what happens when you leave the company if you want to continue the insurance on an individual basis. This is particularly important if you are coming up to retirement, where your age and past medical treatment could result in very high individual premiums. Some insurers offer a discount when you move from a group scheme to a private plan.

Where your employer does not provide a scheme, check with your trade union or professional association to see if they offer discount terms.

---

**cool advice**   Private medical insurance (PMI) is a complex product and contract conditions can be lengthy. With over 20 companies each offering a range of options, it is wise to seek independent financial advice.

# How PMI works

PMI is a complex product and contract conditions can be lengthy. With over 20 companies each offering a range of options, it is wise to seek independent financial advice. An adviser should identify the best plan for your needs and price range and will know which insurers offer good service and are prompt with payments. Some advisers are able to offer better terms than are available if you buy direct from the PMI company.

It is important to understand what conditions PMI does and, in particular, does *not* cover. PMI pays for private treatment for *acute curable conditions* – that is, cases where an operation or a short-term course of treatment can put right things right permanently. It does not pay for emergency treatment, nor does it pay for chronic illness.

> You're a 71-year-old man who has lost interest in sex. Does your doctor have anything to help you?
>
> Peter Marshall, *The Hollywood Squares* (1966)

This can lead to confusion. For example, under your policy you may qualify for private treatment to have a condition investigated and diagnosed, but if it is a long-term illness rather than an acute curable condition you could find yourself back under the NHS.

The premiums you pay for your PMI will depend on the level of cover you require, your age and medical history. It will also depend on the type of hospital you choose to attend. Most insurers group hospitals into three bands – London teaching (the most expensive), national and provincial. Your adviser can help you to choose the appropriate band for your area.

## Different types of PMI

It is very hard to compare PMI policies because they all seem to offer something slightly different. However, most fall into three broad categories:

- standard
- budget
- over-sixties.

Standard cover should pay for virtually everything, but if you want private alternative medicine, GP and dental treatment, among other features, you will probably have to pay for a deluxe version.

> ❄ c o o l
>    advice    Standard cover should pay for virtually everything, but if you want private alternative medicine, GP and dental treatment, among other features, you will probably have to pay for a deluxe version.

Budget plans limit the insurer's risk in several ways. Each carries a risk, so do consider your priorities carefully. For example, a plan might restrict the treatment to a 'menu' of the most common operations. If your condition qualifies then you receive prompt treatment. If it doesn't, tough. A second method of reducing the insurers' costs is to set a monetary limit either per annum or per treatment. PMI companies claim these limits are usually generous enough to cover most major operations, but there is always the concern that you might run out of money halfway through a course of treatment, particularly if complications set in.

An alternative budget concept is the 'six-week' plan that provides standard levels of cover, but only if you cannot be treated under the NHS within six weeks of the consultant's diagnosis. A six-week wait may not sound too onerous, but do bear in mind that you may have a long delay between your GP's referral and actually seeing your consultant – unless of course you pay for a private consultation, which is unlikely to be covered by this type of policy.

Name: Richard Kimble.
Profession: Doctor of medicine.
Narrator: *The Fugitive* (1963)

Finally, some insurers contain costs by asking you to agree to pay an excess – that is, the first £100 or so of every claim. This is probably the most acceptable method of cutting premiums, although the reductions achieved are not so dramatic as under the other budget plans.

Over-sixties plans cover the 60 to 75 age range and offer basic rate tax relief on premiums. Anyone can pay the premiums and claim the tax relief, so you could pay for your parent's policy or even for someone who is not a relative. If you want to apply for medical insurance when you are over 75, you are unlikely to have any success. At this stage it's a case of using your capital wisely if you need a comparatively straightforward operation like a hip replacement, where the NHS waiting lists can be very long.

## Managed care

One of the latest trends in PMI is the use of managed care to contain costs. With managed care the insurer monitors the claim from the outset, before treatment has started and before the first penny has been spent. This means you have to check the insurer will pay up before you actually start treatment (this is known as pre-authorisation). You may also be asked to use certain groups of hospitals where the insurer has negotiated special rates.

# Medical history

Unless you are in a top-of-the-range group scheme run by your employer, the PMI insurer will exclude most pre-existing conditions. This will be done in one of two ways. Where the contract is *fully underwritten* you must disclose your complete medical history and the insurer may impose exclusions as a result. If there is a *moratorium clause* you would not need to disclose your medical history but all pre-existing conditions would be excluded for a period of time – typically two years – after which they would also be covered. Some pre-existing conditions – heart disease and psychiatric illness, for example – may be permanently excluded.

 **Where the contract is *fully underwritten* you must disclose your complete medical history and the insurer may impose exclusions as a result.**

# Premium increases

When selecting your plan, your adviser should consider the PMI company's track record on premium increases. As with any form of general insurance, when your policy comes up for renewal each year insurers can increase premiums without warning. If you are unhappy with the new premium your only option is to vote with your feet and leave. However, if you already have a claim underway it may be impossible to switch insurers. It will also be awkward if you have made claims in the past five years since a new insurer would class any recent health problems as pre-existing conditions and exclude them. If your health has been particularly poor, you might even find yourself uninsurable.

## Further information

The best way to buy protection insurance is through an independent adviser. See Chapter 4.

Bedrooms do not matter. But I must have a big garden. I am a peasant at heart and I want to grow roses in my old age.

Colonel Stark, *Funeral in Berlin* (1966)

# 8

# Long-term care:
# At the end of the day

After reading this chapter you will

*build a granny annex and save a fortune*

*build an old people's home and make a fortune*

*grow old in Scotland – it treats its elderly better*

**THE PROBLEM OF SUPPORTING** a growing elderly population is not confined to the UK, although Germany is the only European country so far to introduce a tax specifically for nursing care. To date the UK government has limited its consultation on long-term care to voluntary insurance and savings plans.

> If you save your breath I feel a man like you can manage it. And if you don't manage it, you'll die. Only slowly, very slowly old friend.
>
> Tuco, *The Good, The Bad and The Ugly* (1996)

Under the NHS and Community Care Act 1993, the responsibility for assessing need and the payment of nursing home fees shifted from the Department of Social Security to the already financially overstretched local authorities. The rules were revised in April 2001. If you have assets and investments worth over £18,000 you must pay your own bills. The value of your house is not included initially in the means test but after three months this will be taken into account unless you have a spouse or other dependent relative still living at home. As a result many single people have to sell their homes in order to pay the fees.

 **cool advice** **If you live in Scotland you may be entitled to higher subsidies towards your nursing home costs.**

The average nursing home in England costs £20,400 a year, rising to £25,000 to 30,000 in the South-East. In England and Wales from October 2001 people in care will be able to claim up to £110 per week to cover nursing care needs but they will still have to pay for their own personal care and residential costs unless they have assets below the means test limit. If you live in Scotland you may be entitled to higher subsidies from April 2002 – £90 per week for personal care and an additional £65 for nursing care.

## Check your options carefully

If you are interested in long-term care (LTC) cover, do seek the help of a specialist independent adviser. Most of these plans are complicated and expensive. Not all of these policies are governed by the strict financial services regulatory system. One organisation well worth contacting is IFACare, which is a voluntary association for independent advisers who agree to adhere to a high standard of ethics and a strict code of practice to ensure best advice is given on LTC. You should also seek legal advice. If you want to act on behalf of an elderly parent, for example, you must have enduring power of attorney in order to appoint a professional adviser to help manage your relative's affairs.

> **Ten thousand in gold cuts an awful lot of family ties.**
> Bishop, *The Wild Bunch* (1969)

Before considering a dedicated LTC policy, check if you are covered under other protection insurance plans. Some critical illness policies pay a cash lump sum if you suffer 'loss of independence'.

If you are tempted to give away all your worldly goods in order to qualify for full financial support under the social services means test, think twice. If you make a substantial gift within six months of entering care your local authority may be able to claw back the assets. Where the gap is longer the authority could take you to court.

There are two ways to insure the cost of LTC. With a 'pre-funded' plan you pay regular premiums or a lump sum ahead of the time when you may need to claim. If you are elderly and not insured, an 'immediate care' plan would guarantee a regular income to pay the nursing home fees but for this you would need to invest a substantial sum.

## Pre-funding plans

At the time of writing only half a dozen insurance companies offered pre-funded plans. The policies pay the benefit to your nursing home or, in some cases, to your carer. You may also qualify for help towards the cost of home alternations where this would enable you to stay put. Annual benefit, which is tax free, is usually limited to about £25,000. However, most people can insure for much less than this if they have other sources of income from pensions and investments.

 **cool advice** An elderly parent might consider an 'impaired life annuity' as this offers a high income if an illness is likely to reduce life expectancy.

To qualify for benefit you must fail two or three 'activities of daily living' (ADLs). ADL tests – also used by social services for those who qualify for state help – include washing, dressing, feeding, continence and mobility. Cognitive impairment should also be on the list, given the rapid increase in the number of sufferers of Alzheimer's disease and similar conditions.

As with income protection you can reduce premiums if you opt for a long 'deferment period' before receiving the first payment. This can be anything from four weeks to two years. You can also reduce premiums if you restrict cover to a limited payment period – for example, two to three years. However, whether you would enjoy peace of mind with this type of policy is questionable. Certainly, conditions that involve cognitive impairment can result in a lengthy stay in care.

The cost of insurance varies, but as a rough guide a man aged 65 who wants to insure an annual benefit of £12,000 would pay monthly premiums of about £70 or a single premium of £9,500.

# Immediate care annuities

If a relative needs to go into a home you might consider an immediate care annuity, although to fund this you may need to sell their house. Where the elderly person could stay at home, provided certain care was available and alterations were carried out, a home income plan might be more appropriate (see Chapter 20).

An annuity provides a regular income for life in return for your lump sum investment. One option for this age group is an 'impaired life annuity' as this offers a higher income if you have an illness which is likely to reduce your life expectancy.

The impairment must adversely affect life expectation and not just impact on the quality of life. Qualifying impairments include AIDS, Alzheimer's, cancer, cirrhosis, coronary disease, diabetes and stroke. Depending on your impairment you could secure an income up to 30 per cent higher than that offered by a standard plan. If you are interested, do go to an annuity special-ist who will select the best terms for your particular circumstances.

Unlike pre-funded plans, the annuity payments are not tax free. Part of the income is treated as a return of capital so this is not taxed. The interest ele-ment is taxed but this reduces with age.

# LTC investment alternatives

LTC is an insurance product, not an investment. Insurance relies on the pool-ing of risk so the benefits of those who need to claim are paid for by the pre-miums of those who do not. This may be a price worth paying for peace of mind, but some investors regard it as money down the drain.

> **This isn't a hospital! It's an insane asylum!**
> Hot Lips Houliahan, *MASH* (1970)

There is an alternative that combines investment and insurance, but it is relatively new and untested. Only a handful of compa-nies offer this type of product. Under an LTC investment plan, you pay a lump sum into a fund from which the insurance company deducts monthly premi-ums to cover the LTC risk. The products currently available use funds that, for one reason or another, are able to offer gross roll up (that is, the fund does not pay income and capital gains tax). This means that if your fund does well and the investment growth covers the cost of the monthly insurance, your LTC premiums are effectively tax free.

 If you make a substantial financial gift within six months of entering care your local authority may be able to claw back the assets.

If you need to claim, initially you draw your agreed annual benefit from your fund and when this is exhausted the insurer picks up the tab for as long as you remain in care. In some cases, for an extra cost, you may be able to protect part or all your fund so that the insurance covers the benefit payments from the outset. However, if you remain healthy to the end and do not make a claim, you can pass your investment on to your dependants.

## Further information

A list of independent firms of advisers who abide by the IFACare code of conduct is available from:
IFACare Administration
Bridge House
Severn Bridge
Bewdley
Worcs DY12 1AB
Tel: 01299 406040
e-mail: **info@ifacare.co.uk**

Other useful organisations include:
The Association of Independent Care Advisers: 01483 203066
(**www.aica.org.uk**)
Age Concern: 020 8765 7200 (**www.ageconcern.org.uk**)
Help The Aged: 020 7278 1114 (**www.helptheaged.org.uk**)
Care and Repair: 0115 982 1527 (**www.careandrepair-england.org.uk**)
UK Home Care Association: 020 8288 1551 (**www.ukhca.co.uk**)

# The money pit

**You know it could be worse. You get a lot more for your money in Bolivia, I checked on it.**

Butch, *Butch Cassidy and the Sundance Kid* (1969)

**Ten shillings in sixpences, forty-two pounds in thruppences, and seven pence. It's going to be a rather rich pudding, but who cares?**

Chef Ivor Clarke, *Do Not Adjust Your Set* (1967)

# 9

# Equities and bonds without tears

After reading this chapter you will

*understand how your local street market works*

*throw out the dodgy jacket that makes you look like a futures trader*

*still go blank when someone mentions derivatives*

**SAVINGS AND INVESTMENT INSTITUTIONS** are adept at dressing up what are essentially quite straightforward assets. As a result, it is easy to fall into the trap of investing in 'products' and to end up with a growing number of plans and schemes which, when examined in more detail, represent anything but a co-ordinated, well-balanced portfolio.

This chapter explains the characteristics of the asset classes you will come across in your quest for the best investments for your requirements. Keep this information in mind when you consider the wide range of products discussed later in Section 4. The aim is to keep a close watch on the underlying asset allocation and only to use the tax efficient product wrappers where they can enhance the return of your preferred investments.

To make the best of the available tax breaks, you also need to understand the basics of taxation from the family as well as the individual point of view and this is discussed in Chapter 18.

## Securities

Investment literature uses a lot of confusing jargon. Commonly used (and mis-used) terms include 'securities', 'stocks' and 'shares'.

'Securities' is the general name for all stocks and shares. What we call 'shares' today were originally known as 'stocks' because they represented part ownership in the joint stock companies – the precursors to today's public limited companies or plcs. So, to some extent the terms stocks and shares are interchangeable, and we still use the terms *stock*markets and *stock*brokers.

Broadly speaking, stocks are fixed interest securities and shares are the rest. The four main types of securities listed and traded on the UK Stock Exchange are:

- **UK ('domestic') equities:** ordinary shares issued by over 2000 UK companies
- **Overseas equities:** ordinary shares issued by non-UK companies
- **Gilts:** bonds issued by the UK government to raise money to fund any shortfall in public expenditure
- **Bonds:** fixed interest stocks issued by companies and local authorities, among others.

## UK equities

If a company wants to raise finance it has two main options. It can sell part of the ownership of the company by issuing ordinary shares (equities) or it can borrow money by issuing bonds, which are a sophisticated IOU. Shares and bonds are bought and sold on the stockmarket.

Equities are the quoted shares of companies in the UK and tend to dominate most private investors' portfolios, whether they are held directly or are pooled through collective funds such as unit and investment trusts or a pension fund. The return achieved by UK equities, when measured over the long term, has exceeded both price and earnings inflation, but in recent years we have entered a period of falling equity returns and gilt yields, so don't take any 'rules' or 'laws' that explain the way securities behave too seriously. Your aim is to invest in companies that will achieve a good return for your money in exchange for an acceptable level of risk.

Companies 'go public' when they are quoted on the Stock Exchange or Alternative Investment Market. In this way a company can raise the money it needs to expand by issuing shares. A share or equity literally entitles the owner to a specified share in the profits of the company and, if the company is wound up, to a specified share of its assets. The owner of shares is entitled to the dividends – the six-monthly distribution to shareholders of part of the company's profits. The 'dividend yield' on equities is the dividend paid by a company divided by that company's share price.

> ❄ cool
> ❄ advice
> It is easy to fall into the trap of investing in 'products' and to end up with a growing number of plans and schemes which, when examined in more detail, represent anything but a co-ordinated, well-balanced portfolio.

There is no set redemption date for equity when the company is obliged to return your original investment. If as a shareholder you want to convert your investment into cash ('to realise its value'), you must sell your shares through a stockbroker. The price will vary from day to day, so the timing of the purchase and sale of shares is critical.

## Share classes

There are different classes of shares. Most investors buy ordinary shares, which give the holder the right to vote on the constitution of the company's board of directors. Since this is the most common type of share, the term 'ordinary' is usually dropped unless it is to distinguish the shares from a different category. Preference shares carry no voting rights but have a fixed dividend payment, so can be attractive to those seeking a regular income. These shares have 'preference' over ordinary shareholders if the company is wound up – hence the name. There are several sub-classes of equities or equity-related investments.

## Convertibles and warrants

Convertibles and warrants are special types of shares that have characteristics which make them attractive in certain circumstances. Convertibles are more akin to bonds (see below), in that they pay a regular income and have a fixed redemption date. However, a convertible confers the right to *convert* to an ordinary share or preference share at a future date. This can be an attractive proposition if the price is attractive on the convertible date.

Warrants confer a right but not an obligation on the holder to convert to a specific share at a predetermined price and date. The value of the warrant, which itself is traded on the stockmarket, is determined by the difference or premium of the share price over the conversion price of the warrant.

## Derivatives

Derivatives, as the name suggests, *derive* their value from the price of an underlying security. This is the generic term given to futures contracts and options, both of which can be used to reduce risk in an institutional fund or, in the case of options, even in a large private portfolio.

A futures contract binds two parties to a sale or purchase at a specified future date. The price is fixed at the time the contract is taken out. These futures contracts can be used by institutional funds to control risk because they allow the manager quickly to increase or reduce the fund's exposure to an existing asset class. Futures have also proved popular as a cost cutting mechanism, particularly in index tracking funds and other funds where there are rapid changes of large asset allocations.

**Lyle Gorch** Silver rings.
**Dutch Engstrom** Silver rings your butt. Them's washers. Damn!
**Lyle Gorch** We shot our way out of that town for a dollar's worth of steel holes?

*The Wild Bunch* (1969)

Options allow you, for a down payment, to have the right but not the obligation to buy or sell something at an agreed price on a specific date. Some private investors use options as a type of insurance policy to protect their portfolio against a fall in the market.

## Overseas equities

These are similar in principle to UK equities but there are differences in shareholder rights. Investment overseas provides exposure to the growth in foreign markets including younger, fast-growing economies. However, these shares also expose you to currency fluctuations. This can be both good and bad, of course, but the point is that it adds an extra layer of risk. The taxation of foreign shares can be less favourable than UK equities. In particular, some or all of the withholding tax on dividends deducted by the foreign country may not be recoverable.

As a rule of thumb, exposure to the major developed economies, for example the European Union countries, the USA and Canada, is considered beneficial but generally is achieved through collective funds – for example investment trusts. Exposure to the emerging economies is high risk and so only suitable for those prepared to take a punt.

## Bonds

UK bonds are issued by borrowers – for example, the government (these bonds are known as gilt-edged securities or just 'gilts') and companies (corporate bonds). Bonds are also issued by local authorities, overseas governments and overseas companies.

In return for the loan of your money, the borrower agrees to pay a fixed rate of interest (known as the coupon) for the agreed period and to repay your original capital sum on a specified date, known as the maturity or redemption date.

UK domestic bonds are either secured on the company's underlying assets – for example, the company's property – or they are unsecured, in which case there is no physical asset backing the bond's guarantee to pay interest and to repay the capital at maturity. Secured bonds are known as debentures and unsecured bonds are known as loan stocks. Since the security offered by debentures is greater than for loan stocks, the former tend to pay a lower rate of interest.

The point to remember about fixed interest securities is that the investment return is determined more by the level of interest rates than the issuing company's profitability. Provided the issuer remains sufficiently secure to honour the future coupon payments (the regular interest) and redemption payment (the return of the original capital), you know exactly what your return will be, as long as you hold the bond to maturity. Gilts offer the highest degree of security because they are issued by the UK government.

## Traded bonds

If you or a fund manager sells a bond before its maturity date, then the value of the future coupon and redemption payments will depend on the prevailing interest rates at the time of sale. So, if interest rates are rising, then the value of the fixed interest security will fall. This is because for the same amount of capital invested you could get a better return elsewhere. Conversely, if interest rates are falling, then the value of the fixed interest security will be higher because it provides a greater stream of income than you could get from alternative sources.

This volatile pattern of behaviour is more apparent with fixed interest securities that have a long period to run to maturity since they are more likely to be traded before redemption date.

---

❄ **cool advice** **The return achieved by UK equities over the long term has exceeded both price and earnings inflation, but in recent years we have entered a period of falling equity returns and gilt yields, so don't take any 'rules' or 'laws' that explain the way securities behave too seriously.**

---

To summarise, as a general rule equities are considered more risky and volatile than bonds because they behave in an unpredictable way whereas, provided the company or government backing a bond is watertight, the return on a bond *held to maturity* is predictable. However, it is not predictable if you decide to sell before maturity.

## Eurobonds

UK companies can raise money outside the UK market by issuing 'Eurosterling' bonds – that is bonds denominated in sterling but issued on the Eurobond market. Contrary to its name, the Euromarkets are not confined to Europe but are international markets where borrowers and lenders are matched.

The main advantage of Eurosterling bonds, from the borrower's point of view, is that they can reach a much wider range of potential lenders. However, this is not a market for private investors in the UK.

# Index-linked gilts

Index-linked gilts are issued by the UK government and guaranteed to provide interest payments (the coupon) and a redemption value which increases in line with annual inflation. For this reason they are one of the lowest risk assets for income seekers. Having said that, in practice they have not proved particularly attractive compared with other income-generating alternatives.

The return on index-linked gilts in excess of the retail price index varies, but usually it is possible to buy these securities in the marketplace at a price which guarantees a real rate of return to the holder, assuming that the stock is held to maturity.

# Cash

Cash does not refer to stacks of bank notes stuffed under the mattress, but usually means a deposit account. Deposits have the advantage that the value in monetary terms is known and certain at all times. What you don't know is the level of interest you will receive and whether this will fall short of the rate of inflation.

# Property

In investment terms, property usually refers to the ownership of land and buildings that are used by a business or other organisation. The owner of the property receives income from the rent charged to the tenant and over time this rent is expected broadly to keep pace with inflation. The dominant factor in the value of a property is the desirability or otherwise of its location.

There are several problems with property. First, it is often sold in large blocks that cannot easily be split for investment purposes. As a result, only the larger institutional funds can afford (or are wise) to own property directly.

Second, property is a very illiquid asset and it can take several years for the right selling conditions to arise. Moreover, unless you invest via a collective fund, you cannot dispose of your investment piecemeal to make best use of your annual capital gains tax (CGT) exemption but instead could be landed with a whopping CGT bill.

# Comparing equities, bonds and cash (deposits)

It is common practice to compare returns on equities with bonds, and both asset classes with cash (deposits). However, as Barclays Capital pointed out in its annual *Equity-Gilts Study*, it is important to view equities over the long term. During a period of just a few years the returns can be volatile and even negative – as happened in 2000 when the total return from equities was –8.6 per cent after adjusting for inflation. By contrast, gilts returned 6.1 per cent in real terms. In 1999 equities performed well, but in 1998 returns on equities fell far short of gilts again.

Barclays pointed out:

*Timing is therefore very important for equity investors. The received wisdom that long-term investors should concentrate their assets in the equity market is an over-simplification. The case for equity investment may be weak if an investor can realise his or her objectives by means of a less risky strategy.*

Investors keen to keep up with the comparative movements of gilts and equities should refer to the *Financial Times*, which publishes the gilt–equity yield ratio. This tracks the yield on gilts divided by the yield on shares. As a rule of thumb the normal range is between 2 and 2.5, so if it dips or soars well out of this range it may indicate that shares are very expensive or that gilts are very cheap. Market analysts use this as one of the signals to indicate that a bull (lower figure) or bear market (higher figure) is imminent.

 **c o o l advice** **Your aim is to invest in companies that will achieve a good return for your money in exchange for an acceptable level of risk.**

It is also important to keep in mind the relationship between inflation and returns. Barclays' guide points out that inflation is a key determinant of investment returns. Stockmarkets may not be prepared for an inflation 'shock' (a sudden and unexpected change) but they adjust over time and provide a long-term hedge against price rises. Gilts and cash are not suitable inflation hedges.

## Period of investment

Clearly, long-term returns on equities, gilts and cash should be viewed with some caution and certainly should not be treated as a guide to the future. While history indicates that equities should provide a better return than bonds over the *medium to long term*, if you go into the stockmarkets for shorter periods you are in danger of getting your fingers burned, either because the markets take a tumble just before you want to get out or because the fixed costs associated with setting up your investment undermine the return over the short term.

## Dividend reinvestment

This is important. The Barclays study states:

*Dividends account for nearly two-thirds of total returns to equities over long periods of time. Gilts have been poor long-term investments but income from them has outweighed the reduction in capital values. Since 1990, however, the capital values of gilts have been improving.*

## Income from equities or gilts?

Chiswell Associates, in its *Compendium of Stock Market Investment*, provided the following succinct argument in favour of equities as a source of income, as well as capital growth (see sources at the end of this chapter):

*Equities represent part ownership of a business. Equity investors provide the core finance for the business and in return they receive dividends paid out of the company's profits. The remainder of the profits are retained by the company for reinvestment in its business, thus building up its assets, earnings power and future dividend paying potential.*

*The value of equities, therefore rests on the value of the dividend flow which investors receive.*

*If dividend payments grow over the years then, all other things being equal, the value of shares will rise too since the income stream will be more valuable and the total return (income plus capital growth) increases.*

*Investors may buy and sell shares for short-term gain but in the final analysis equity investment is really about income.*

The interest on gilts will look attractive compared with the current income from equities, but since gilt income is fixed, the flow of income from the gilt cannot rise over time in the same way as equity dividends (unless the gilt is index linked – but here the initial income would be quite low).

*Eventually the cash value of the rising equity dividend will catch up and exceed the value of the fixed interest payment. Furthermore, the rising dividend flow will have pulled up the value of the shares whereas the capital value of the gilt will not have changed.*

*This process is accelerated by inflation. By and large companies are able to absorb the costs of inflation by passing on cost increases to customers in the form of higher prices. This preserves the profitability of the business, whereas with fixed interest gilts your capital and income are exposed to inflation.*

## Different styles of institutional fund management

Stock selection refers to the process where the investment manager or private investor chooses individual securities. This topic is covered in Chapter 13.

It is rarely wise for a private investor to imitate the style of an institutional fund manager. The large pension funds, for example, are worth millions of pounds. Some run into billions. This means they can make money on minor price changes due to the sheer volume of their transactions.

> Always keep your bowler on in times of stress, and watch out for the diabolical masterminds.
>
> Emma Peel, *The Avengers* (1961)

Moreover, compared with a private client, institutional funds benefit from very low dealing costs and, in the case of pension and charity funds, almost complete exemption from income and capital gains tax. This means that what might trigger a buy or sell transaction in the institutional market often should be interpreted as a much more cautious 'hold' position by the private investor.

## Active managers

Active investment managers aim to increase a fund's value by deviating from a specific benchmark – for example, a stockmarket index. There are two basic techniques used in active stock selection.

The starting point for active managers who adopt a bottom-up approach is the company in which the manager may invest. The manager will look at in-house and external research on the company's history and potential future prospects. This will include an examination of the strength of the balance sheet, the company's trading history, the management's business strategy and the price/earnings ratio (the market price of a share divided by the company's earnings/profits per share in its latest 12-month trading period).

> **cool advice** It is rarely wise for a private investor to imitate the style of an institutional fund manager. The large pension funds, for example, are worth millions of pounds. Some run into billions. This means they can make money on minor price changes due to the sheer volume of their transactions.

From the company analysis the manager will proceed to look at the general performance and prospects for that sector (for example, oil, retailers and so on) and then take into consideration national and international economic factors.

The top-down manager works in reverse, looking first at the international and national economic factors that might affect economic growth in a country, geographic area (for example the 'Tiger' economies of South East Asia) or economic category (emerging markets, for example) and gradually work down to the individual companies.

Among private investors, the fundamental analyst focuses almost exclusively on individual companies and would tend to disregard the economic climate and market conditions. The technical analyst, also known as a chartist, concentrates on historical price movements and uses these charts as a way of reading future movements in share prices.

## Passive managers

Passive managers aim to track or replicate a benchmark. This style is also known as index tracking. It may sound simple, but in practice this is a complex process based on emulating the performance of a particular stockmarket index by buying all or a wide sample of the constituent shares.

> That was transmigration of object. There's a great deal of difference between that and pure science you know.
>
> The Doctor, *Doctor Who* (1963)

The passive manager does not consider the merits of each stock, of different sectors and economic cycles. If it is in the index then it must be represented in the fund. To date index-tracking funds have done very well compared with actively managed funds, largely because the passive manager's charges are very low in comparison with the active manager.

Passive management becomes very complex when the process tries to outstrip the index returns by deviating in a specific way. This is known as quantitative management.

## Other styles

Specialist active managers may use a specific style that will affect their returns. They may, for example, focus on small companies (SmallCap), larger companies, undervalued businesses (value investors) or those with potential for rapid growth (growth investors).

 **cool advice** The point to remember about fixed interest securities is that the investment return is determined more by the level of interest rates than the issuing company's profitability.

## Further information

*Barclays Capital Equity-Gilt Study 2001*: www.barclaysglobal.com

Chiswell Associates
No. 4 Chiswell Street
London EC1Y 4UP
Tel: 020 7614 8000
www.chiswell.co.uk

The London Stock Exchange publishes many useful information leaflets and books. For details contact:
The Public Information Department
London Stock Exchange
London EC2N 1HP
Tel: 020 7797 1372
Fax: 020 7410 6861
www.londonstockex.co.uk

**Miller**  Captain, I'm concerned about this vessel. It's taking on water.
**Mallory**  Why does that concern you?
**Miller**  I can't swim.

*The Guns of Navarone* (1961)

# Nightmare on Wall Street

After reading this chapter you will

*understand investment risk and be afraid ... very afraid*

*never look a gift horse in the mouth before checking out the rest of its anatomy*

*appreciate why those who look after the pennies end up with, er, pennies*

**THIS CHAPTER IS LARGELY DEVOTED** to asset allocation and should help you decide which type of assets best meet your needs before you move on to the selection of individual shares and bonds or collective funds. But first we take a look at that four-letter word 'risk'.

 The two chief dangers for private investors are capital loss and inflation.

Risk is very subjective. Like beauty, it is in the eye of the beholder. The technical definition of risk, in financial terms, is 'the standard deviation of the (arithmetic) average return', but we won't worry about that for now. The two chief risks for private investors are capital loss and inflation.

The reward for investors who take a risk is the total return, which is usually expressed as a percentage increase of the original investment. This may be a combination of income (or yield) plus capital growth (or rise in the market price).

## Inflation risk

Savings and investments that expose you to inflation risk usually fall into the 'safe' category. For example, we all tend to think of building society deposit accounts as risk free. But are they? If you are worried about the risk of losing your original capital then, provided you stick to the well-regulated UK building societies, you can put your money on deposit and your original capital will indeed be safe.

> **Dragline** Nothin'. A hand full of nothin'. You stupid mullet head. He beat you with nothin'.
> **Lucas (Luke) Jackson** Yeah, well, sometimes nothin' can be a real cool hand.
>
> *Cool Hand Luke* (1967)

Your capital will not diminish and should grow, assuming income is reinvested. However, the growth will be modest and in real (that is, inflation-adjusted) terms, it may even be negative, depending on the rate of inflation.

This does not mean you should ignore deposit accounts. In practice they play a very important part in providing you with an easy access home for emergency funds and for short-term savings where capital security is your primary goals (see Chapter 11). But as a general conclusion, over the medium to long term, deposit accounts are synonymous with capital erosion.

Bonds, which are issued mainly by the government (gilts) and companies (corporate bonds), can offer the prospect of higher returns than a deposit account, but there is a risk that the borrower may dip into your capital in order to maintain the flow of income. Also, like deposits, conventional bonds do not offer any guaranteed protection against increases in inflation.

## Capital risk

Historically, if you wanted to match or beat inflation over the long term you would have had to invest in equities. However, with equities, unless your fund offers a guarantee (and these can be costly – see Chapter 16), your capital certainly is at risk. So, when you see the statutory wealth warning that your investment can go down as well as up, take it seriously.

## How to manage risk

Risk can be managed in different ways. You can concentrate it in a single investment or spread it over a wide range. For example, if you invest all your money in a single share and it does well you will be in clover. If the company goes bust you could lose the lot. As a general rule it is wise to spread risk by investing in a range of shares either directly or through collective funds such as unit and investment trusts.

Even with collective funds the risk rating varies considerably. At one end of the spectrum are the higher risk specialist funds, which tend to be small and managed on an aggressive basis. At the other, more comfortable, end are the large UK equity or international funds that offer greater immunity to the capricious whims of stockmarkets. Bear in mind, though, that even the most broadly diversified funds will be hit when stockmarkets crash.

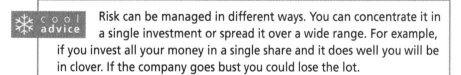

cool advice | Risk can be managed in different ways. You can concentrate it in a single investment or spread it over a wide range. For example, if you invest all your money in a single share and it does well you will be in clover. If the company goes bust you could lose the lot.

You can protect yourself further from risk if you diversify into different asset classes – for example, instead of just investing in different types of equities, you could include some bonds, gilts, deposits and, possibly, property in your portfolio. These behave in a different way from equities and therefore do not share the same vulnerabilities to certain economic cycles.

## Your risk assessment kit

Before you consider the various investment options outlined in the following chapters, you need to get acquainted with a set of benchmarks which help you judge the merits of an asset class, product or scheme and to compare it with other alternatives.

It doesn't matter if you are looking at deposit accounts, collective funds, direct equity and bond investments or high-risk investments such as enterprise investment schemes, which invest in the shares of unquoted trading companies. In each and every case the benchmarks will help you judge whether this is right for you.

 **You can manage risk by diversifying across different asset classes and different styles of investment management.**

The benchmarks will also help you to focus on the important fundamentals as opposed to the bells and whistles, which are used so successfully in marketing literature to make products and services look more attractive, safer, tax efficient, or ethical than they really are. The risk analysis guide suggests the most important questions you should always ask before investing.

## Asset allocation

Later in this book we take a closer look at stock selection and how market cycles affect market sectors and individual companies. Here we explain how to reduce risk through diversification using direct equity investment, bonds and gilts, and a range of collective funds.

Your starting point is an asset allocation plan. For a private investors, the 'liabilities' can cover a wide range of objectives. For example, your children's or grandchildren's school fees fall due each term and represent a known cost, which must be paid on specific dates in the future. Another liability is the mortgage repayment. If you have an interest-only loan, typically you might

## Risk analysis guide

■ **Aims**  What are the stated aims and benefits of the investment? Do these fit in with your own aims and objectives?

■ **Returns**  Compare the potential net returns of the investment with after-tax returns on very low-risk products such as 120-day notice building society deposit accounts, short-term conventional gilts and National Savings. Is the potential outperformance of your chosen investment really worth the additional risk?

■ **Alternatives**  Which other investments share similar characteristics? Are they simpler, cheaper, or less risky?

■ **Investment period**  For how long can you genuinely afford to invest your money? Compare this with the stated investment term and then check how the charges undermine returns in the early years. Also make sure you know about any exit penalties and remember that anything described as a 'loyalty bonus' usually acts as a penalty in disguise if you don't stick out the investment for the required period.

■ **Risk**  What is the risk that the investment will not achieve either its own stated aims or your own private objectives? What is the most you can lose? Is your capital and/or income stream at risk? What is the likely effect of inflation? Find out how the investment is regulated and what happens if the firm/investment manager goes bust.

■ **Cost**  Look at the establishment costs and ongoing charges. Watch out for high annual management charges on collective funds, particularly for long-term investments, as these will seriously undermine your return. With direct equity portfolios watch out for the high transaction charges and turnover costs associated with 'portfolio churning'.

■ **Tax**  The way the fund and you, the investor, are taxed is important because it will affect your ultimate return. Check for income and capital gains tax implications and consider how these might change over the investment period and remember, never invest purely for the sake of obtaining tax relief. Your investments must be suited to your circumstances and must be able to stand up with or without the tax breaks.

need to save over a 25-year term at which point you need a large lump sum to repay the outstanding debt.

In a similar way your pension scheme or plan builds up a fund that may be used at retirement to buy an annuity, which guarantees to pay you a regular income for life. Alternatively, if you decide to keep your fund fully invested in retirement (see Chapter 25) your objective is to provide a regular stream of monthly income.

In addition to these more obvious liabilities you may have several other aims which require different periods of investment – for example, an expensive holiday abroad, a new car, or a temporary income to cover the time between when you leave work and when you want to start drawing on your pension scheme.

> **Cole Thornton** I'm paid to risk my neck. I'll decide where and when I'll do it. This isn't it.
>
> *El Dorado* (1967)

You can see from these examples that while your overall objective may be capital growth, you also need to manage the liquidity of your assets in order to pay off the big debts on time, and the cash flow in order to meet more regular income needs, where relevant. If this exercise is particularly complicated in your circumstances then a good financial planner or stockbroker should be able to help you draw up a plan and review it on a regular basis.

## What is your starting point?

Your portfolio should reflect your current financial position (and that of your family), your current and future investment objectives, and your tax status. It may also reflect your ethical views, which might prevent you from investing in a range of companies with whose business goals or methods you disagree (see Chapter 15).

Make sure you have a clear perception of your tolerance to risk. Whether you use an adviser or deal direct, this is critical. Don't settle for a vague sentiment, but consider each investment in turn in the context of your overall asset allocation, and use the risk analysis guide on page 96 to determine which investments are appropriate for you and which ones you should avoid.

# Risk strategies

The problem with risk is that usually there is a wide grey margin between the worst that could possibly happen and the likelihood of this actually taking place. For example, in theory, if you invest in equities you could lose the lot if the company goes bust. As a shareholder you are last in the line of creditors so it quite likely that you would get little or nothing back if there are insufficient assets to go round.

So, how likely is it that a company will go bust? Clearly this depends to some extent on the companies you select and the state of the economy. But in practice the risk is a lot more tangible than you might think and many people who invest in smaller companies see one or two of their choices go bust over a long period of time. Your task then is to quantify the level of risk and decide whether you feel comfortable with it. In other words, to what extent are you prepared to trade off higher risk against higher potential expectations – and conversely, higher potential losses?

This does not alter the case for equities. It just means that you have to choose with care and spread risk. Despite the low inflation environment of recent years, it is not safe to build investment policy on the assumption that inflation has been beaten for good. An inflation rate of just 3 per cent halves the value of money in just over 20 years so it seems advisable to continue to place the emphasis on equities, but perhaps with a higher weighting of bonds, gilts and other assets like property, given the volatility of markets at present.

> **cool advice** Never invest purely for the sake of obtaining tax relief. Your investments must be suited to your circumstances and must be able to stand up with or without the tax breaks.

A defensive approach might, for example, invest 30 per cent of the portfolio in fixed interest, index-linked gilts, foreign bonds and cash. A further 50 per cent could be held in UK equities and 20 per cent in overseas equities. However, do bear in mind that any model portfolio is aimed at the mythical *average* investor. Clearly, each individual needs a private benchmark which reflects his or her own requirements, both short term and over the longer term. For example, some investors may avoid foreign bonds due to the currency risk, while others will regard them as an important diversification into overseas markets.

Diversification is not such a big issue within the conventional gilt market because all gilts are issued by the same source, namely the government. This does not mean that gilts are free from volatility. The nominal coupon and redemption date are known but the real value or price during gilt's life cycle are not known.

If you are interested in corporate bonds because they pay a slightly higher income than gilts it is important to diversify in a similar way to an equity portfolio. It is rare for a company to fail to the extent of its equity capital but not its loan capital. Therefore in practice the prior charge of a loan stock provides little protection and a loan stock is best viewed as equity risk.

## Reweighting your portfolio

If you take your existing portfolio to a stockbroker, be prepared to allow your broker to sell some of your existing shares if he or she believes they are inappropriate for your investment aims or that they represent too large a proportion of your portfolio and therefore create a concentration of risk. Consider, for example, the type of portfolio you may have if you responded to privatisation offers, received free 'windfall' shares from a building society or life assurance company, and you applied for cheap shares through your employer's share option scheme.

Your portfolio may have done very well in the past but it will not have a good spread of shares in the main All-Share sectors. Instead it is likely to consist of utilities (privatisation issues), financials (windfalls) and whatever category your employer happens to fall into. In this case your portfolio could lack representation in important sectors like foods, pharmaceuticals and retailers, among others.

It is also important to remember that if you intend to invest a large sum – for example, an inheritance, or the proceeds from a pension or endowment plan – there is no need to complete the process in a matter of days. In practice this could be a very unwise approach. Timing is critical to successful investments and in practice it could take six to twelve months to construct or rebalance your portfolio. During this period, keep any uninvested capital in an easy access account and be sure to shop around for the best rates.

Your stockbroker will also have to consider your tax position – particularly the capital gains tax implications of selling large chunks of shares. If you have not been making use of your annual capital gains tax exemption (£7700 for the 2001–2002 tax year), then your larger holdings could well carry a hefty CGT liability (see Chapter 18). Tax may become more complicated if you are retired or close to retirement. At this point, in addition to your income tax and CGT concerns, you should give careful thought to inheritance tax (IHT) planning.

## Collective funds for overseas exposure

Don't be surprised if you end up with a large chunk of your money invested in collective funds, even if you have a substantial sum to play with. It makes sense to adopt this route if you want to gain exposure to certain markets – smaller UK companies and overseas markets, for example. It can be risky or impractical to invest in one or two smaller companies (there are 368 in the SmallCap index) – unless, of course, you really are convinced of a company's merits.

Overseas markets can be more expensive to enter and individual share prices too large. In this respect the UK is quite unusual in having a relatively low price per individual share (this characteristic is maintained by companies which split shares when they become unwieldy).

Swiss companies, for example, commonly have a share price of £5000 each, so if you have £100,000 to invest overseas it is not sensible to have, say, two shares in one Swiss company. Rather, you should have £10,000 in units in a collective Swiss blue chip fund if you are keen on Switzerland – or possibly £20,000 in a European blue chip fund, which would invest in a selection of leading European companies.

## Achieving the right asset allocation

To give you an idea of how the experts approach the task of asset allocation for private investors, you can look at the private investor indices constructed by FTSE International in conjunction with the Association of Private Client

Stockbrokers and Managers (APCIMS). These are published at the weekend in the *Financial Times* Money section.

Although each investor's objectives will be different, for the sake of simplicity, the three models we consider here are for income, growth and balanced portfolios. The asset allocation of each model portfolio is based on research from a wide range of private client fund managers and stockbrokers. The weightings are amended on a regular basis, so the figures in Table 10.1 will not necessarily be up to date, but nevertheless they serve to highlight the different strategies used to achieve the three most common investment goals.

**TABLE 10.1** ■ Private Investor indices' asset allocation

| Asset class | Growth % | Balanced % | Income % |
|---|---|---|---|
| UK equities | 60 | 55 | 50 |
| International equities | 25 | 20 | 5 |
| Bonds | 10 | 20 | 40 |
| Cash | 5 | 5 | 5 |

*Source:* FTSE International/APCIMS published in Saturday's *Financial Times*

As you can see from Table 10.1, the difference in the UK equity weighting is not so great as you might expect, but the individual shares would be selected with different priorities in mind. Growth would be achieved by taking a slightly more aggressive approach. While you would expect a fair number of blue chips, there would also be some small and medium-sized companies to boost growth prospects.

## The income seeker

By contrast the income portfolio would focus on higher yielding shares. Some investors might have a preference for the larger companies (for example, the FTSE 100 companies), which tend to have a steadier track record on dividends payments than some smaller companies. The point to bear in mind here is that size and risk do not go hand in hand but represent two different decisions for income seekers. Some smaller, higher risk companies can provide a high yield but might not be appropriate for a retired income seeker.

However, many retired investors are looking not just for short-term income but also for income over 10 to 20 years. During this period the bond and cash element would provide a stable guaranteed income, but equities are needed to provide an element of capital growth to maintain the real value of the portfolio.

Don't assume, though, that just because you are growing older you should switch part of your portfolio out of equities and into gilts, bonds and cash. Many investors who retire early cannot or do not want to draw their pension immediately – either because it will not be paid until the employer's official pension age of 65 or because the pension would be substantially reduced. In this case you might be looking for an immediate and high income from your portfolio rather than long-term income and growth.

## International equities

International equities play an important part in the growth portfolio. This would provide exposure to foreign markets with good growth prospects. Of course, the level of risk would depend on where you invested. There is a big difference between, say, the European Union countries or North American, and the Japan/Pacific region or the emerging markets of South America, Africa, and Central and Eastern Europe, for example.

Bear in mind that foreign investment also exposes you to currency fluctuations and, in some countries, exchange control problems. Political instability and hyperinflation may also be features of emerging economies.

## Bonds and cash

Finally, the weighting of bonds and cash is probably the clearest indication of the portfolio's aim. In this case the income portfolio has almost half its assets in this class, while the growth portfolio has only 10 per cent. A younger investor with a robust attitude to risk might not even bother with this amount but go wholly for UK and foreign equities. Some investors might also include property.

## UK equities

For most investors, whether looking for income, growth or a balance of the two, at least half of the portfolio will be invested in UK shares. Although there is a tendency to regard the FTSE 100 companies as somehow 'safer' than medium and small companies, it is not true to say that the big is synonymous with secure.

A common strategy is to invest directly in FTSE 100 companies because these are well diversified and often have overseas interests. Exposure to the FTSE 250 (the 250 largest companies by market capitalisation after the top 100) and in particular to the SmallCap (the remaining 368 shares in the All-Share) can be achieved through collective funds, or direct, depending on your attitude to risk and confidence in your ability to research less well known companies adequately.

> A Sherman tank can give you an ... edge.
>
> Oddball, *Kelly's Heroes* (1970)

The FTSE All-Share, which covers about 99 per cent of the companies that are listed on the London Stock Exchange, has 36 sectors. Some include a large number of companies representing a broad spectrum of industry – Engineering and General Retailers, for example. Others are designed to categorise just a few important companies in a very specific market. Gas distribution, for example, has only six companies but this includes the enormous Centrica.

## Overseas equities

Since 1979, when UK exchange controls were abolished, the average pension fund has increased its weighting from 5 per cent to 25 per cent in overseas equities. Private investors have also demonstrated a keen interest in overseas stocks and have been rewarded with generally good returns. As mentioned above, in practice, for many investors the need for diversification argues against direct overseas equity investment except where the portfolio is very large. Specialist unit and investment trusts represent a cheaper entry and a good way to gain exposure to these important markets without undue risk of over-specialisation.

Having said that, if you are interested in certain sectors – say, car manufacturing – the choice of UK shares is very limited and you may wish to buy US shares, for example, to obtain the level of exposure you desire.

> Always compare an investment with a low risk benchmark like
> gilts or deposits to determine whether the potential for
> outperformance is worth the risk and the cost.

Some stockbrokers believe that investing overseas is very important from the point of view of diversification. In other words the benefits lie with reducing risk rather than increasing return. However, with the increasing globalisation of UK companies the degree of diversification overseas need not be as high as in the past.

# Market cycles

As a general rule the companies in a sector share certain characteristics, which make them respond in a certain way to changes in the market cycles. This is why it is important, although not essential, to build a portfolio which spans all the major sectors. This helps to spread risk and avoids your portfolio crashing in a nasty way as the economy enters or emerges from a recession. (Economic cycles, including some help with bear markets, are discussed in Chapter 16.) Remember though, that many of the blue chip companies which form the FTSE 100 index have considerable exposure overseas and so are not only affected by economic cycles in the UK. As mentioned above, this is generally seen as a plus point for investors keen to spread risk.

# Further information

Details about the FTSE International/APCIMS Private Investor Indices can be found at the FTSE International web site (**http://www.ftse.com**) where a service called On Target will allow you to analyse the performance of the portfolios free of charge. Alternatively, the indices are reported in the *Financial Times*, other financial newspapers and publications and on a number of data vendor terminals.

# A fistful of dollars

Why this whole country is run on epidemics. Where you been? Big business, price fixing, crooked TV shows, income tax finagling, souped up expense accounts. How many honest men do you know?

Hud Bannon, *Hud* (1963)

**Michael**  And now here's Denise to show you how to tell your friends' fortunes.
**Denise**  Ask their bank managers.

*Do Not Adjust Your Set* (1967)

# 11

# Rainy days and Mondays

After reading this chapter you will

*steal your grandson's piggy-bank*

*still smoke and buy risky investments, despite the warnings on the packages*

*feel very confused*

**THIS CHAPTER IS AIMED PRIMARILY** at those with short-term savings needs and investors looking for income. Here you will find details of the various savings and investment opportunities where important guarantees are offered – but at a price. The trick is to recognise the guarantees for what they are, use them wisely, but avoid the trap of investing too much in products that are not designed to provide capital growth.

## Easy access deposits for rainy days

All investors need an immediate access emergency fund to pay for unforeseen events such as sudden repairs on the house and car. However, this is not a role for equity-based investments. If you have to pull out of an equity fund in a hurry you could lose money, particularly in the early years when your investment is 'working off' the effect of initial charges or when the investment manager may impose an exit charge. You also need to time sales of equities carefully due to the volatility of markets.

The traditional home for cash is the building society. Stick with it but avoid the common mistake of keeping too large a reserve when part of your money could be earning a potentially better return elsewhere.

> **cool advice** The traditional home for cash is the building society. Stick with it but avoid the common mistake of keeping too large a reserve when part of your money could be earning a potentially better return elsewhere.

The size of your emergency fund should be determined by your monthly expenditure, your liabilities and the level of padding you feel is appropriate for your lifestyle and peace of mind. As a very rough guide it is worth keeping three times your monthly outgoings in an account that has one week's notice. Accounts offering a higher rate of interest with, say, three months' notice, can be used for known future capital expenditure – for example a new car, a holiday or school fees. If you manage your cash flow carefully then you can feed money from your other investments to your high interest rate account well in advance of the dates upon which these more substantial bills fall due. Keep a watchful eye on your longer-term deposits as rates change frequently. Postal and internet accounts tend to offer the best rates.

Probably the best source of up-to-date information on savings products is the monthly *Moneyfacts* guide to mortgage and savings rates, which covers savings accounts, children's accounts, cheque accounts, credit cards, store cards, bonds, gilts, mortgages, National Savings, and loans. *Moneyfacts* also publishes a separate monthly guide to life assurance and pension products. Subscription details are provided at the end of this chapter.

You can also find useful information on the best rates for a variety of savings accounts in the personal finance pages of the weekend newspapers. Most papers publish useful summaries of best buys for different types of products and accounts (many of which are provided by *Moneyfacts*).

# Safety at a price

Before you lock in to a fixed income product, remember that if interest rates rise you will have committed yourself to a low rate of return. Of course if the reverse happens and you lock in before rates plummet you will congratulate yourself on doing the right thing. However, if the experts consistently make errors in their predictions of interest rate trends, the chances of you getting it right are slim.

> It's not the money I love, it's the not having it I hate.
>
> Molly, *The Unsinkable Molly Brown* (1964)

For most people, some form of inflation proofing is an essential element in their income-generating portfolio of investments. The purchasing power of £100 will be worth just £64 after 15 years of inflation at 3 per cent and £48 if the inflation rate is 5 per cent.

The hidden cost of income guarantees is a reduction in the real purchasing power of your capital. As a rule, guaranteed income products limit or exclude altogether any prospect of capital growth. With some products, part of your capital could be used to bolster income if returns are lower than expected. Exposure to this type of investment should be limited. If investing for income *growth* is a better way of describing your requirements, then you should include at least some equity investments within your portfolio. Clearly this introduces risk, but provided you aim for diversity and avoid the exotic your main concern will be fluctuations in income rather than the fear of losing everything.

# Tax status

This is a crucial factor in your choice of savings products. For example, the income from National Savings Pensioners' Bonds is paid gross but the income from insurance company guaranteed bonds in effect is paid net of basic rate tax and you cannot reclaim this. In theory this should make the NS bonds a clear winner for non-taxpayers, but the slightly higher income available on the insurance bonds can offset this tax advantage. Depending on rates at the time, non-taxpayers should consider both products.

In the following pages we outline some of the most popular savings and investment options for income seekers – and one or two unusual opportunities you may come across in your research.

# Income earners

## National Savings

National Savings (NS) offers a wide range of accounts and bonds designed for every age and tax status. Income bonds, for example, have a three-month notice period for withdrawals and the bonds must be held for a minimum period of one year. If you don't give the required notice you lose 90 days' interest.

 For most people, some form of inflation proofing is an essential element in their income-generating portfolio of investments.

NS savings certificates can be either fixed rate or index linked and both run for five years. All returns are tax free even with early repayment, although if you don't go the full five years the interest rate drops. NS Pensioners' guaranteed income bonds can be bought by anyone over age 60 and offer a monthly tax-free income guaranteed for five years. NS also offers two accounts with a passbook – the investment account, which requires one month's notice, and the ordinary account that offers instant access at post office counters.

One of the attractions of NS products is that you can buy them through the post office and there are no charges. Bear in mind though that NS changes its interest rates less frequently than building societies so you should always compare rates before committing yourself.

For details of the complete range of NS products ask at your local post office or use the contact details provided at the end of this chapter. Remember, NS does not pay commission to advisers – which may explain why many commission-based advisers fail to recommend them.

## Tax-exempt special savings accounts (TESSAs)

TESSAs were withdrawn for new investment after 5 April 1999 but if you have an existing account that is coming up to maturity you can reinvest the capital in an individual savings account (ISA). The amount transferred does not count towards your annual ISA allowance.

TESSAs were not specifically designed to generate income but it is possible to make partial withdrawals of the interest and retain the tax-exempt status. Most TESSAs pay a variable interest rate although a few providers offered a fixed rate for either one year at a time or for the full five years.

## Cash Individual Savings Accounts (ISAs)

ISAs are discussed in more detail in Chapter 12, but briefly, up to £3000 of your £7000 annual subscription can be paid into a deposit account. You can hold this in a cash-only or mini-ISA but if you take out one of these you can't invest the rest of your subscription in a separate equity ISA.

Despite the low maximum annual limit the cash ISA is a tax-efficient way to boost your savings and for many investors the tax break on the mini ISA is more valuable than that associated with the equity maxi-ISA. This is because cash ISAs give a complete exemption from income tax on the interest, while investment ISAs are still liable for some income tax on dividends, although they have a complete exemption from capital gains tax (CGT) and no income tax is paid on bonds or bond funds.

Interest rates tend to be attractive on the top ISAs (see *Moneyfacts* for the best rates) but do keep an eye on providers that offer a special rate for just a few months in order to entice you in, then drop back to a much more mundane level of interest. If you are prepared to tie up your money, you can get an even better rate on notice accounts.

Watch out for inflexible clauses that penalise you if you want to transfer your fund elsewhere, for example. If you stick to CAT-marked ISAs then the accounts must offer you instant access, among other features. CAT stands for charges, access and terms.

## Gilts and bonds

Gilt-edged stocks are bonds issued by the UK government via the UK Debt Management office (DMO), an executive agency of the Treasury. If you buy gilts you are lending the government money in return for a tradable bond that promises to pay a fixed regular income for a specified period, at the end of which the government repays the original capital. Investors can buy and sell gilts throughout the lifetime of the issue.

Gilts play an important part in a defensive or income-producing portfolio although investors might also look at corporate bonds to improve their yields.

You might also consider bond funds that include bonds issued by stable governments – for example US Treasury bonds and German Bunds have been popular in recent years. For more information on gilts and how to buy them, see Chapter 14.

## Corporate bond funds

Historically, gilts have played an important part in the more defensive portfolio and particularly as a safe, interest-generating asset for the retired. However, given the comparatively low rates of interest currently on offer, many private investors are turning to corporate bonds for a slightly better return.

There are risks, of course. Gilts are guaranteed by the government and are considered ultra secure. Corporate debt is guaranteed by companies. Some of it may be secured on assets but generally speaking the security is much lower than for government stock. This is reflected in the company's credit rating. A very low credit stock can have a very high yield. However, the potential for capital loss is equally high.

> **Henry Gondorff** You not gonna stick around for your share?
> **Johnny Hooker** Nah. I'd only blow it.
>
> *The Sting* (1973)

Collective funds such as corporate bond unit trusts can be held in an ISA. Corporate bond funds offer potentially higher yields than guaranteed income bonds (see below), but neither the capital nor the income is guaranteed. Here it is vital for you and your adviser to examine the underlying bonds held to achieve the yield and to check the charges. A GIB provider should invest in top-quality debt, which is likely to be given a double-A or triple-A rating by leading analysts of loan risk like Standard & Poor's and Moody's. Some of the bond funds that offer a high yield achieve this by buying lower quality debt instruments that can expose the investor to the risk of capital loss.

Advisers do not recommend corporate bond funds for the short-term investor due to the buying and selling costs. They also suggest that you should avoid bond funds which deduct the annual management charge from capital instead of income as this structure may be used to artificially inflate the potential yield.

## Guaranteed income bonds (GIBs)

GIBs offer a fixed rate of interest over a specific term. Most investors go for three years or less. As a rule of thumb, therefore, you could use GIBs as comparatively short-term investments and corporate bond funds for the medium to long term. You can invest anything from about £5000 in a GIB and at maturity you get back your original capital plus interest, unless you elect to have interest paid out during the term of the bond. Unlike a corporate bond fund, with a GIB your capital and income is guaranteed.

In addition to the one to five year bonds, AIG Life and GE Life offer 'odd-term' or made to measure GIBs for wealthy investors who need to fix for a specific period. AIG Life also offers variable rate accounts for those who need total flexibility of access, although obviously here the income is not guaranteed.

With such a variety of terms available, the made-to-measure bonds are considered ideal for two very different types of investor: risk averse older people who need a regular income from savings, and wealthier individuals who want a first-class cash management system. The odd-term bonds are often used to hold cash set aside to pay large income and capital gains tax bills each year on 31 January.

---

✳ c o o l
advice
Gilts play an important part in a defensive or income-producing portfolio although investors might look at corporate bonds to improve their yields. You might also consider funds that include bonds issued by stable governments.

---

The taxation of life assurance funds is complicated, but broadly if you are a higher rate taxpayer, a deposit account rate of 5 per cent gross will actually yield £3 for every £100 invested, whereas the GIB will yield £3.28. Remember that GIB providers are forced to quote their rates net of basic rate tax whereas the banks and building societies quote gross rates. To compare like with like, a higher rate taxpayer will need to deduct 40 per cent from the building society rate and only 18 per cent from the GIB rate.

GIBs pay interest net of basic rate tax and if you are a non-taxpayer you cannot reclaim this. For this reason GIBs are generally considered unsuitable for non-taxpayers. However, since these bonds generally pay slightly higher rates of income than the tax-free NS products, it pays to consider both options.

A higher rate taxpayer who owns a GIB can defer any additional liability until the end of the investment term. Furthermore, once a bond matures, if you want to reinvest your capital you can defer the tax liability if the insurance company issues a formal offer to you to reinvest the entire proceeds in a new bond.

Given the fluctuating yields on the underlying assets, GIB rates change frequently so it is wise to seek advice on the timing of your investment. Most GIB providers will only sell through independent financial advisers. The rates usually assume a commission payment so where the adviser arranges for this to be reinvested, your income will be even higher.

## Permanent income bearing shares (PIBs)

An alternative to gilts and corporate bonds is PIBs. These form part of the permanent capital of a building society but have no repayment date and are more like an irredeemable loan than ordinary equities.

The thing to remember about PIBs is that they are not on offer from building societies but instead are quoted on the Stock Exchange and must be bought through a stockbroker. Their prices are similar to gilts but they offer slightly higher yields because they do not have the same high level of security as the government. Nevertheless PIBs offer a useful income bearing investment at competitive rates.

## Premium bonds

National Savings premium bonds are considered unsuitable for income seekers as no income as such is paid and you have to rely on the probabilities of winning to earn the equivalent of interest on your investment.

## Guaranteed equity bonds

Guaranteed equity bonds use derivatives to guarantee a percentage of stock-market growth or to guarantee the unit value of fully invested funds. A few of these funds offer to pay an income, but only when the relevant index has achieved a specific return.

# Halfway houses

Many investors, particularly pensioners, need to squeeze as much income as possible from their savings and are reluctant to take any risks with the capital. The trouble with this approach is that over time inflation eats into the real value of both capital and income. This is why most advisers recommend that income seekers should have at least a portion of equity-based investments in their portfolios.

But if you genuinely believe you cannot afford the risk of ordinary shares it is worth considering a halfway house – that is, investments which offer some capital protection plus a rising income. This category of investments includes index-linked gilts and the stepped preference shares of split capital investment trusts.

## Index-linked gilts

These bonds are issued by the government and guarantee to increase both the six-monthly interest payments and the 'nominal' or original capital investment that is returned to you on the redemption date. The capital increases in line with the retail prices index (RPI).

Since the starting RPI figure used is eight months before the date of issue, the final value of the investment can be calculated precisely seven months before redemption (RPI figures are published a month in arrears). But, as we discussed earlier in this chapter, guarantees offered by gilts and corporate bonds only apply if you hold the bonds to maturity. Like conventional gilts, the index-linked variety are traded actively, so the price and real value can fluctuate significantly between the issue and redemption dates.

> I admire his manners and I admire the speeches he makes and I admire the house he lives in. But if you're saving it all for him honey, you've got your account in the wrong bank.
>
> Ben Quick, *The Long Hot Summer* (1958)

Investors seeking absolute guarantees from their income yielding portfolios may be tempted to put all their money in gilts. In this case you might be better off with a balance between conventional gilts, which offer a comparatively high fixed income but no index linking of the capital value, and index-linked gilts, which offer a low initial income but protect both the income and capital from rising inflation.

## Stepped preference shares of split capital trusts

These offer an income that is supposed to be guaranteed to rise each year at a fixed rate, plus a fixed redemption price for the shares when the trust is wound up. Each trust offers a different yield and annual increase, depending on the nature of the underlying assets.

 **The taxation of income-producing products is a crucial factor in your choice of savings products.**

Over the past year or so there has been an increasing level of concern about the ability of some of these investment trusts to meet their guarantees, so do not invest without independent advice. The factors to consider are the risk profile, the current dividend yield, and the gross redemption yield – that is, the total return expressed as an annual percentage, assuming the share is bought at the present price and held to maturity.

The best source of general information on all types of investment trusts is the Association of Investment Trusts (AITC), which publishes useful fact sheets and a Monthly Information Service, which provides a breakdown of all the member trusts and performance statistics.

## Purchased life annuities

Annuities, sold by insurance companies, guarantee to pay a regular income for life in return for your lump sum investment. The annuity 'rate' – or the level of regular income you secure in return for your lump sum – will depend on several important factors, including your life expectancy and interest rates. Women tend to live longer than men so usually receive a lower income in return for the same level of investment. If you are in ill health you may be able to get a better rate if the insurance company thinks your life expectancy is less than the average for your age. This is known as an ill health or impaired life annuity. The main point to remember with annuities is that unless you pay extra for a capital guarantee, once you hand over your money it is gone for good, even if you die the following day. Annuity rates are interest rate sensitive and fluctuate considerably so do seek expert advice over the timing of the purchase and the annuity company.

## Further information

*Moneyfacts* is available in larger libraries and by subscription. You can also buy a single copy by credit card – 01603 476476. Price at the time of writing was £5.95.

For information on gilts visit the Debt Management Office website (**www.dmo.gov.uk**). The site includes an online version of the informative 'Private Investors Guide'.

You can contact the Bank of England brokerage service on freephone 0800 818614 or go to the website (**www.bankofengland.co.uk**). A link appears on the DMO site.

The Association of Investment Trust Companies is on 020 7431 5222 (**www.aitc.org.uk**).

I got one rule: never go to bed without making a profit.

Tully Cow, *The Comancheros* (1961)

# Strength in numbers

After reading this chapter you will

*understand more jargon than is healthy for normal people*

*find the tax aspects of collective funds fascinating*

*never be invited to dinner parties again*

**THIS CHAPTER DESCRIBES THE FOUR** most popular types of collective funds in the UK: unit trusts, open-ended investment companies (OEICs), investment trusts, and life assurance funds. Many of these funds can be held in a tax-efficient wrapper, known as an individual savings account (ISA), which replaced personal equity plans (PEPs) for new investment from April 1999.

Although these funds share many features in common and offer a similar broad investment scope, there are differences in structure and taxation. Your choice will depend on the finer details.

Tax efficient vehicles like ISAs do not offer a magical solution to investment performance. What they do offer is a shelter from income tax, capital gains tax (CGT), or both. If you run your own pension plan or ISA then you can invest in most asset classes and the returns will be enhanced due to the tax breaks. The important point here is to set your investment goals first and only then

**c o o l
advice**    Tax efficient vehicles do not offer a magical solution to
investment performance. What they do offer is a shelter from
income tax, capital gains tax, or both.

to decide which types of assets are best held in the different tax efficient
plans.

# The internet

These days there is a wealth of information available on funds on the internet.
Some of the most useful sites are mentioned in Appendix 1, which also gives
details of several fund supermarkets. These sites allow you to mix and match
different funds and managers all within an ISA.

# The selection process

When it comes to selecting a good fund, there is plenty of advice on what not
to do and very little on positive selection criteria, so what follows is to some
extent subjective. No doubt over the years you will develop your own favourite
theories.

The financial press and several firms of consultants produce annual surveys
that highlight the best and worst in the various categories of funds. You must
take great care when you examine past performance statistics because these
can be very misleading. What the surveys do offer is some ideas on how to
screen funds, so it is well worth checking out the methodology used in the
most authoritative examples. You can also look at how the ratings agencies –
Standard & Poor's Fund Research, for example, or Moody's – rate the funds.
Top funds in terms of research capability and the investment management
team, among other features, get an A, double-A or triple-A award. Fund
objectives should be clearly defined and the objectives should be measurable,
so that there are clear benchmarks against which performance can be judged.
The investment processes – asset allocation and stock selection – should also
be set out clearly.

The Financial Services Authority (FSA), the chief regulator, does not require companies to disclose past performance details. This is something of a cop-out because, although it is difficult to police the use of statistics, to ignore past performance altogether is unwise. In many cases past performance statistics are a useful aid to gauge the future potential of a manager or fund, *provided* you bear in mind the following important caveats:

- They must be coupled with a clear understanding of how past performance was achieved.

- They must be combined with an assessment of the current investment style of the management team.

- The individuals responsible for past performance must still be in place.

## Unit trusts and open-ended investment companies (OEICs)

Although there are differences between the unit trust and OEICs structure, as far as the private investor is concerned these two types of fund can be treated as identical. For the sake of simplicity where we refer to a unit trust, this covers both products.

A unit trust is a collective fund with a specific investment aim. Unit trusts are 'open ended', which means they may create or cancel units on a daily basis depending on demand. Investors purchase units in the fund, the value of which fluctuates in line with the value of the underlying assets. Most funds invest mainly or wholly in equities, although the number of corporate bond funds, which invest in corporate bonds, preference shares and convertibles, among other assets, is growing rapidly.

> Money is like the sun we walk under. It can kill or cure.
>
> Dolly, *The Matchmaker* (1958)

Some ISAs based on unit trusts offer capital guarantees or guarantee to provide part of the rise in a stockmarket index and protect you from the falls. The guarantee is 'insured' through the use of derivatives – financial instruments which are used to protect a fund's exposure to market fluctuations.

For the more cautious investor these 'protected' unit trusts, as they are called, when held within an ISA could represent a tax-efficient method of gaining a high exposure to equities without the usual risks. However, it is important to remember that protection carries a cost (see Chapter 16).

# Investment trusts

An investment trust is a British company, listed on the UK stock exchange, which invests in the shares of other quoted and unquoted companies in the UK and overseas. As public companies, investment trusts are subject to company law and Stock Exchange regulation. The prices of most investment trusts are published daily in the *Financial Times*.

> **cool advice**   Take great care when you examine past performance statistics – they can be very misleading.

Investment trusts are different from unit trusts in several important ways and offer the active investor additional opportunities. However, these opportunities also make investment trusts potentially more volatile than unit trusts. For example, investment trust companies have a fixed number of shares so, unlike unit trusts, 'units' cannot be created and cancelled to meet increased and reduced demand. As with any quoted company, the shares are only available when other investors are trying to sell.

This means there are two factors that affect investment trust share prices. The first is the performance of the underlying assets in which the company invests. This factor also affects the price of units in a unit trust.

However, where unit trust prices directly reflect the net asset value of the fund, investment trust share prices may not. This leads to the second factor, which is that the market forces (supply and demand) to which investment trust shares are subject may make the shares worth more or less than the underlying value of the company's assets. If the share price is lower than the value of the underlying assets, the difference is known as the discount. If it is higher the difference is known as the premium.

Investment trusts can borrow money to invest, an activity known as gearing. This adds extra flexibility and if the shares purchased with the borrowed money do well, the company and its shareholders will benefit. A poor return on the shares will reduce the profitability of the company.

'Split capital' investment trusts can have two types of shares – one that has a right to all the income and one that has a right to the capital growth. There are several other types of share, each offering different features, for example, stepped preference shares, which offer dividends that rise at a predetermined rate and a fixed redemption value which is paid when the trust is wound up.

## Taxation outside an ISA or PEP

In terms of taxation, the unit and investment trust route is very similar. Where these investments are held outside of an ISA (or a PEP), in both cases the CGT liability falls on the investor who can offset any tax liability against the annual CGT exemption (£7500). (See below for taxation within an ISA or PEP).

Charges on investment trusts are generally lower than on unit trusts, with the exception of index tracker unit trust ISAs/PEPs. However, tracker funds available as ISAs are confined to the UK stockmarket and therefore do not offer such broad diversification as the larger and older international investment trusts.

In conclusion, unit trusts, with the exception of the index trackers, are generally considered slightly more expensive than investment trusts but less sensitive to market movements.

# Insurance funds

Like unit trusts, a lump sum premium in an insurance company bond buys units, which directly reflect the net asset value of the fund's underlying investments. The charges for the two types of collective funds are broadly similar. However, the tax treatment is quite different (see below). Despite the confusing array of investments offered by insurance companies to the public, most fall into one of three main categories.

With maximum investment plans and insurance company investment bonds, your premiums are invested in a choice of funds, most of which are unit linked, similar in concept to unit trusts in that your premiums buy units in a collective fund and the value of those units rises and falls in line with the value of the underlying assets.

Although sold by life assurance companies, most of these regular and single premium plans offer minimal life cover, as their main purpose is invest-

## Insurance funds

- **Maximum investment plans (MIPs)** are regular monthly or annual premium investments and usually run for ten years. Once this term is complete you can either take the proceeds or leave the fund to continue to benefit from investment growth. You can also make tax-efficient annual withdrawals.
- **Insurance company investment bonds** are similar to MIPs, but here you invest a single premium or lump sum.
- **Endowments** combined investment with a substantial element of life assurance.

ment. If you die the company might pay out 101 per cent of your original investment or the value of the fund, whichever is greater.

The traditional endowment is most commonly used as a repayment vehicle for a mortgage, although sales have slowed following a recent misselling scandal. As mentioned above, the distinguishing feature of an endowment is that it combines a significant element of life assurance with your savings plan so that if you die during the term of the policy the combination of the value of your fund plus the life assurance is sufficient to repay the debt. It is possible to buy second-hand endowments where people have sold a policy to a market maker in order to get a higher price than would be available from the insurance company. Contact details are provided at the end of the chapter.

Unit linked life assurance funds offer a similar range of investment opportunities as unit trusts. You can also select a with profits fund, which invests in a mixture of equities, bonds and property and have a rather idiosyncratic method of distributing profits. This is discussed below.

## Taxation of life assurance policies

Insurance company bonds pay tax broadly equivalent to the basic rate on income and capital gains. The income tax cannot be reclaimed so, generally, these bonds are not considered suitable for non-taxpayers. Moreover, the CGT paid by the fund cannot be offset against an individual's exemption.

At the end of the investment period, the proceeds of a life assurance policy will be treated as though the fund had already paid the equivalent of basic rate tax. For lower and basic rate payers that is the end of the story. But what happens next for higher rate payers depends on whether the policy is classed by the Inland Revenue as 'qualifying' or 'non-qualifying'.

With a qualifying policy there is no further tax liability for higher rate payers. However, to attract this special tax status the policy must abide by various conditions. First, it must be a regular premium plan where you pay a predetermined amount each month or each year. Second, it has to be a long-term plan – usually a minimum of ten years. Third, it has to provide a substantial amount of life cover.

This means that single premium investment policies are non-qualifying but the regular premium MIPs may be classed as qualifying depending on the term and level of life cover provided. Mortgage endowments, which tend to be long-term regular premium plans, usually are qualifying due to the substantial element of life cover.

## Unique tax feature of bonds

There are circumstances in which the unique features of investment bonds can be attractive to certain investors. With bonds there is no annual yield as such since income and growth are rolled up within the fund. But up to 5 per cent of the original capital can be withdrawn each year for up to 20 years. The Inland Revenue treats these withdrawals as a return of capital and therefore at the time of payment they are free of tax so the higher rate tax liability is deferred until you cash in your policy. (Withdrawals above 5 per cent are treated by the Inland Revenue as though they are net of basic rate tax – so the higher rate liability must be paid, not deferred.)

Even if you invest in a non-qualifying life policy, you may be able to reduce or avoid the deferred higher rate tax bill due to the effect of top slicing relief. Top slicing relief averages the profit over the number of years the bond has been held and adds this profit slice to an investor's income in the year the bond matures. If part or all of this falls into the higher rate bracket, it would be taxed. However, with careful tax planning investors can avoid this liability by encashing the bond when they become basic rate taxpayers – in retirement, for example.

Higher rate taxpayers who have used their full CGT allowance may also find bonds and MIPs attractive because the 5 per cent withdrawals do not have to be declared for income tax purposes in the year of withdrawal.

## Low-cost fund switching

One advantage of bonds over most unit trusts is that insurance companies generally offer a low-cost switching facility between a large range of funds and these switches do not give rise to a CGT liability, even where the new sub-fund is run by a different asset manager. Otherwise the charges for the two types of funds are broadly similar, although the tax status of life offices usually allows them to operate with slightly lower annual charges and this can have a significant effect on your fund's growth over the long term.

## Investment choice

The investment choice under life assurance policies is as follows. *'Unit linked'* plans offer a very wide choice, ranging from UK and international equities to UK and international fixed interest securities, index-linked gilts, property, and commodity and energy shares. Your money buys units in the fund's assets and the unit price rises and falls directly in line with the performance of these assets.

*'With profits' funds* are simply heavenly if you thrive on jargon and obscurity – which is a pity really because they can play an important role in a more cautious investor's portfolio. The with profits fund is the fund of the life office itself and invests mainly in a range of international and UK equities, bonds and property. To avoid dramatic fluctuations, insurance companies 'smooth' their bonus rates, holding back some of their profits in the good years to maintain a reasonable return in the bad years.

In addition to the annual bonus you also receive a final or 'terminal' bonus at the end of your investment period or when you die. The final bonus is discretionary (that is, voluntary on the part of the insurance company) and tends to reflect recent performance.

With profits funds have a 'market value adjuster', which allows the insurance company to reduce the value of your units if there is a run on funds – during a period of falling markets, for example. This means that your fund value is never totally guaranteed, as policyholders have discovered in recent years, particularly if they were with Equitable Life.

In recent years bonus rates have fallen, partly due to falling returns and partly to compensate for what many commentators regard as over-generous bonuses paid in the late 1980s. This does not mean that with profits policies represent poor value – some companies continue to achieve very good results over the medium to long term. However, it does mean that you cannot rely on bonus levels of the past continuing in future.

## Early surrenders of life policies

Long-term life assurance investments tend to deduct the commission costs for the entire investment period during the first year or two. This is why so many people have got back so little from their policies if they have pulled out during this 'initial' period.

An endowment – or indeed any investment – is portable when it comes to mortgage repayment. If you buy another house and need a larger mortgage, it may be best to keep the policy you have already and top up with a repayment or interest only mortgage backed by the savings plan of your choice. You do not need to take out another endowment – an ISA may be a more tax efficient alternative if you are not already using up your annual allowance.

> Morons. I've got morons on my team. Nobody is going to rob us going down the mountain. We have got no money going down the mountain. When we have got the money, on the way back, then you can sweat.
>
> Percy Garris, *Butch Cassidy and the Sundance Kid* (1969)

If you simply cannot continue a policy for some reason, don't just stop payments without first considering the alternatives. You could, for example, make the policy 'paid up' which means you no longer pay premiums but you do not withdraw your fund until the maturity date. You should still benefit from investment growth, but do check the ongoing charges and what penalties apply before taking this step.

If you need the capital, you might be able to take a loan from the insurance company, based on the surrender value of your policy. Alternatively, you might get up to 30 per cent more than the surrender value if you sell your policy on the second-hand endowments market. In this case an investor buys it from you and takes over the commitment to continue the premiums in the hope that the final payout will be well in excess of the purchase price plus the cost of the outstanding premiums.

The two main options are to auction the policy or to sell it to a market maker, who naturally will charge a fee or take a percentage of the profit. (The profit is the difference between what you would have got as a surrender value from your insurance company and the actual price achieved.)

## Alternative investments / hedge funds

Investments are described as 'alternative' where the risk and returns of the fund or asset do not correlate with (or behave in a similar way to) more traditional investments such as equities and bonds. Hence they are described as having a 'low correlation' with traditional equity and bond markets.

> ❄ cool
> advice    Investment trusts offer the active investor additional opportunities, but they are also potentially more volatile than unit trusts.

The most common alternative investment you are likely to come across is the hedge fund. Hedge funds aim to produce 'absolute' returns – that is a positive return in all market conditions – and to eliminate market risk. The way they achieve this varies and the fund strategies are complicated. Hedge funds are discussed in more detail in Chapter 16.

## Friendly society policies

Friendly societies are often snubbed as the small fry of the investment industry. However, in contrast to life assurance funds, which have to pay both income and CGT, friendly society funds are tax free. Unfortunately, the amount you can invest is small – £270 a year (£300 if you pay your premiums on a more regular basis than just once a year) and most plans run for ten years. There are societies that accept a lump sum investment to cover payments for the full ten years. Look carefully at past performance and charges and compare these with what is on offer from ISA managers and unit and investment trusts which offer low contribution regular savings plans.

## Offshore funds

In certain cases for more wealthy, risk tolerant investors it may be appropriate to consider offshore funds (but not before you have used up your annual ISA allowance). Whether an offshore fund would be suitable will depend on the tax jurisdiction of the fund, the way the fund itself is taxed and your own tax position as an investor.

Points to consider with offshore funds include the charges, which often can be very high compared with UK funds, and the regulation – for example, if it is outside of the UK, what protection do you have if the company collapses or the fund manager runs off with your money?

> American millionaires must be all quite mad. Perhaps it's something they put in the ink when they print the money.
>
> Charles Bonnet, *How to Steal a Million* (1966)

As a general rule for a UK investor investing in UK securities, once you have used up your ISA allowance, unit and investment trusts are likely to prove more cost effective and simpler than offshore funds. There are two main types of offshore insurance bond – *distribution bonds*, which pay a regular 'income' and *non-distribution bonds*, which roll up gross.

Investors who may gain by going offshore include UK and foreign expatriates who are non-resident for UK tax purposes and who can benefit from gross roll-up, non-distribution bonds if they do not pay tax in the country where they live. Higher rate taxpayers may also benefit from the gross roll-up but you do have to pay tax when you bring the money back into the UK, although of course you may have switched to the basic rate tax bracket if you have retired by the time the non-distribution bond matures.

## Personal equity plans (PEPs)

Over the 12 tax years from January 1987 up to April 1999 that personal equity plans were available, you could have invested a maximum of £85,000. After April 1999 you could no longer contribute to a PEP but any existing funds you built up through your plan can remain in the tax-efficient wrapper and be managed as a separate portfolio.

**cool advice**  If you want the facility to invest directly in equities and bonds, and access to the full range of collective funds you need a self-select ISA.

There used to be different categories of PEP and some geographical restrictions, but these rules have been abolished so you can merge your investments and change their asset allocation to create a more international spread of investments.

In practice many investors who took advantage of the PEP rules from the beginning are now coming up to retirement. In this case they may prefer to change the asset allocation to reflect an increased income requirement. PEP investors also have access to a wider range of corporate bonds and, for the first time, to gilts and other fixed interest securities issued by European governments.

If you would like to make some changes to your PEP – including transfers to other managers – it is best to seek independent advice to make sure you fully understand the more flexible rules.

# Individual savings accounts (ISAs)

ISAs were introduced in April 1999 and replaced PEPs for new investments. The range of investments you can hold within an ISA is very broad and includes a wide selection of collective funds. You can also use a 'self-select' ISA to hold a portfolio of funds and individual shares and bonds.

Clearly, if you have comparatively small amounts to invest it does not make sense to run your own portfolio because trading in small volumes is disproportionately expensive. For many investors, therefore, buying into collective funds through packaged ISAs is cost effective.

Moreover, if you are happy to stick within a range of unit trusts and OEICs you can split your £7000 allowance between several managers if you buy through a fund supermarket. This enables you to get round the one ISA per year rule (see Appendix 1).

## The ISA rules

Currently you can invest £7000 a year in an ISA if you are 18 or over and a UK resident. There is no tax relief on the contribution but gains and income in the ISA fund build up free of tax. You do not pay tax on dividend income or interest. It is the fund manager's job to claim back the tax you are 'deemed' or treated as though you had paid on all UK company dividends. At present the credit is 10 per cent on share income although this will be reduced to zero in 2004. You can get back 20 per cent on bond income. There is no CGT liability for ISA investors (although this means you cannot offset a capital loss within an ISA against other gains).

There are two types of ISA plan, known as the mini and maxi. You cannot take out both in the same tax year. You can invest in three separate mini-ISAs run by different managers. The limit is £3000 in a cash mini ISA, £3000 in shares and £1000 in life assurance funds.

Alternatively you can take out a single maxi-ISA with one manager and still invest in shares, cash and life funds but you can, if you wish, put the whole £7000 into shares. Fund supermarkets allow you to invest across a range of managers within the single maxi plan.

## CAT-marked ISAs

'CAT' stands for charges, access and terms. If you buy a CAT-marked product you are not guaranteed that it will be better than non-CAT-marked ISAs but you can be sure the manager has agreed to certain conditions.

## CAT-marked equity ISAs

- Annual management maximum charge of 1 per cent.
- Minimum regular saving from £50 per month or a minimum lump sum of £500.

## CAT-marked cash ISAs

- Must not have charges except for additional services – for example, if you ask for an extra statement.
- Must allow savers to pay in or withdraw as little as £10 on no more than seven days notice.
- Must not impose other conditions such as how frequently you can make withdrawals.

If interest rates go up, the ISA rate must follow within a month.

## CAT-marked insurance funds

■ Maximum annual management charge of 3 per cent.

■ Minimum premiums from £25 per month or £250 per year.

■ Must not apply a penalty if you cash in your account.

■ After three years if you surrender your account (cash it in) you must get back at least all the premiums you paid in.

## Self-select ISAs

If you want maximum flexibility, the facility to invest directly in equities and bonds, and access to the full range of unit trusts, OEICs and investment trusts in your collective ISA funds, then you need a self-select plan. Self-select ISAs are offered by many firms of stockbrokers (the Association of Private Client Investment Managers' website is at **www.apcims.co.uk**) and a few independent financial advisers, for example, certain members of the Association of Solicitor Investment Managers (**www.asim.org.uk**).

Apart from the wider investment choice, one of the immediate benefits of the self-select structure is that it enables you to make changes to your portfolio on the same day. With packaged ISAs it can take weeks and sometimes even months to switch between managers. This can be frustrating and costly in a rising market. You can also hold cash within the self-select plan and earn interest on this while you are waiting to reinvest the money.

The cost of your self-select plan will depend on the stockbroker's or adviser's charges. This might be a flat annual administration charge, which could suit the larger portfolios, or the fee might be linked to the value of the fund (for example, 0.5 per cent per annum plus VAT). Some will have no annual fees, but will charge for dividend collection, which on a large portfolio could add up quickly. One thing to look out for is high dealing charges, especially on shares. What can appear cheap because of a low or zero annual management charge can prove costly if there is little or no discount on unit trust purchases and if sharedealing charges for buying and selling are in excess of 1 per cent.

> $15,000,000,000 in gold bullion weighs 10,500 tons. Sixty men would take 12 days to load it onto 200 trucks. Now, at most you're going to have two hours before the Army, Navy, Air Force, and Marines move in and make you put it back.
>
> James Bond, *Goldfinger* (1964)

Finally, don't forget that the self-select route can provide you with as much or as little advice as you want depending on whether you opt for a discretionary service, where your stockbroker makes all the investment decisions for you; an advisory service, where you and your stockbroker discuss your options before you make a decision; or execution only, where you make all the decisions yourself and your stockbroker simply carries out your instructions (see Chapter 4).

## Further information

If you are interested in buying or selling an endowment policy contact the Association of Market Makers on 020 7739 3949 (**www.money-world.co.uk.apmm**).

The Association of Investment Trust Companies can be contacted on 020 7431 5222 (**www.aitc.org.uk**).

The Investment Management Association is on 020 7831 0898 (**www.investmentuk.org**).

You read the profit and loss statements like a vulture, and you play the stockmarket like a fox but you store your nuts like a squirrel.

Angel, *Good Morning and Goodbye* (1967)

# 13

# Keep good company

After reading this chapter you will

*talk with confidence about stockmarket ratios*

*know more about the companies your friends work for than they do themselves*

*join an investment club because you desperately need some new friends*

**WHEN INVESTMENT STRATEGIES GO WRONG**, active fund managers are quick to point out that stock picking is an art not a science and that markets are, by their very nature, unpredictable. Passive management (index tracking) is a different kettle of fish and aims to eliminate the risk of individual stock selection. So, if your portfolio or collective fund holds a sample of different stocks or actually replicates every stock in an index (the FTSE 100, the 250 or the All-Share, for example) over the long term, you can't lose *provided* your benchmark is the index itself. Of course this does not mean your portfolio is guaranteed to rise. If the index takes a tumble, your portfolio will follow. Nevertheless, low cost index tracking unit trusts are very popular and worth considering if you are after a broad exposure to the UK market.

The fact that stock picking is an art does not mean you should abandon the pursuit of knowledge and select your individual shares by sticking a pin in the Companies and Markets section of the *Financial Times*. What it does mean is that you are never guaranteed success; nor is your stockbroker. This is why investing in shares can be very risky, particularly over the short term when the volatility of markets can temporarily depress the share price of even the best of companies.

> I use my gun for money, and I don't like to work for nothing. But you trouble me again and I might have to break my rule.
>
> John Gant, *No Name on the Bullet* (1959)

The difference between good stock picking and the pin-sticking exercise is information and strategy. Pin sticking is all about pure luck, stock picking is all about making informed decisions in the light of your investment aims. Those who put in the leg work just have to accept that the pin stickers sometimes hit lucky.

## Your starting point

If you have over £100,000 to invest (some stockbrokers put the figure much higher) you could consider including direct equity investments in your portfolio. The optimum minimum number of shares depends on what you are trying to achieve.

Opinions vary greatly on this point, but as an absolute minimum you should aim to hold 10 different shares, however, 20 or 30 would be even better since this would help achieve a better diversified spread of risk, provided each holding was a sensible minimum size. Again opinions vary, but as a very rough guide you could consider a minimum holding as anything between £1000 and £5000, depending on the costs involved. To avoid over-exposure to the risks inherent in smaller companies, some advisers recommend you put at least half of your capital destined for equities in FTSE 100 companies.

An alternative is to achieve your exposure to the FTSE 100 companies through index-tracking unit trusts. On top of this you can buy a handful of carefully selected individual equities to boost your portfolio's potential growth.

## Investment aims

Whatever your starting point, it is important to have an objective and to stick to it. A very simplistic approach is to determine whether you are looking for growth, income or a mixture of the two – and over what time frame. You then need to determine the level of risk you are prepared to take and decide the features you are looking for in a company. If you ask the right questions before you buy and stick to your strategy, while there is no guarantee of success (always remembering that this is art not science), nevertheless you will avoid the fads like the technology stocks in the late 1990s.

 **Remember that one of the most obvious pitfalls for private investors to avoid is frequent dealing where the costs can quickly outweigh minor gains.**

Always remember that one of the most obvious pitfalls for private investors to avoid is frequent dealing where the costs can quickly outweigh minor gains. As a very rough guide you will find that the price of shares you buy will need to rise by about 4–5 per cent before you work off the purchase costs.

In addition to a selection process you need a selling strategy. It's no good selecting your shares with care if you do not have a policy for weeding out the losers at the right time. Loyalty is a misplaced emotion in the private investor.

## Buying and selling

How you buy your shares (this includes investment trust shares) will depend on the nature of the agreement you have with your stockbroker. If you have a discretionary or advisory stockbroker, the firm will act on your behalf once you have completed a terms of business agreement and paid a cash and/or stock deposit. The firm will automatically provide a tariff of charges.

The choice of stockbroker services was discussed in Chapter 4. You may prefer and need a traditional discretionary or advisory service from a stockbroker but if you are looking for convenience and low cost *and* you have the expertise to make your own share selection, an online execution-only firm will be adequate, provided it offers a good combination of price and service. For a guide to online services, see Appendix 1.

## Company share schemes

With the increasing cost of retirement it is wise to build up different sources of capital and income rather than to rely solely on your company pension scheme or individual pension plan. Shares purchased through an employee share ownership scheme can also provide a lump sum when you leave and want to start your own business, for example.

However, like any equities, if you buy shares in your company you are taking a risk, particularly if you are a director or senior employee and the shares form a significant chunk of your total remuneration. Things can get complicated if you leave a company earlier than expected and you should seek expert advice on the timing of your share purchases and any tax implications.

Moreover, with falling markets there is a genuine concern that the value of shares you purchase may plummet. As a general rule, therefore, it is wise to consider how well the company's shares fit in your overall portfolio before you take a major stake.

With the general schemes, however, there is little or no risk until you decide whether to buy. Moreover, buying shares through a company scheme is also tax efficient if you make a capital gain above the annual exemption as these shares are classed as business assets and the rate of CGT can be as low as 10 per cent (see Chapter 18).

There are over 5000 companies in the UK with Approved Employee Share Schemes with about 3.5 million participating employees. These schemes offer tax benefits for employees who participate. The best source of information on the range of company share schemes is ProShare.

## How shares are grouped

Shares fall into all sorts of different categories and each label tells you something important about the investment prospects. Size and type of business are the two most obvious categories.

## Does size count?

The simple answer is yes, and this is as good a starting point as any. The London Stock Exchange has more than 2000 listed companies and is the main securities market in the UK. It acts as a primary market for new issues and also as a secondary market. (Gilts and bonds are also listed on the Stock Exchange – see Chapter 14.)

In theory, large companies that are well diversified should be more stable than smaller companies, partly because of their sheer size and deep pockets, but also because through diversification in the UK and overseas, they should be less vulnerable to market cycles and economic factors such as a rise or fall in interest rates or a recession. If one part of the company is affected by a fall in retail sales, for example, other parts of the group might still be thriving. In this way an investment in a blue chip company carries an inherent spread of risk, whereas a small, specialist company is much more vulnerable to economic conditions and market sentiment.

 **c o o l  advice**   It's no good selecting your shares with care if you do not have a policy for weeding out the losers at the right time. Loyalty is a misplaced emotion in the private investor.

Clearly, the reverse is also true. If you pick a small, growing company that doubles its turnover in one year then your shares could boom. Larger companies are less likely to experience sharp rises as well as the sharp downturns, although there are always exceptions to this rule. In practice, of course, a large company can get into serious trouble or even go bust unexpectedly. It is always a nasty shock to discover in retrospect just how well the directors can hide what should have been clear signs of impending doom.

Finally, income seekers need to decide what risks they are prepared to take. A high income-generating portfolio can also be highly speculative – it does not have to be confined to larger companies.

# The FTSE International Indices

The quickest way to assess the size of a company is by looking at the FTSE International Indices, published each day in the *Financial Times*. It is helpful to consider the chief characteristics of the main equity indices that are likely to contain your most popular shares. Bear in mind though that these are *theoretical* characteristics. In practice markets may move in a totally unpredictable fashion so it is important to look at *actual* trends, not just the theory.

The FTSE Actuaries indices are arithmetically weighted by market capitalisation so that the larger the company, the greater the effect its share price movement will have on the index. 'Market capitalisation' is the stockmarket valuation of the company, which is calculated by multiplying the number of shares in issue by their market price.

## The FTSE All-Share

This is the most comprehensive UK index and consists of just over 718 companies with a total market capitalisation of about £1463 billion. The All-Share is regarded as the professional investor's yardstick for the level of the UK equity market as a whole and represents about 99 per cent of UK stockmarket capitalisation. Within the All-Share, companies are allocated to 36 different categories of shares according to industrial sector. There are also sub-indices, for example the FTSE 100 and Mid-250.

## The FTSE 100

This index consists of the 100 largest UK companies by market capitalisation and is the standard reference point for defining Britain's blue chip companies (blue chip being the highest value chip in a game of poker). The FTSE 100 companies together represent about 84 per cent of the UK stockmarket capitalisation. These are large companies, many of which are multinationals with substantial overseas exposure. Companies in this index tend to do better in a recession than smaller companies and their size and diversification tends to make them fairly stable investments.

> Real diamonds! They must be worth their weight in gold!
>
> Sugar Kane, *Some Like It Hot* (1959)

Some advisers recommend that once you have your portfolio of collective funds, this is the best place to start with direct equity investments. To further enhance your spread of risk, make sure you choose your shares from a wide range of sectors (see below).

---

**cool advice** — Large companies that are well diversified should be more stable than smaller companies, partly because of their sheer size and deep pockets but also because they tend to be well diversified in the UK and overseas.

---

If you are more adventurous and want to spend your time hunting down value for money among the smaller companies in the All-Share, you could always buy units in a UK tracker fund which replicates the FTSE 100 and gain your blue chips this way, leaving you free to spend time researching smaller companies.

## The FTSE 250

This index consists of the next 250 companies below the FTSE 100 and can include or exclude investment trusts. The Mid-250s are companies capitalised at between £250 million and £2.3 billion. Together, these companies represent about 13 per cent of the UK stockmarket capitalisation (including investment trusts). These companies may have less exposure to manufacturing in overseas markets although they may rely heavily on exports. During an economic recovery, companies in this index tend to experience higher returns than the FTSE 100, but still manage to avoid exposure to the volatility experienced by some of the smaller companies in the All-Share index: a good bet, therefore, after you have built up your collection of blue chips – but do make sure you research the individual companies well before taking the plunge.

## The FTSE SmallCap

This index does not have a fixed number of constituent companies but instead it comprises all the remaining companies in the All-Share which are too small to qualify for the top 350 (about 368 at the time of writing). Together they account for about 3.2 per cent of the total UK capitalisation. Clearly, All-Share companies that fall outside of the FTSE 350 (the FTSE 100 and Mid-250 combined) are potentially more risky and volatile than the larger companies. However, this is an area in which private investors traditionally have done well. These companies are less sought after by the professionals because very large funds cannot trade in these shares easily since the size of the deal might in itself push up or depress the share price. As a result, these companies usually are less well researched that the FTSE 350.

Certainly, if you have local knowledge of a company and you believe it has a good management team and is in an up and coming market, you could do very well. However, beginners and the risk averse should not commit too much money to any one company because this would concentrate the risk in your portfolio.

## Fledgling index

The Fledgling market covers all of the companies that are too small at present to be in the All-Share index but are otherwise eligible to join the Exchange (about 640 companies at the time of writing). Together the SmallCap and Fledgling indices are known as the All-Small index. Once you get down to this level you really have to be careful. Whatever their business, the share price of small companies can be extremely volatile. A company that specialises in one or two products is very vulnerable to price competition and a sudden reduction in demand. Moreover, a signal from a tip sheet to buy a small company's shares could be enough to send the price through the roof, while a panic to sell on the part of very few investors can be enough to force the share price down into the doldrums.

> You want to come out of this territory with a profit ... you're gonna have to hunker down and talk business with a man who's cleaning out his pigsty. That's where the sales are made ... and it can't be done in a New York suit.
>
> Rubin Flood, *The Dark at the Top of the Stairs* (1960)

In conclusion, intensive research and a strict ceiling on the amount you invest in any one company are essential. Also, these shares may not be very liquid so buying, and in particular, selling, can be a problem. If you plan to use a stockbroker, find one that specialises in smaller companies to save you some legwork.

## Alternative Investment Market (AIM)

AIM replaced the Unlisted Securities Market (USM) in 1995 and lists about 608 companies. It allows small and relatively new companies that are growing quickly to go public without having to go through the expensive and time-consuming full listing procedures required for a Stock Exchange main listing. Private investors should also note that AIM companies are not regulated so strictly as fully listed companies. In due course a successful AIM company may move into the All-Share. These are risky companies. As with the smaller company shares listed on the exchange but outside of the All-Share, you must be sure you have done your research well before parting with your cash. Again you should watch out for lack of liquidity with AIM companies.

## Companies ineligible for the All-Share

Some companies are not eligible to join the All-Share or the Fledgling market. This is not usually a question of size but of some other characteristic. For example, the following are ineligible:

- Foreign companies (which would also be listed on their home country stockmarket), for example, Americans, Canadians and South Africans, which are listed after the AIM countries in the *FT* Companies and Markets section.
- Subsidiaries of companies already in the All-Share.
- Companies with less than 25 per cent of shares in 'free float' (that is, over 75 per cent is held by the family or directors).
- Companies whose shares were not traded for a minimum number of days in the previous year.
- Split capital investment trusts.

# Classification by sector

The sectors used by the FTSE International categorise the All-Share group companies according to what they do. In theory this helps because the companies in a sector are likely to be affected by a similar range of economic factors. For example, if we are in a dire recession people still need to eat, so companies in the 'Retailers, food' sector might be a good place to find some defensive stocks, while 'Breweries pubs and restaurants' and 'Leisure and hotels' might feel the pinch as consumers cut back on non-essential items.

However, stock picking purely by sector is not necessarily a good technique. Some sectors represent a very concentrated market whereas others – transport, for example – represents a diversified range of companies. The point to remember here is that you must consider the profile of the sector and the company itself. Just because one company is experiencing good growth does not mean that you can pick any company in the sector and be guaranteed a winner.

Where the sector classifications can help is in determining your investment position relative to the 'market'. If your aim is to beat the All-Share index, for example, you need to have a clear idea of how the index is constructed and deviate where you feel a sector is likely to perform well under the current market conditions.

## Shareholder perks

Some shares offer certain perks – for example, a discount at the company's stores or free tickets to certain events. In most cases these are no more than the free gift in the cereal box but for some sport, entertainment or other enthusiasts the perks may well swing it. Do check, however, whether you will qualify for the perks, particularly if you use a nominee account where you are the beneficial owner but the shares are held in the nominee company's name.

## New issues

These might include government's privatisations of previously public sector companies and the major building societies and life assurance institutions, which have converted from 'mutual' status, where they are owned by their members, to public limited companies owned by shareholders. Most demutualisations have been characterised by the large windfall share payments, where free shares in the new company were given to existing savers and borrowers.

## What the company will tell you

Clearly the first place to start is with the company itself. By law a company listed on the Stock Exchange must produce a considerable amount of documentation for its shareholders (and of course the regulators and accountants, among others). Typically, this will include two sets of profit figures at six-monthly intervals. The first set in the company's financial year is known as the interim results while the second set, the final results, is produced at the company's financial year end.

> **cool advice** Income seekers need to decide what risks they are prepared to take. A high income-generating portfolio can also be highly speculative – it does not have to be confined to larger companies.

These figures provide a detailed analysis of the company's trading year and its profits or losses. In addition you should get hold of the annual report and accounts, which are available to existing and prospective shareholders.

## The FT London Share Service

A very useful source of information is the *Financial Times* London Share Service. In the Companies and Markets section you may see a symbol after the company name. A club symbol indicates that you can obtain the current annual or interim report free of charge. All you have to do is phone a 24-hour number quoting the reference provided in that edition of the *Financial Times*.

## How to value shares

Once you have identified the shares that appeal to you and seem to fit well in your portfolio, it is time to take a closer look at the mathematics. Alternatively, if ratios leave you cold then this is one of the best reasons going for appointing a stockbroking firm, which employs its own analysts.

There are two basic exercises here. First, you need to make a general assessment of how well or otherwise the company is doing compared with the market as a whole and with its peers within the appropriate sector.

Check the company's recent history. There are several online sources of information (see Appendix 1), while the *Financial Times* share service in the Companies and Markets section of the paper provides recent news stories about the company, profit forecasts plus a five-year financial and share price performance review, among other details. Follow up this information with a thorough reading of the annual report and accounts, but do remember that this document will be out of date and should be supplemented with any recent news.

> X squared to the power of two minus five over the seven point eight three times nineteen is approximately equal to the cube root of MCC squared divided by X minus a quarter of a third percent. Keep that in mind and you can't go very far wrong.
>
> Eric, *Do Not Adjust Your Set* (1967)

The second exercise is to consider how the market views the share price. This is a more precise activity and requires an understanding of how professionals make their calculations. For some companies it is necessary to look at the net asset value (investment trusts and property companies). Gearing – or the amount the company has borrowed compared with what it actually owns – is also an indicator of the company's security and an investor's sensitivity to company performance. (Gearing is known as leverage in the USA.)

## The dividend yield

This is a method of examining the income from an investment based on historic information. It is the annual gross dividend as a percentage of the market price. The figure shows the rate of gross income a shareholder would receive on an investment at that particular share price – rather like the way you might describe the before tax interest paid on a deposit account. As with an ordinary deposit account, there is no guarantee that the dividend yield will be maintained.

The Barclays Capital Equity-Gilt Study (see page 86) explains that a low dividend yield is associated with a high valuation for the stockmarket because it tends to be followed by low returns, whereas high dividend yields tend to be followed by high real returns, especially over the following 12 months.

The trouble is that we must never assume the past is a guide to the future. Much will depend on the economic environment. The study explains:

*A prolonged period of low inflation and sustained economic growth could maintain the stockmarket at levels that might appear high by past standards … The lesson of history is that the benchmarks for valuation can and do change.*

*Investment is therefore more about gauging the direction of markets and hence appreciating the new valuation norms than relying on past guidelines. Changes in the economic environment are the main determinant of changes in valuation standards. In particular, changes in the inflation rate are a major influence on the markets.*

## Key indicators in practice

Clearly, there are no hard and fast rules with dividends because they reflect the current state of the business. If the company is prone to follow the dips and peaks of market cycles (see Chapter 16), this will be reflected in the dividend payments. Even some of the larger companies – including those on the FTSE 100 – have been cutting dividends lately, so do keep an eye on the company's record. Dividends form an important element in the 'total return' – that is, dividends reinvested plus capital growth.

As mentioned above, analysts tend to assume that a higher dividend indicates the shares are likely to produce above average total returns over the long term, while some very successful investors only invest in high yielding shares.

However, a comparatively high dividend is always worth checking out to make sure there is nothing untoward going on behind the scenes. Look at the company's gearing (debt) to see if it is borrowing to shore up its dividend commitment. Very high dividends can be a sign that the company is in trouble.

You might also come across the term 'dividend cover'. This is a stock market ratio that quantifies the amount of cash in a company's coffers. If the dividend cover is high, this means the company could afford to pay out the dividend several times over from earnings per share. This indicates that profits are being retained for the business. When the cover is low it means the company had to struggle to scrape together the dividend announced and may even have subsidised it from reserves.

## The price/earnings (P/E) ratio

This is the market price of a share divided by the company's earnings (profits) per share in its latest 12-month trading period. As a very rough guide, a high ratio means the market considers a company is likely to produce above average growth, while a low P/E ratio means the opposite.

P/E ratios are a handy benchmark to use when comparing shares of similar companies within a sector – two supermarket chains, for example. You also need to check the ratio against the average for other sectors because it could be that at a particular point in the market cycle all shares in the sector in which you are interested might be marked down if they move in line with economic trends.

Both the dividend yield and the P/E ratio are shown in the *Financial Times* share prices pages.

## Net asset value

This is an important feature for certain types of company, particularly property companies and investment companies. Take investment trusts, for example. These are UK companies that invest in the shares of other companies. Investment trusts have a fixed number of shares that are subject to the usual market forces, so the share price does not necessarily reflect the total value of the shares which the trust owns.

If the share price is lower that the value per share of the underlying assets, the difference is known as the discount. If the share price is higher, the difference is known as the premium. As a general rule, an investment trust share trading at a discount may represent good value.

## Financial gearing

This is the ratio between the company's borrowings and its capitalisation – in other words, a ratio between what it owes and what it owns. You should find out why a company is highly geared before you invest, particularly if interest rates are high, because servicing the debts could cause a considerable strain on its business and profits. However, do consider the gearing in the context of the company's business plans. If interest rates are low, a highly geared company which is well run can make good use of its debts – for example, to expand into a new and profitable market.

Another way of looking at gearing is to consider how the profits compare with the interest payments made to service the company's debt. The number of times profits can cover the interest payments is known as 'interest cover'. Company analysts suggest that in very broad terms a ratio of four times profits to interest owed is healthy. A ratio of 1:1 is definitely not.

## The acid test

Analysts also refer to something called the 'acid test', which is a ratio of the company's current assets (excluding stock) to its current liabilities. The reason stock is excluded is that if a company is in serious trouble its stock may not be worth the full market value. Sales and auctions following liquidation usually sell at knockdown prices.

> **cool advice** The real point about stockmarket ratios is to use them to spot where the market ratings are inappropriate to the company's actual prospects.

Analysts reckon that the ratio ought to be about 1:1, so that if the company did get into trouble it could meet all its liabilities (including payments to bond holders and shareholders) without having to rely on whatever the liquidator could raise by selling off its stock cheaply.

## Asset backing

This is another way of looking at what the company would be worth if all else failed and it went bust. In practice this test is a common exercise in the analysis of a takeover bid. The aggressor and the shareholders need to know the real value of assets per share in order to calculate an attractive price for the bidding process. Clearly, the acquiring company needs to persuade the shareholders to either transfer their loyalty to the prospective new management team or simply to grab the money and run.

## The pre-tax profit margin

This is the trading profit – before the deduction of depreciation, interest payments and tax – as a percentage of turnover. The pre-tax profit margin is considered a useful guide to the company's general performance and the management team's competence because it reveals the profits earned per pound of sales.

## The return on capital

This is the profits before tax, divided by the shareholders' funds, and indicates the return the company is making on all the capital tied up in the business.

# Making comparisons

All of these ratios and measures must be considered in the context of a full financial picture of the company. Obviously if you rely on just one or two, you may miss something very important or get an unbalanced view of the company.

Don't fall into the trap of thinking that just because the figures indicate a company will pay out high dividends in future or will experience capital growth that this will automatically follow. There are no guarantees. All you can achieve is an informed prediction.

Also, remember that the real point about ratios is to spot where the market ratings are inappropriate to the company's actual prospects. Clearly, to identify this situation you would require a good deal of knowledge about the company itself and to understand why the market has got it wrong. In conclusion, for most investors it is important to use as many sources as possible for information about markets, inflation, the economy and individual companies.

# Further information

The FT London Share Service provides a wealth of useful data for very little outlay. See the Companies and Markets Section of the paper.

ProShare's *Introduction to Annual Reports & Accounts*, £4.95 from
ProShare: 020 7720 1730 (**www.proshare.org**).

Two books on interpreting financial pages in the *Financial Times* are *How
to Read the Financial Pages* by Michael Brett, published by Random House,
and *The Financial Times Guide to Using the Financial Pages*, by Romesh
Vaitilingam, published by FT Prentice Hall.

The Stock Exchange publishes useful leaflets on buying and selling
shares. For copies telephone 020 7797 1000 or write to The Stock Exchange,
London EC2N 1HP (**www.londonstock-exchange.com**).

## Company share schemes

Your employer should provide clear details of the various ways you can buy
shares in the company. Where the share option is part of your total remuneration then this information should have been set out in a contract when you
joined. You can also contact your local Inland Revenue office for leaflets on
the subject.

A useful guide to employee share ownership is published by ProShare.
The website covers all the main arrangements (**www.proshare.org**).
ProShare
Library Chambers
13–14 Basinghall Street
London EC2V 5BQ
Tel: 020 7220 1730

**Blofeld**  They told me you were assassinated in Hong Kong.
**Bond**  Yes, this is my second life.
**Blofeld**  You only live twice, Mr Bond.

*You Only Live Twice* (1967)

# The name is bond

After reading this chapter you will

*realise that no investment is safe*

*put your money in bricks and mortar*

*pray your aunt remembers you in her will*

**GILTS AND CORPORATE BONDS** have always been popular with investors seeking income but in these days of volatile markets many investors are turning to these assets as a safe haven for capital that might otherwise be invested in equities.

 Gilts play an important part in a defensive or income-producing portfolio although investors might also look at corporate bonds to improve their yields.

Before we look at these investments it is important to understand the rather complex relationship between equity returns and bonds and how this can change. Historically there has generally been an inverse correlation between equity returns and the yields on bonds. In theory, then, if equity returns are falling, bond yields should rise, and vice versa. However, if demand for bonds increases dramatically bond prices will go up and the yields will fall – possibly at the same time that equity returns are falling.

> Reminds me of that fellow back home that fell off a ten-storey building ... As he was falling people on each floor kept hearing him say, "So far so good!"
>
> Vin, *The Magnificent Seven* (1960)

We have experienced this worrying trend in recent years and it is attributed to the fact that private investors have been piling into this asset class, as have maturing occupational pension funds, which weight their asset allocation more heavily towards bonds in order to pay the guaranteed pensions. The combined impact of these two developments could change the long-term relationship between equity returns and bond yields.

## What is a bond?

If you put your money into gilts and bonds the borrower promises to repay the loan in full at a fixed date in the future. With conventional gilts and bonds the borrower pays interest, known as the coupon, twice a year at a fixed rate. As a general rule, the longer the term, the higher the income – but also the greater the drop in the real value of your capital at the maturity or redemption date.

Both gilts and qualifying bonds (not convertibles and preference shares) are free of capital gains tax on any profits because the 'return' is classed as income. However, this is not a win–win situation since you cannot offset a loss against capital gains in excess of the exemption.

## Government bonds

Gilt-edged stocks are bonds issued by the UK government via the UK Debt Management Office (DMO), an executive agency of the Treasury. If you buy gilts you are lending the government money in return for a tradable bond that promises to pay a fixed regular income for a specified period, at the end of which the government repays the original capital. Investors can buy and sell gilts throughout the lifetime of the issue.

Gilts play an important part in a defensive or income-producing portfolio, although investors might also look at corporate bonds to improve their yields. The DMO website (see further information below) is an excellent source of information for private investors and maintains an up-to-date list of all the gilts in issue. The most common category is the conventional gilt, which behaves like a conventional bond and pays interest twice a year. You can also buy index-linked gilts, which pay a dividend that rises each year in line with the retail price index. The third category listed – rump gilts – refers to issues where there are very few gilts in circulation.

> **cool advice** Both gilts and qualifying bonds are free of capital gains tax on any profits because the 'return' is classed as income. However, this is not a win–win situation since you cannot offset a loss against capital gains in excess of the exemption.

Private investors can buy gilts in several ways. You can purchase through a bank or stockbroker that is a member of the Gilt Edged Market Makers Association (GEMMA). If you buy and sell in this way the bank or stockbroker will charge a commission for the transaction. You can also buy through the Bank of England brokerage service direct (see further information below) or via the post office. Information on gilt prices and yields is published in the second section of the *Financial Times* on weekdays and in the first section on Saturdays.

## How to assess bond income

To assess the income from gilts and bonds you need to look at three figures.

- The *nominal* value represents the original purchase price (which is not necessarily the price at which you buy). This is the amount you receive at redemption.
- The *coupon* tells you the interest rate that applies to the nominal value throughout the loan period.
- The *market price* is the present value if you buy or sell.

The coupon and nominal figures determine the level of interest but the actual return or yield will depend on the buying price. If the buying or market price of a gilt or bond goes up, the yield goes down because you have paid more than the nominal value and therefore the interest rate will be smaller in comparison. So, if the nominal price is 200p and the interest rate is 10 per cent but you buy at 240p, then the interest is still only 10 per cent of 200 – that is 20p, so the yield is 8.33 per cent (20p as a percentage of 240p).

If the situation was reversed, so the nominal is 240p, the interest rate 10 per cent and you buy at 200, you will still get 10 per cent of 240p, which is 24p – a yield of 12 per cent.

## The safety of your investment

The important difference between gilts and other bonds is the nature of the guarantee. If you buy gilts you are lending money to the UK government, which is the safest borrower in terms of credit worthiness. Other bonds might be guaranteed by banks, companies and foreign governments, so there is an element of credit risk. This is reflected in the slightly higher yield – often about 0.3 per cent above gilt yields – offered to compensate you for the higher risk.

> He won't touch 'em. The croupier at Gilman's says he never plays anything he can't win.
>
> J.J. Singleton, *The Sting* (1973)

One other point on the security of corporate bonds. Issuers and advisers may make much of the fact that in the event of a company going bust, bonds rank before shares in the creditors' pecking order. Frankly, it is unlikely that a company in these circumstances could afford to repay bond holders but not shareholders. In most cases, therefore, it is wise to take this apparent additional security with a pinch of salt.

## Price fluctuations

Gilts and bonds can be traded during the loan period, and there are no guarantees on the return of capital if you sell before the redemption date. Prices tend to reflect the market's view on future interest rates. This means that although in general gilts and bonds are less volatile than shares, there have been many exceptions that disprove this rule. Over an unusual period in 1994, for example, gilts fell by as much as 15–20 per cent.

Gilt interest is paid in arrears so the price will also take into account whether a recent interest payment has been made to the holder – in which case the price is ex-dividend. If the interest is still to be paid, the price is cum-dividend. The price quoted in the *Financial Times* is the mid-point between buying and selling prices.

## Index-linked gilts

Many investors, particularly if they are retired, need to squeeze as much income as possible out of their assets and are reluctant to take any risks with the capital. Advisers usually recommend that even an income-orientated port-folio should contain at least some equity-based investments. These, they argue, should provide some capital protection plus a rising income.

If you are not comfortable with ordinary shares, it may be worth consider-ing a half-way house, namely investments which offer a rising income plus some capital protection. The most common choice is index-linked gilts, which pay interest at a certain percentage above the rate of the retail price index (RPI).

> **c o o l**
> **advice**
> The important difference between gilts and other bonds is the nature of the guarantee. If you buy gilts you are lending money to the UK government, which is the safest borrower in terms of credit worthiness.

Index-linked gilts guarantee to increase both the six-monthly interest pay-ments and the 'nominal' or original capital investment due at redemption in line with increases in the RPI. Since the starting RPI used is eight months before the date of issue, the final value of the investment can be calculated precisely seven months before redemption (RPI figures are published a month in arrears).

Like conventional gilts, the index-linked variety are traded actively so the price and real value of the yield can fluctuate significantly between the issue and redemption dates. However, there is no inflation (RPI) risk for the investor in index-linked gilts other than the eight-month period without indexation at the end of each stock's life.

## Comparisons with other investments

So, how does this compare with the yields on equities? The income on index-linked gilts is guaranteed to grow in line with inflation over the years but cannot grow more quickly. Equities, however, offer no guarantees but historically have grown more quickly than the rate of inflation. However, under unfavourable economic conditions, such as those experienced over the past few years, equities can lag behind inflation. A similar comparison can be made with conventional gilts, which have a fixed income throughout their term.

> So it's from a finance company. So, it's better that no letter at all! So they want the third payment on the Plymouth. [*Dropping each letter on the floor in turn.*] So they want the fourth ... the fifth ... the sixth ... the seventh ... So they want the Plymouth.
>
> Shapiro, *Stalag 17* (1953)

Index-linked gilts have not offered particularly competitive returns compared with equities, conventional gilts or cash since they were first issued in 1981, but in today's volatile climate it is important to remember that index-linked gilts have provided their return for a much lower level of risk than the other two categories. If you make adjustments for tax, their net return is a little more competitive.

Investors seeking absolute guarantees from their income-yielding portfolio may be tempted to put all their money in gilts. If you are in this position, do go for a balance between conventional gilts, which offer a comparatively high fixed income but no index linking of the capital value, and index-linked gilts, which offer a low initial income but protect the income and capital from rising inflation.

## Corporate bonds

One of the most popular ways of holding corporate bonds is through a unit trust, but there is no reason why experienced investors should not buy direct provided they can achieve a sensible spread of risk.

For the bulk of bond funds that do not offer a capital guarantee it is important to view with caution the assumption made by some promoters that these funds offer investors absolute safety and security. With some funds your capital could be eroded to maintain high-income payments.

Rather like index-tracking funds, charges are a more significant factor in the corporate bond fund selection process than is the case with equity funds. With a bond fund the gap in performance between the best and the worst is small, so differences in charges are highly significant.

## Charges and yields

The Investment Management Association has co-ordinated the way in which corporate bond fund yields are calculated by its members so that managers show yields on a consistent basis. The yield figures should not be examined without reference to the way the annual management charge is deducted. If this is taken out of capital, as opposed to the usual practice of deducting it from income, then the yields will look artificially high.

When it comes to the yield, there are two figures to consider: the gross redemption yield and the running yield.

■ The *gross redemption yield* or *projected total yield* takes into account both the income received and changes in the capital value of the bonds if they are held to maturity.

■ The *running yield* or *projected income yield* only takes into account the current rate of income received from the bonds. No allowance is made for any changes in the capital value so this could mask capital erosion, for example, if the annual charge is deducted from capital.

---

**cool advice** For the bulk of bond funds that do not offer a capital guarantee it is important to view with caution the assumption made by some promoters that these funds offer investors absolute safety and security.

---

As a general rule the gross redemption yield is the better measure of the total expected investment return. A high gross redemption yield might be accompanied by a higher credit risk and often greater volatility in the capital value of the fund. The running yield is important for investors concerned about the income they will receive. A high running yield is often associated with capital erosion.

## Further information

The DMO website is at **www.dmo.gov.uk** and includes an online version of the informative Private Investors Guide.

The Bank of England brokerage service is on freephone 0800 818614 or go to **www.bankofengland.co.uk**. A link appears on the DMO website.

**Your evil is my good. I am Sutekh the Destroyer. Where I tread I leave nothing but dust and darkness. I find that good.**

Sutekh, *Dr Who* (1963)

# 15

# Farewell to arms

After reading this chapter you will

*still want your aunt to leave you her mink coat in her will*

*get rich by investing in illegal drug trafficking, guns and gambling*

*support the right to arm bears*

**IF YOU ASK TEN PEOPLE** what they think is ethical you will get ten different answers. Ethical views, by their very nature, are subjective. Nevertheless, in this chapter we consider how, as an investor, you can put your ethical and environmental views into practice – if you have any, that is.

> ❄ cool advice
> The major exclusions in ethical funds tend to be arms, alcohol, tobacco, gambling, animal testing, environmental damage and the payment of exploitative wages in developing countries.

As an ethical investor you will have to use your personal opinion to decide which companies are worth investing in and which should be shunned. Whether you make your own selections or you wish to set guidelines for your financial adviser, it is important to be able to explain your views clearly.

You also need to appreciate the impact any ethical screening process will have on a fund's annual returns. An ethical fund will not have broad exposure to the FTSE All-Share, for example, which is the benchmark used to judge the performance of most general equity funds. An ethical fund, therefore, needs to have an appropriate performance benchmark and should not be expected to reflect market movements as a whole.

> But the essential arithmetic is that our young men will have to shoot down their young men at the rate of four to one, if we're to keep pace at all.
>
> Air Chief Marshall Sir Hugh Dowding, *Battle of Britain* (1969)

Fortunately, the launch in 2001 of the ethical stockmarket indices – FTSE4Good – makes it much easier for you and your investment manager to assess a company's approach to the environment or social issues like exploitative wages, for example.

Bear in mind that some advisers are much more sympathetic than others when it comes to ethical investment. An adviser who takes the matter seriously will have considerable research at his or her disposal. A cynic will probably try to dissuade you, pointing out the significant constraints on the choice of shares and how this can undermine performance. Don't dismiss the cynical approach. Remember, any strong ethical views you may have are likely to go against your adviser's natural instinct to help you make as much money as possible.

## Ethical Investment Research Service

Ethical investment is a complicated subject and not helped by the difficulty and cost of obtaining sufficient data upon which to form a view about the ethics or otherwise of a company. A good source of information for people interested in this subject is the Ethical Investment Research Service (EIRIS), which maintains a database of ethical funds and individual companies.

EIRIS was set up in 1983 by a number of organisations including Quakers, Methodists, Oxfam and the Rowntree Trust. It monitors the screening and performance of the ethical and environmental unit trusts, so if you are interested in collective funds this is the best place to start.

It also offers a screening process for direct equity investors. The simplest way to use EIRIS research is to request an 'acceptable list' – a list of companies which meet your ethical or environmental criteria. A 'portfolio screen' enables you to find out more about the shares you hold, while for the real enthusiast EIRIS fact sheets provide all the information on the database on the companies in question.

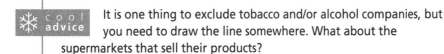

cool advice    It is one thing to exclude tobacco and/or alcohol companies, but you need to draw the line somewhere. What about the supermarkets that sell their products?

EIRIS researches over 1000 companies. The list of screening options from which you can choose gives you an idea of why this is such a complicated topic:

- alcohol
- animals (meat production and sale, leather/fur manufacture and sale)
- arms and sales to military purchasers
- community involvement
- corporate governance
- directors' pay
- environmental issues
- equal opportunities
- gambling
- greenhouse gases
- health and safety convictions
- human rights
- intensive farming
- military contracts
- newspaper production and television
- nuclear power (fuel, components and construction of plants)

- overseas interests (wages exploitation in emerging economies, deriving profits from countries with poor human rights records)
- ozone-depleting chemicals
- pesticides
- political contributions
- pornography
- Third World involvement
- tropical hardwood
- tobacco
- waste disposal
- water pollution.

## Defining an ethical policy

The major exclusions in ethical funds tend to be arms, alcohol, tobacco, gambling, animal testing, environmental damage and the payment of exploitative wages in developing countries. But the list could extend almost indefinitely.

Some funds take a proactive approach and aim to invest in companies that are working towards a desirable goal – 'green' companies involved in recycling or environmentally-friendly waste disposal, for example. Environmental funds can also be regarded as ethical. Here the choice of shares will depend on a company's environmental policy in terms of pollution, ozone depletion, deforestation and waste management, among other criteria.

> Let me see if I've got this straight: in order to be grounded I've got to be crazy and I must be crazy to keep flying. But if I ask to be grounded, that means I'm not crazy any more and I have to keep flying.
>
> Yossarian, *Catch 22* (1970)

If you have strong ethical views you need to decide where to draw the line. It is one thing to exclude tobacco and/or alcohol companies, but what about the supermarkets that sell their products? Gambling is also a typical exclusion, but does this mean all the outlets that sell tickets for the National Lottery should be avoided? Some ethical investors might favour pharmaceutical companies because of their groundbreaking research in the war against cancer and AIDS, for example. Others might exclude the same companies on the grounds that they carry out experiments on animals.

In an extreme case, even apparently innocuous products like National Savings and gilts can cause problems because they are effectively 'sold' by the UK government. The same government is responsible for the massive expenditure on arms and animal experiments, via public and private sector agencies and universities. You must decide whether these factors outweigh the benefits of expenditure on education, health and social security (see Table 15.1).

**TABLE 15.1** ▦ Large companies commonly avoided by ethical investors

| Company | Stockmarket weighting % | Arms | Alcohol | Tobacco | Gambling |
|---|---|---|---|---|---|
| Allied Domecq | 0.27 | | * | | |
| Bass | 0.37 | | * | | |
| BAT | 0.64 | | | * | |
| BAe Systems | 0.66 | * | | | |
| Cobham | 0.06 | * | | | |
| Diageo | 1.48 | | * | | |
| Gallaher | 0.15 | | | * | |
| GKN | 0.29 | * | | | |
| Greene King | 0.02 | | * | | |
| Hilton | 0.18 | | | | * |
| Imperial Tobacco | 0.21 | | | * | |
| Marconi | 1.15 | * | | | |
| Rank | 0.05 | | | | * |
| Rolls Royce | 0.18 | * | | | |
| Scottish & Newc | 0.18 | | * | | |
| Smiths Industries | 0.26 | * | | | |
| Spirent | 0.32 | * | | | |
| Tomkins | 0.07 | * | | | |
| Wetherspoon | 0.04 | | * | | |
| Whitbread | 0.16 | | * | | |
| Wolverhampton & Dudley | 0.02 | | * | | |
| **Total** | **6.76** | | | | |

*Source:* Chiswell Associates

## Broad-brush approach

In practice many investors settle for a broad-brush approach that eliminates the obvious villains but does not go into too much detail. Using the analogy above, this would exclude the tobacco companies but not the supermarkets that sell cigarettes. This approach would also screen out the companies whose primary business is armaments but could leave you with companies with a minority interest in arms.

Probably some element of compromise is called for, but you have to decide how far you are prepared to go to identify the ethical stars and whether you are willing to accept the resulting restriction in investment choice. If you take ethical investment to its natural conclusion you will end up investing purely in property. This is not a good idea.

> **Garage manager** You must have shot an awful lot of tigers, sir.
> **Charlie C** Yes, I use a machine gun.
>
> *The Italian Job* (1969)

You also need to decide whether to limit your ethical investment views to your private portfolio of shares and funds or whether to take it further. For example, if you are in a company pension scheme, what influence, if any, can you have over the investment aims of the pension fund?

The chances are that this would be limited to your freedom to express your views to the trustees. Ultimately, you could decide to leave the scheme and set up your own ethical personal pension plan, but this could be a very high price to pay because the company scheme is a very valuable benefit for you and your dependants (see Chapter 22).

# Impact of ethical screening on returns

Critics of ethical investment argue that performance suffers due to the exclusion of many major FTSE 100 companies, most of which have something distinctly unethical somewhere among their diverse operations. If a fund excludes the very obvious unethical villains it would lose access to about 8 per cent of the stockmarket by value. This figure grows if you add animal testing, nuclear power, and environmental damage, for example. The full EIRIS screening, shown above, disqualifies up to 60 per cent of the FTSE 100 companies.

This means that an ethical fund is likely to have a disproportionate weighting towards smaller, more risky companies. As far as performance goes, smaller companies have the ability to outperform their larger counterparts. They are also inclined to be more volatile and must be selected with great care, as the performance of the FTSE 250 and SmallCap (the smallest 368 in the FTSE All-Share index) have demonstrated over the past few years. Bear in mind that when the SmallCap does well it is often due to the stunning outperformance of a handful of companies rather than a consistently good performance across the board.

---

> **cool advice**   An ethical policy may leave a fund over-exposed to certain sectors which are only be ethical by default – the hotels and leisure industry, for example.

---

In addition there is a danger that the ethical policy leaves a fund overexposed to certain sectors that may only be ethical by default – the hotels and leisure industry, for example. Moreover, the fund would be unable to reap the rewards of a boom in other sectors such as chemicals, engineering or pharmaceuticals.

A good year to illustrate this point is 1997, when most general ethical funds underperformed the market as a whole because they had limited exposure to the sectors that outperformed. Typical exclusions that proved regrettable from the performance point of view included banks (most lend money indiscriminately to non-ethical companies and countries with poor human rights records), integrated oils (environmental damage) and pharmaceuticals (animal testing and, occasionally, exploitation in tests on humans in emerging countries).

## Alternative investments

EIRIS provides details of investments that it believes offer a distinct social value but which are not listed on the Stock Exchange. Examples include investment in a company that imports tropical hardwood from sustainable sources, or one involved in fair trade with developing economies.

The attraction here is that by investing in these companies you help them to grow. However, the downside is that the shares may not pay dividends and can be difficult to sell. Moreover, all the usual warnings about small companies apply with a vengeance.

> **cool advice** Critics of ethical investment argue that performance suffers due to the exclusion of many major FTSE 100 companies, most of which have something distinctly unethical somewhere among their diverse operations.

## Further information

The EIRIS website is at **www.eiris.org**. Information on the ethical indices is available from **www.ftse4good.com** or phone 020 7448 1810. *Life and Pensions Moneyfacts* lists ethical and environmental life assurance funds, pension funds and unit trusts: 01692 500765.

**You'll need something to protect you from the cold.**

Dr Craven, *The Raven* (1963)

# 16

# Cycles and bears

After reading this chapter you will

*realise that nothing is safe*

*run from equities to bonds and from bonds to cash and from cash to panic*

*run away and join a circus*

**THE EVENTS OF SEPTEMBER 2001** – the bombing of the World Trade Centre in New York – and the subsequent political and economic uncertainty – added fuel to the gloomy predictions of a prolonged bear market. In turn this has focused the attention of cautious equity investors on the bewildering array of products that aim to provide the holy grail of 'steady growth' or, as the alternative investments providers would put it, 'absolute returns' – that is, positive returns throughout all market cycles.

But despite marketing claims, there is no magic formula that puts the 'steady' in the growth formula and the 'absolute' in the return.

Protection against volatility carries a cost and with products that appear to rely on little magic black boxes, like with profits funds, protected funds and hedge funds, it is usually quite difficult to establish what that cost will be in terms of the reduced annual return. Equally unclear is the potential downside. With profits bonds, for example, have been criticised for the lack of clarity in profit distribution and guarantees, but the real issue here is that investors do not understand the risks and the penalties that can apply under adverse market conditions.

> ❄ c o o l
> advice    Despite marketing claims, there is no magic formula that puts the 'steady' in the growth formula and the 'absolute' in the return.

If you want to manage equity risk through a financial product as opposed to asset allocation, you need to assess whether the underlying structures and techniques will meet the marketing claims. This 'look through' approach will also help you to make comparisons between apparently very different products.

One of the most worrying aspects of stockmarket investment is the tendency of professional and private investor alike to behave like lemmings under certain economic conditions. Mass hysteria can trigger a dramatic fall in equity prices. In practice crashes are few and far between. Of more concern – and a much more likely contingency – is a slow slide into a long bear market.

At the risk of over-simplification, a bear market is where share prices are falling, while a bull market is where shares are rising. If you are feeling bearish you believe share prices are due to take a tumble, while if you are bullish you believe the opposite.

## How bubbles burst and markets crash

To understand the lemming-like activity associated with a market crash (or 'burst bubble', as in 'South Sea' and 'Mississippi') it is useful to consider the period leading up to these events to spot the common denominators. This is not a technical exercise. The most obvious features of the pre-crash market mentality are those well-known human characteristics greed and fear. In a wise little volume called

> If we crash I can't win!
> Speed, *Speed Racer* (1967)

*Bluff Your Way in Economics* (Ravette Publishing, 1996), Stuart Trow describes the bubble mentality and what happened when the Mississippi bubble burst:

*A speculative bubble occurs when people become obsessed with a particular investment. Fear plays a large part in the bubble's build-up, with investors desperate not to miss the boat and willing to buy at any price, completely disregarding logic.*

History provides some examples that are both illuminating and, due to the passage of time, quaintly amusing. Take the Mississippi Bubble. In the early eighteenth century, the Mississippi Company held a monopoly on all French territories in North America. The king of France and the French government were enthralled by the prospect of untold riches promised from the New World to the extent that they allowed the Royal Bank to issue bank notes backed not by gold or silver, as was common at the time, but by shares in the Mississippi Company.

 **The most obvious features of the pre-crash market mentality are those well-known human characteristics greed and fear.**

Trow explains: 'When the company crashed in 1720, the entire French monetary system was wiped out. Even people who had not invested in the company lost out as the bank notes became worthless.'

Britain escaped a similar fate but nevertheless thousands of investors suffered terribly when the South Sea Bubble burst after the collapse of the extraordinarily speculative South Sea Company in the eighteenth century. This followed a period of extreme stockmarket activity so the sudden loss of confidence in one company appeared to trigger a loss of confidence in the entire market.

As we can see, market crashes are devastatingly indiscriminate. For tumbling along with the bubble company's shares go the share prices of some of the most respected companies in the economy. Nor do markets always recover quickly – hence the need to take a long-term view with equities. The Wall Street Crash of 1929, for example, saw US stocks lose almost 90 per cent of their value. They did not regain their pre-crash levels until the mid-1950s.

Turning to more recent history, in October 1987 the UK stockmarket crashed. Although pundits still argue about the precise cause, the essential point is that once again greed and an unbridled speculative frenzy had overtaken logic. Investors continued to buy shares because they failed to see that the prices could not go on rising indefinitely. The bubble mentality does not just apply to shares. Other assets are equally vulnerable. A similar frenzy was characteristic of the UK housing boom in the late 1980s when people paid silly prices only to find themselves in the negative equity trap once the housing bubble had burst.

We are just as vulnerable today as we were in 1987. Some would argue more so due to the increased number of leveraged investors – those who take out a loan in order to invest in the stockmarket. It sounds highly risky yet this is precisely what homeowners do when they arrange an interest-only mortgage backed by an endowment or individual savings account (ISA). For this arrangement to succeed you need to achieve sufficient rates of return to service the loan and make a profit.

> **Bialystock** What's the matter with you?
> **Bloom** I'm hysterical! I'm having hysterics. I'm hysterical. I can't stop when I'm like this. Oh my god. Ah-la-la-la. [*Bialystock throws a bucket of water on him.*] I'm wet. I'm wet. I'm hysterical and I'm wet. I'm in pain and I'm wet and I'm still hysterical! No, no, no, don't hit, don't hit. It doesn't help. It only increases my sense of danger.
>
> *The Producers* (1968)

## Your survival kit

To survive and indeed thrive during bear market cycles you need a clear strategy. Fortunately, this is one time when private investors can score over the professionals because there are no clients waiting for their next quarterly figures and there is no pressure on you to follow the market trend.

Think first why you are in the market at all. If you are typical of most private investors, you will purchase shares for the long-term income and gains and will recognise that it is inefficient, time consuming and costly to change or churn your portfolio on a regular basis. So, in theory at least, if you invest in the right type of shares – even if it is at the wrong time – your portfolio should be able to ride market cycles. If, after careful research, you thought a company was worth investing in two weeks ago, its shares will still be worth holding today. And in most cases it should still pay out dividends, even if there has been a sudden switch from a bull to a bear market. Provided you chose wisely in the first place, the capital growth will return.

This logic is fairly sound when applied to blue chips because these businesses are themselves well diversified and represent a spread of risk across markets (and often continents too) within just one share holding. However, the logic does not necessarily extend to smaller, more speculative companies. In the run up to October 1987, for example, some companies came to the stockmarket which were very speculative and considerably overpriced. They did not recover. In this case you would have got the worst of all worlds. You paid dearly for your shares in the first place, their price fell and they never recovered capital value. Moreover, you did not even benefit from a decent run of dividends.

Remember also that certain market sectors are cyclical. Shares in engineering or construction companies, for example, usually do well when the general economy is flourishing, while shares in consumer goods companies and retailers will do well while consumer spending is expected to rise.

> **c o o l advice**  Interest rates are important because they may directly affect the amount a company is charged for borrowing, although the extent will depend on the structure of the debt.

So, while the following explanation attempts to demystify some of the economic jargon, do bear in mind that these are generalisations only and if you bought a tin-pot company in the first place, no amount of economic alchemy is going to turn it into a crock of gold.

## How to read economic information

This is going to be a *very* brief lesson in economic cycles and how they affect your shares. If it sounds theoretical, that's because it is. No sooner do we spot a clear trend for certain companies (categorised by size or sector, for example) to behave in a certain way during a certain stage in the economic cycle, we are proved wrong. This is when we have to remember yet again that investment is an art, not a science. So, while it is handy to know the theory, never expect reality to mirror it.

First, let's get to grips with some handy vocabulary. The economics reports in newspapers rely on just a few key phrases and with these manage to mystify most of the people most of the time. Regard the jargon as no more than a form of shorthand and remember that it is one thing to understand the theory, but entirely another to interpret economic events correctly. Economics is a very imprecise science (rather like investment) and the experts usually get it wrong but nevertheless are paid a great deal for their views.

# The essential jargon

Before you start you need to understand what is meant by 'the economy'. Think of it in terms of old-fashioned home economics – which was all about making the housekeeping last for the entire week and boiling the Sunday roast bones for soup on Thursdays. Nowadays of course we all have credit cards so we don't have to make income meet expenditure – or at least not very often.

The economy is the financial state of the nation. The *state* of the economy tells us how much housekeeping is coming in and whether we are being prudent and boiling bones for soup, or borrowing in order to spend what we do not have.

Certain statistics known as economic indicators show the state of the economy at a particular time. The most important economic indicators to remember are interest rates and inflation because whatever happens to the UK economy or the world as a whole usually ends up affecting one or both of these rates. This in turn has an effect on government lending policy and companies' performance, which in turn affect your investments.

## Interest rates

Interest rates are important because they may directly affect the amount a company is charged for borrowing, although the extent will depend on the structure of the debt.

The Bank of England is responsible for setting short-term interest rates and uses them to curb or encourage spending. If we are all spending far too much ('we' being both individuals and companies) then the Bank will increase interest rates to stop us borrowing to spend. Likewise, if we are saving too much and not spending enough, the Bank might lower interest rates to encourage more borrowing and spending.

## Retail Prices Index (RPI)

This is published by the Office for National Statistics every month and is the most common measure for inflation. It is calculated by constructing a so-called 'basket' of goods and services used by the typical household (based on a sample survey of about 7000 households throughout the country). The basket includes housing and household expenditure, personal expenditure, travel and leisure, food and catering, alcohol and tobacco. The most recent base date was January 1987, which had a value of 100.

You may come across other types of inflation. For example, underlying inflation is the unofficial term given to the inflation rate in an economy measured by RPI minus mortgage interest payments. Headline inflation is the full RPI, including mortgage interest costs.

## Impact on companies and share prices

So, how does all this come together to affect your investments? Well, rising interest rates increase the cost of borrowing for the companies in which you invest. The profits of a company which is highly geared (that is, it has a high ratio of borrowing to assets) naturally will suffer if the cost of servicing its debts increases. This cost will be passed on to shareholders because it will lower the profits out of which it pays the dividends.

At the same time the dividends available from equities will start to look uncompetitive to income investors who will find better sources elsewhere if interest rates are high. Double-digit rates of interest on deposits are very appealing no matter what the rate of inflation. Moreover, high interest rates may damage a company's growth prospects because they will encourage it to keep its spare cash in deposits rather than to take a risk and invest in expanding the business.

Low interest rates have the opposite effect and can be good for companies because the cost of borrowing comes down and the share value rises. So, although a fall in interest rates sounds gloomy because it follows news of high unemployment or a slowdown in the economic growth (usually expressed as the gross domestic product or GDP – see below), for equity investors it can be good news.

Gilts react to fluctuations in inflation. A rise in inflation usually forces gilt prices down and therefore yields go up. This is because there is less demand for fixed interest securities at these times. An improvement in gilt yields in turn can have a detrimental effect on the stockmarket because gilts become more attractive relative to equities.

The public sector borrowing requirement (PSBR) also has an impact on the gilt market. The PSBR is the public sector deficit – the amount by which government spending (including local authorities and nationalised industries) exceeds the income from taxation, rates and other revenues. One of the main methods the government uses to finance this debt is to sell gilts. If the PSBR is higher than expected, the price of gilts may fall, as there will be a greater supply.

The budget deficit is similar to the PSBR but also includes income from occasional 'extraordinary revenue' – for example, from privatisations of public sector companies. So a cut in the budget deficit or PSBR will be good news for gilts because supply is more limited and so prices rise. However, if the government has achieved the cut by increasing corporate taxation, this will be generally bad news for shares.

Other factors include the health or otherwise of retail sales, which obviously largely affects the retail stores and supermarkets and housing starts (the number of new homes being built) which are generally viewed as a leading indicator of a future pick-up in the economy.

## The market cycles

Everyone knows that the timing of investment decisions is critical. Getting it right is not easy though, even for the experts. As Mark Twain once said, 'October is one of the peculiarly dangerous months to speculate in stocks. The others are July, January, September, April, November, May ...'.

> **Field reporter** Are they slow-moving chief?
> **Sheriff McClelland** Yeah, they're dead. They're all messed up.
>
> *Night of the Living Dead* (1968)

What follows is again a very brief overview of the main features of market cycles and their impact on share prices. Please remember, this is the *theory* and should not unduly influence your decisions.

If you have a large lump sum to invest then almost certainly you would be wise to drip-feed it into the market over a period of, say, six months to a year. In this case you would want to check how the economy is behaving at the particular times you invest in order to determine the effect on companies and sectors.

But to switch from one sector to another in the hope of cashing in on the market's weakness or, even more risky, to keep one step ahead is almost certain to fail all but the most dedicated full-time investor. Moreover, it will prove very costly.

Remember also that all the institutional investors will interpret economic trends and anticipated changes in market cycles ahead of you, so share prices will reflect both the current and expected future trends. Trying to spot the change in cycle well before the professional analysts is not a game for the novice or indeed for anyone who values their capital.

Finally, do remember that when it comes to shorter-term investment decisions all things are relative. Shares are only worth the additional risk if they offer returns well above what you can get from gilts, bonds and deposits, taking into account tax and the dealing costs.

## Phase 1: Early stage of a recovery

At this point interest rates are high and economic activity is at a low ebb. Inflation is falling and interest rates also begin to fall – perhaps anticipated by rises in the bond markets. Blue chip companies begin to improve but interest in smaller companies is non-existent.

The first shares to benefit are interest rate sensitive shares such as banks, property and building and construction companies – some of which previously may have been very depressed. However, analysts view this as a dangerous phase because banks may regard their problem clients as more valuable if they go into liquidation. More companies go bust in the early stages of a recovery than in the depths of a recession.

*Which shares may do well?* Banks and well-financed property companies.

## Phase 2: Well into recovery

This is when the recovery gathers pace and short-term interest rates continue to fall. As a rule, at this point the recovery ought to begin to feed through into consumer spending. Share prices rise.

*Which shares may do well?* Retailers, car dealers, and manufacturers of durable goods such as furniture, should begin to improve.

## Phase 3: Recovery

Interest rates have now reached the bottom and investors fear they may rise. At this point the market may see a major 'correction' to its generally upward trend.

*Which shares may do well?* Capital goods, engineering and other heavy industry.

## Phase 4: Heading for recession

The flow of money into the markets is rather like an oil tanker – it keeps going for quite a while after the signal to stop. So the market makes sharp gains on heavy volume (in other words, there is a lot of money coming into the markets) despite rising interest rates. Smaller companies prove very popular. Conglomerates, 'people' businesses and 'concept stocks' are all the rage. Commodity prices are booming and stoking up inflation for the future. (Commodities are raw materials and foodstuffs, among other items.)

*Which shares should do well?* While there will be money to be made in the stockmarket at this phase of the market cycle, it is important to recognise that this is the period which generally will precede a fall. You might consider taking steps to anticipate a fall by gradually but steadily shifting some of your assets out of shares and into cash or other more defensive investments. Avoid trendy companies like the plague.

## Phase 5: Into recession

The stockmarket falls, possibly in response to an external event but in any event interest in shares dries up. Commodity shares might do well at this point because the underlying economy still has to turn down.

*Which shares do well?* Defensive shares like food, manufacturers and brewers will tend to do better than the market as a whole but may still drop in price.

## Achieving a balance of sectors

No combination of investments will be absolutely suited to a particular phase of the market. Even if you plan ahead, you will find that each successive market cycle displays different characteristics. Nevertheless, a diversified portfolio is more likely to hold its value or at least limit the blows, compared with a portfolio that is weighted towards just one or two sectors.

# How to deal with bears

If you are confident that your portfolio contains good quality shares and are prepared to hold for the long term, you are probably as well placed as any to sit out a bear market. Even so, it is worth watching for opportunities to buy into quality companies at depressed levels. If you want to take further action to prepare your portfolio for a bear market, then there are certain steps you might consider. At all times keep in mind the aims of your portfolio.

## Change your asset allocation

Gilts and bonds may be more appealing if you are concerned about the equity markets. If you are already looking for income then you might consider moving more of your portfolio into conventional gilts. Gilts and bonds are discussed in Chapter 14.

There are alternatives. You can try to reduce risk by including overseas as well as UK equities in your portfolio. In addition you could build in a 'protection' by using more predictable investments (not all of which will be low risk), such as zero dividend preference shares, National Savings certificates and gilt and corporate bond funds. Remember though, if you invest directly, gilts and bonds are only predictable if you hold them to maturity. If you need to sell before this date you will find these instruments can be almost as volatile as equities.

## With profits

With profits funds aim to reduce volatility by diversifying across a range of asset classes, but in addition they use an actuarial smoothing mechanism to try to ensure consistent returns over the long term. As a with profits policyholder you may also be exposed to the profits and losses of other lines of the company's business. This can be both good and bad, as Equitable Life's policyholders now appreciate.

## Protected and guaranteed funds

Protected or guaranteed funds are quite different. Typically, these guarantee the original capital and provide part of the rise in a stock market index, while limiting the potential falls. Instead of using asset allocation techniques to sustain returns through poor equity markets, the guarantee is provided through a derivatives contract – an insurance policy if you like. The fund manager can exercise this contract if the market falls beyond a certain point.

---

❄ **cool advice**   If you have a large lump sum to invest then almost certainly you would be wise to drip-feed it into the market over a period of, say, six months to a year.

---

Given their high costs, protected funds are perhaps the least effective equity-based structures for the long term. They do, however, provide a halfway house between cash and equities and can be used to consolidate gains a few years before you want to retire or repay the mortgage, for example.

The success of these products depends on the investor's expectations and this is a very important point. Most protected funds outperform cash so if you were an investor who would otherwise have put money in a building society account or premium bonds then you would have been perfectly happy with the performance. Investors who want a stockmarket-linked investment and are prepared to pay a premium to restrict large potential losses or to reduce uncertainty in the form of volatility would also most likely be happy. Investors who want guarantees that cost nothing or full stockmarket potential with no downside will be disappointed.

Having said that, products which base your return and the capital guarantee on the performance of a complex series of indices or an unrepresentative basket of individual shares are very high risk indeed and have no role in the cautious investor's portfolio – or indeed in *any* portfolio.

## Alternative investments

Alternative investments are the latest 'black box' product. Investments are described as alternative where the risk profile and the return of the fund or asset do not correlate with conventional equity and bond markets. This can mean an asset class like property, but is more likely to mean something very risky – for example, private equities that are not quoted on a stock exchange.

Probably the most common example of an alternative investment is the hedge fund. There is no statutory definition of a hedge fund but, as the consultant PricewaterhouseCoopers points out, most of these funds will share the following characteristics:

- aggressive leverage – that is heavy borrowing to invest
- the use of 'short' selling – that is buying and selling assets the fund doesn't own (see below)
- performance-related fees – typically an annual fee of 1 per cent to 2 per cent of the assets plus anything from 5 to 25 per cent of the profits
- short-term strategies
- opaque financial information – in other words, you never really know how much you are paying.

The classic hedge fund holds undervalued stocks for the medium to long term in the same way as any active manager might do. This is the 'long' element in a long/short fund. For a small premium, hedge fund managers also 'borrow' stocks which they believe are becoming overpriced from the major institutional pension and insurance funds, many of which indulge in stock lending to boost their own returns. The hedge manager sells high and repurchases the stocks when the price drops so they can return them to the stock lender on the due date. This technique is known as 'short' selling and allows managers to pocket the profit if the price of the stock drops. In this way these funds can sustain the annual return in falling markets – but only where the manager has outstanding skills. In theory it exposes the investor to an unlimited liability if the price of the stocks that are sold short shoots through the ceiling.

There are as many different styles as there are hedge fund managers. Some are comparatively low risk, but others are very risky indeed, particularly where the fund is highly geared – that is, it has borrowed heavily to invest. Charges can be much higher than for conventional funds and more complex – for example, there is usually a performance-related element for the fund manager. It is also important to realise that you are investing in the skills of a specific manager, and these managers tend to change jobs quite frequently

The fund of hedge funds approach has proved most popular to date. This is where the fund invests in a range of hedge funds with different styles and strategies, reducing the exposure to any single hedge fund or manager – but at the expense of another layer of costs.

## Bear in mind …

Before you consider any specific products you need to be clear about your investment horizon and your attitude to risk. There is nothing intrinsically wrong with a risky investment as long as you understand the risks and have the capacity to take that risk. Most investors have a poor perception of risk – for example, many would define a tracker fund as low risk, or they might perceive a high-income bond with a guaranteed return of 10 per cent as a free lunch with no regard to risk to capital.

> **Joe** You're *not* a girl! You're a guy! Why would a guy want to marry a guy?
> **Jerry** Security.
> *Some Like It Hot* (1959)

One of the most obvious points to clarify when you examine any product is just how much you can lose if markets go pear shaped (which they do) and/or everyone tries to get out at once (ditto). In 'black box' products, somewhere in the small print the company will explain its powers to cut the value of your investment or to renege on its guarantees under certain conditions, but it may make the likelihood of this actually happening look very remote indeed. A good rule of thumb here is to avoid any product that depends on markets or interest rates behaving in a predictable way.

If you prefer to stick to the more standard collective equity funds, such as unit trusts and unit-linked life funds, you can manage risk to some extent through careful asset allocation so that you are diversified across sectors as well as markets and across styles as well as fund managers. Even sophisticated investors may find upon examination that they are well diversified in geographical terms but concentrated in certain sectors, while the portfolio as a whole is geared towards growth funds with no allocation to value investing.

> **cool advice** Given their high costs, protected funds are perhaps the least effective equity-based structures for the long term. They do, however, provide a half way house between cash and equities and can be used to consolidate gains a few years before you want to retire or repay the mortgage, for example.

The structure that appears best designed to capture the essence of diversification is the multi-manager or fund of fund approach. Where this is offered by a well-resourced company with a first-rate fund manager database, the approach can manage risk in three important ways: by diversifying across asset classes, investment managers and investment styles. However, do bear in mind that this approach will add an extra layer of cost.

## Further information

ProShare, *The Private Investor's Guide to the Stockmarket*, was the main source for the guide to economic cycles (**www.proshare.org**).

**The only performance that makes it, that makes it all the way to the top, is the one that achieves madness.**

Turner, *Performance* (1970)

# 17

# Performance

After reading this chapter you will

*appreciate that the fund manager's style has an impact on returns – as well as his dress sense*

*understand why statistics and damned lies are so easily confused*

*never again believe what you read in the papers*

**TO ASSESS THE PERFORMANCE** of your portfolio you need to compare it with a range of suitable benchmarks. Equally important is to set your own performance targets. These should be realistic and refer specifically to the aims and objectives of your investment choice.

Don't feel daunted by the mass of detail in the *Financial Times* (*FT*) Company and Markets section. This is the best starting point for any investor who wants to check the progress of a private portfolio of shares and funds and provides a wealth of useful information once you learn to read the language. This chapter gives you a quick course in how to interpret the pink pages.

# Compare with 'safe' investments

Before you consider the performance of your choice of shares, it is always a good idea to check what returns you could achieve from comparatively 'safe' investments. For the purpose of comparisons with equities, a 'safe' benchmark would be one that offers a high degree of capital protection.

 **cool advice** **Before you consider the performance of your choice of shares, it is always a good idea to check what returns you could achieve from comparatively 'safe' investments that offer a high degree of capital protection.**

So, take a look at what the after tax returns have been on 60- and 120-day building society postal deposit accounts, internet accounts and short- to medium-term gilts. These benchmarks will reveal whether over these periods the returns from equities have been worth the additional risks to your capital. You can find these figures in the *FT*.

## Compare with inflation

There are several ways of evaluating the performance of your portfolio. The simplest measure also has the most serious drawbacks. This is an absolute benchmark. Let's say, for example, that retail price inflation is 3 per cent and

> No, there's no terrible way to win. There's only winning.
>
> Jean-Pierre Sarti, *Grand Prix* (1966)

your portfolio, which is designed to achieve a balance of income and growth, returns 6 per cent over the year. Considered in isolation you might be quite satisfied that your capital has grown by 3 per cent in real terms – that is, 3 per cent above the rate of inflation.

However, you might be less satisfied if you discovered that the FTSE All-Share (the main yardstick for the UK stockmarket as a whole) had risen by 12 per cent, or that many other investors with similar portfolio aims to your own had achieved 13 per cent. The point is that when markets are rising most professional investors and private amateurs can achieve what look like reasonable results. The real skill is in achieving above-average returns.

## Compare with an index or peer group

To measure performance in this way you need a benchmark relative to an index or peer group. As mentioned, the most relevant index for a portfolio of UK shares is the FTSE All-Share, which contains about 770 companies listed on the UK stockmarket.

If you specialise in medium sized or smaller companies you might also measure against a more specific index such as the SmallCap (the companies in the All-Share which are outside the top 350) or the FTSE 250 (the largest 250 companies after the FTSE 100). This is fine provided you keep the results in context. Whatever your specialisation, it is always worth checking your progress compared with a broad benchmark. If you are in smaller companies and the best performing shares are in the FTSE 100 you may decide that taking the extra risk associated with small companies isn't worth it. For internet fans, the FTSE International website is packed with useful information about the FTSE indices (**www.ftse.com**).

## Collective funds

With collective funds it is comparatively easy to measure against a peer group because the funds are categorised according to investment aim. For example, managed (a combination of equities, bonds and sometimes property), UK equity income, international fixed interest and so on.

> **cool advice** The most relevant index for a portfolio of UK shares is the FTSE All-Share, which contains about 718 companies listed on the UK stockmarket.

Having said that, within the managed fund sector for life assurance and pension funds there is a wide range of different risk levels, so do check the asset allocation and types of shares selected by the manager. You might find, for example, that the manager has achieved an outstanding performance only because he or she took bigger risks than are typical for the fund sector as a whole. A good example is a managed fund where the manager invests almost wholly in equities during a bull market, when most of the other funds are, say, 70 per cent in equities with the rest in bonds and gilts to reduce risk.

It is also important to check performance on a discrete basis. Discrete results show year-on-year rather than cumulative performance. This is important because a good cumulative result over five years might hide an outstanding (possibly lucky) short-term performance followed by several years of mediocrity. Unfortunately, most published results for collective funds are cumulative and discrete results are difficult to analyse without access to a major statistics database such as Standard & Poor's Micropal. However, your stockbroker or financial adviser certainly should have access to these statistics.

## Performance measurement services

In the past private investors did not have any recognised scientific and independent performance measurement service comparable to what is available in the institutional market. Recently, two independent services for private investors were launched that both aim to provide a benchmark against which you can measure your portfolio. The first is the Private Investor Indices from FTSE International and the stockbrokers' association APCIMS. The second is from WM, one of the leading performance measurers in the institutional market. Details of both services are provided at the end of this chapter.

> I'd like to make one good score and back off.
>
> Pike, *The Wild Bunch* (1969)

You can use the FTSE International indices (income, growth and balanced), which are published in the *FT*, in several ways:

- to make a direct comparison with your own portfolio
- to use as the basis for a review of the asset allocation and structure of your portfolio with your investment adviser
- as a benchmark against which you can compare and assess the performance of discretionary stockbrokers.

The FTSE/APCIMS indices show what happens to a portfolio which is run like a collection of index-tracking funds – each element representing the appropriate index for UK equities, various overseas equity indices, cash and so on. Clearly, the asset allocation of any 'model' portfolio is to some extent arbitrary but, given the expertise of the providers, this is as good a benchmark as any and will show whether your own or your manager's deviations from the indices actually improved returns or undermined performance.

WM's service is slightly different. This shows whether you and/or your manager did better or worse than your peers and is based on asset mix information from over 20 managers and brokers, combined with the returns on the appropriate investment indices over the quarter measured.

Both services are very useful, but remember that benchmarks are only intended to provide guidelines and should not be regarded as an absolute measure of performance. The FTSE indices, for example, are designed to relate to the average UK-based investor with a sterling denominated pool of savings.

FTSE International pointed out that investors may have potential capital gains tax liabilities which must be taken into account, as must any advisory fees. Also, investors may hold particular stocks for a variety of reasons.

## Collective funds

The online websites that provide useful information on funds are shows in Appendix 1. Chase de Vere publishes an annual guide to ISAs and updates its performance supplement every six months (**www.chasedevere.co.uk**). For the confident and experienced investor this represents a practical and authoritative DIY kit.

Another excellent source of informed commentary on ISA performance is Bestinvest's ISA guide (**www.bestinvest.co.uk**). In addition to its recommendations, in a refreshingly brisk manner the company also publishes a 'Spot the Dog' guide that lists all the funds you should consider avoiding or selling and explains why.

---

c o o l
advice

Discrete results show year on year rather than cumulative performance. This is important because a good cumulative result over five years might hide an outstanding (possibly lucky) short-term performance followed by several years of mediocrity.

---

For investment trusts, probably the most useful source of performance data is the monthly information sheet (MIS) from the Association of Investment Trust Companies, which shows the results of £100 invested in each investment trust share and the performance of the underlying net assets. The latter is considered a far better measure of the company's investment expertise because it disregards the impact of market forces on the company's share price.

If you have the time, you could build up a more detailed record of performance fluctuations by monitoring your fund's price changes, although this would not show the impact of dividend reinvestment. With unit trusts, for example, your unit trust manager should send you a quarterly or six-monthly valuation that will show the unit price. For more frequent updates you can check the price in the authorised unit trusts pages in the *FT*. On Saturdays the information appears in the *FT* Money section, while on weekdays you will find these figures in the Companies and Markets section. Compare percentage price changes with changes in an appropriate benchmark. Again, the FTSE All-Share is the best general index for UK equity-based unit trusts.

If you find reading the pink pages rather daunting, a basic description of the column headings is provided in the *FT* itself but a more detailed source is the *Financial Times Guide to Using the Financial Pages* by Romesh Vaitslingam (Pearson Education).

## Periods of measurement

The costs of buying shares, whether direct or through a unit or investment trust, combined with the short-term volatility of markets, has meant that performance tends to be measured over the medium to long term – typically over a minimum period of five years. While this is a sensible approach for private investors, it should be backed up by more regular monitoring that will pick up on changes in fund management style or personnel.

With equity investments clearly past performance is an imperfect guide to the future – whether you hold them directly or through collective funds. However, performance can give a good indication of a share's prospects where it is examined in conjunction with other essential data about the company and its investment processes.

> **Mike** I don't think $200 is gonna do us any good if we're dead!
> **Micky** Yeah, man. We shoulda asked for $250.
> *The Monkees* (1966)

Once you have identified the funds that are appropriate in terms of asset class and allocation it is important to assess different managers' investment style. For example, was the performance achieved through a consistent ability to pick the right stocks or did the total returns rely on occasional periods of outperformance based on a high-risk strategy?

It is also important that you or your adviser keep track of the actual management team responsible for the performance. Investment teams have a nasty habit of defecting to rival companies and if this happens in an investment house where star managers rule the roost, you might consider a similar move. Very sensibly, some investment houses keep a tight lid on individual managers and insist on a team mentality that provides a more stable environment.

# Guide to reading the financial pages

The sections below on 'How to Read the Figures' were drawn from the material mentioned in the source material at the end of this chapter plus details provided in the *FT* 'Guide to the London Share Service' which is published at the end of the share prices in the Companies and Markets section. For investment trust performance data, the AITC was the main source.

## *Financial Times* services

The *FT*'s London Share Service includes various investor services indicated by a symbol after the company name. A club symbol indicates that you can obtain the current annual or interim report free of charge. All you have to do is phone a 24-hour number quoting the reference provided in that edition of the *FT*. Up-to-the-second share prices are available by telephone from the *FT* Cityline service at 020 7873 4378 (**www.ftcityline.com**).

# Share prices information

Share prices, including investment trusts, are quoted each day in the *FT* Companies and Markets section. This includes companies in the All-Share, the Alternative Investment Market (the market for new smaller companies) and the foreign companies (Figure 17.1).

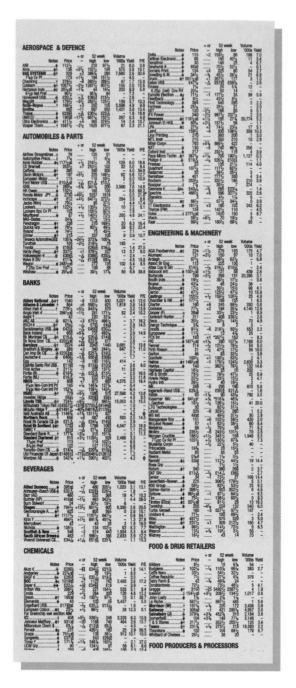

**FIGURE 17.1** ■ Example share prices

Source: Financial Times

## How to read the figures

The column headings used in the *FT* are shown in brackets.

### Name and notes (Notes)

The first column lists the company name or its abbreviation. The various symbols represent particular features of its shares. For example, a diamond indicates that a merger, bid or reorganisation is in process, while a club indicates that there is a free annual or interim report available. A heart symbol indicates a stock not officially listed in the UK. Many shares of overseas mining companies fall into this category. A spade symbol indicates an unregulated collective investment scheme.

These are some of the main symbols used but for a comprehensive list refer to the 'Guide to London Share Service' in the Companies and Markets section of the *FT*.

### Market price (Price)

The second column shows the average (or mid-price) of the best buying and selling prices in pence quoted by market makers (the financial institutions that actually buy and sell shares) at the 4.30 pm close of the market on the previous trading day. If trading in a share has been suspended, perhaps because the company in question is involved in a takeover, the figure shown is the price at suspension and this is indicated by a hash symbol (#). The letters 'xd' following a price mean ex-dividend and indicate that a dividend has been announced recently but buyers of the shares will not be entitled to receive it.

### Price change (+ or -)

The third column gives the change in the closing price compared with the end of the previous trading day.

### Previous price movements (52 week high/low)

Columns four and five show the highest and lowest prices recorded for the stock over the past year.

### Trading volume (Volume '000s)

This shows the trading volume at the end of each day and is a good indication of a share's liquidity. Both buying and selling figures are counted so divide by two to get the number of shares that changed hands.

### Yield

Column seven shows the percentage return on the share. It is calculated by dividing the gross dividend by the current share price.

### Price/earnings ratio (P/E)

The final column is the market price of the share divided by the company's earnings (profits) per share in its latest 12-month trading period. In effect this is a measure of investor confidence since it compares the price of a stock with the amount which the company is earning in profits. Generally, the higher the figure, the higher the confidence, but you should only measure against companies in the same sector.

Yields and P/E ratios move in opposite directions. If the share price rises, since the gross dividend remains the same, the dividend yield falls. Also, if the share price rises, since the earnings per share are constant, the P/E ratio increases. Expect a big change in these figures when important company announcements are made on earnings and dividends.

## Weekly summary

On Mondays the *FT* provides information on the following (see Figure 17.2):

- *Price change*: the weekly percentage change.
- *Dividend*: the dividends paid in the company's last full financial year. A double dagger symbol indicates that the interim dividend has been cut in the current financial year, while a single dagger indicates an increase.
  - *Dividend cover*: this shows the number of times the dividend could have been paid out of net profits. The figure is a ratio of profits to dividends, calculated by dividing the earnings per share by the gross dividend per share. Analysts regard this as a key figure in assessing the security of the company and its ability to maintain the level of future dividend payments (see page 149).
  - *Market capitalisation*: this is an indication of the stockmarket value of the company in millions of pounds sterling. It is calculated by multiplying the number of shares in issue by their market price. In order to calculate the number of shares in issue from the figures listed, you can divide the market capitalisation figure by the market price. However, if there are other classes of share capital in issue, their value would also need to be added in order to calculate the company's total market capitalisation.

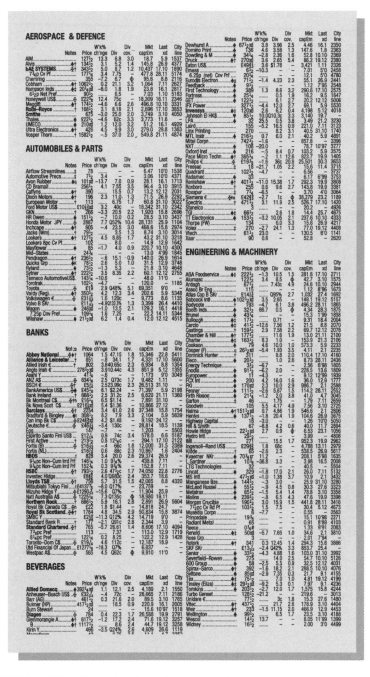

**FIGURE 17.2** ▦ Example of weekly summaries

Source: *Financial Times*

   – *Ex-dividend date*: the last date the share went ex-dividend (see page 199).

   – *Cityline*: for-up-to-the-minute information call Cityline (see page 197).

## Unit trust and open-ended investment company prices

Unit trust and open-ended investment company (OEIC) prices appear under 'Managed Funds Service'. These are funds authorised by the Financial Services Authority and therefore can be marketed direct to the public. Unauthorised trusts are not sold to the public but are used as internal funds by the financial institutions.

    Unit trust and OEIC management groups are obliged to provide certain information to unit holders and the accepted practice is to publish unit prices together with other important information in the *FT* and other national news-papers (Figure 17.3).

## How to read the figures

### Name of the investment group, its pricing system and trust names

This is shown as, for example, 'ABN Amro Fund Managers Ltd (1400)F' fol-lowed by the company's address and telephone number for dealing or enquiries. (Use this number if you want to get a free copy of the management group's most recent report and scheme particulars.) Under each company heading are listed its authorised unit trusts.

    The figure in brackets in the heading is the basis of the company's pricing system. The figure refers to the time at which the price was measured (using a 24-hour clock) and the basis of calculation. 'F' refers to forward pricing, which means orders are taken from investors and the price of units is deter-mined by the next valuation. All larger groups have a valuation point each day, often at noon. So, if an investors phones through their order at 10 am, the price will be struck at noon that same day. An investor who phones at 1 pm will have to wait for a price until the following midday valuation.

    Some groups still deal on an historic price basis, indicated by 'H'. This means they buy and sell using the price agreed at the last valuation point.

### Initial charge (Init chrge)

Column two indicates the percentage charge deducted from your investment to cover certain costs – for example, administration and the sales commission

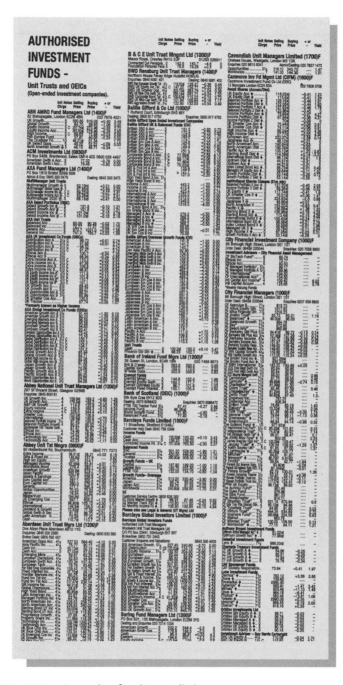

**FIGURE 17.3** ■ Example of unit trust listings

*Source: Financial Times*

paid to advisers, if applicable. If the charge is 5 per cent, then £95 out of every £100 will actually be available to be invested in your chosen fund.

### Notes

The symbols and letters in column three indicate particular features of a unit trust. For example, 'E' indicates that there is an exit charge when you sell your units. 'C' indicates that the manager's annual charge is deducted from capital, not income. A full list of notes, some of which may appear against figures in other columns, can be found at the end of the *FT* Managed Funds section.

### Selling price

This is also called the bid price and is the price at which investors sell units *back* to the manager.

### Buying price

This is also called the offer price and is the price at which investors buy units.

### Price change (+ or -)

The sixth column compares the mid-point between the bid and offer prices with the previous day's quotation.

### Yield (Yield)

The last column shows the income paid by the unit trust as a percentage of the offer price. The quoted yield reflects income earned by the fund during the previous 12 months and therefore relates only to past performance.

## Investment trust prices

Investment trusts are quoted in the London Share Service section. Most of the information is the same as for other companies, with the exception of the last two columns (Figure 17.4).

### Net asset value (NAV)

This is the approximate value of the underlying assets owned by the company. As with the share price, the NAV is shown in pence.

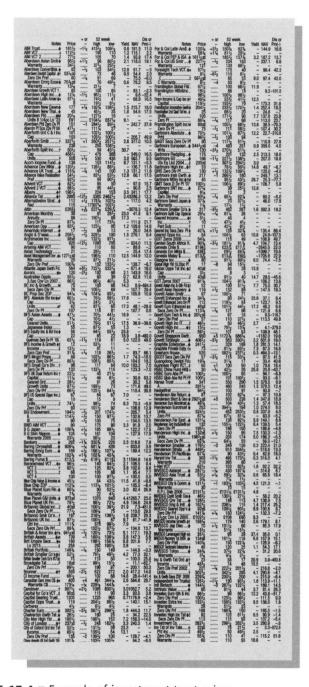

**FIGURE 17.4** ■ Example of investment trust prices

Source: Financial Times

**Discount or premium (Dis or PM(-))**

The premium is shown as a minus sign. If the value of the underlying assets is higher than the share price, then the trust is said to be at a discount. In other words, assuming there is nothing untoward about the trust, the shares are likely to be good value because their underlying value is worth more than the price you pay. If the NAV is lower than the share price the shares are at a premium and generally should be avoided.

## AITC Monthly Information Service

For a more detailed guide to investment trust performance, use the AITC's Monthly Information Service. If you are new to the service you will find it helpful first to read the user's guide which explains how the MIS is organised and what the various figures represent.

> ❄ cool advice   It is important to assess different managers' investment style. For example, was the performance achieved through a consistent ability to pick the right stocks or did the total returns rely on occasional periods of outperformance based on a high-risk strategy?

The monthly service shows the performance of all the trusts over several time periods and includes a comparison of trust performance measured against various indices and other important benchmark figures such as unit trusts, building societies and the retail prices index.

Bear in mind that with the AITC it is the trust itself, not the management group, that is the member. The AITC covers most of the investment trust market by volume.

## Further information

Apart from the ever-growing online resources (see Appendix 1) there are several useful print sources. For shares read the *FT* and *Investors Chronicle*. The *FT* also covers collective funds, but there are several additional sources of reference, for example, the useful articles, surveys and statistics which appear in specialist publications such as *Money Management*, *Planned Savings*, *Bloomberg Money* and *Moneywise* – all of which are available from newsagents. The Consumers Association publishes best buys for personal pensions, among other savings and investment plans, in its *Which?* magazine.

The Private Investor Indices, including their construction and management and back histories, are available free of charge from FTSE International's internet site at (**www.ftse.com**). These indices are shown in the Weekend Money section of the *FT* on Saturdays.

WM's Private Client Indicators are available from:

WM

World Markets House

Crewe Toll

Edinburgh EH4 2PY

Tel: 0131 315 2000; fax 0131 315 2999

**www.wmcompany.com**

*The Financial Times Guide to Using the Financial Pages*, by Romesh Vaitilingam, published by Pearson Education.

For a free sample copy of the AITC Monthly Information Service, write to:

Association of Investment Trust Companies

Durrant House

8–13 Chiswell Street

London EC1Y 4YY

**www.aitc.org.uk**

**I trust I make myself obscure**

Sir Thomas Moore, *A Man for all Seasons* (1966)

# The taxman cometh

After reading this chapter you will

*realise that tax avoidance can be fund, if a tad risky*

*persuade your spouse to put the share portfolio in your name –*
*for tax planning reasons*

*wonder how accountants ever get a date*

**SMART TAX SAVING BEGINS AT HOME**. Here you can redistribute income and assets to make best use of each family member's annual personal allowances and exemptions. You should also consider making appropriate inheritance tax arrangements to help you retain your wealth within the family when you die. Where necessary it might be appropriate to use a trust – an arrangement that allows you to specify who will receive the benefit of certain assets but without giving the beneficiaries total control.

The hallmark of good tax planning is that it will pass the Inland Revenue's scrutiny with flying colours, even where complicated family trust arrangements and considerable wealth are involved.

## Keep it legal

The hallmark of good tax planning is that it will pass the Inland Revenue's scrutiny with flying colours, even where complicated family trust arrangements and considerable wealth are involved.

The Revenue distinguishes between our various attempts to minimise our tax liability. In particular you need to understand the terms 'evasion', 'avoidance' and 'mitigation'. Although these tend to be used indiscriminately, their meanings are *very* different.

- *Evasion*: if you deliberately omit something from your tax return, or give a false description, that's evasion. You have not just been dishonest – you have acted criminally and could be fined or imprisoned.

- *Avoidance*: this is on the right side of the law but can include arrangements that use tax loopholes – that is, procedures the Revenue may frown upon but has not yet got around to closing down.

- *Mitigation*: if your tax saving has been encouraged by the government – for example, you put your investments into an individual savings account (ISA) or a pension scheme, that is mitigation and it is most definitely on the right side of the Revenue.

Among other services, your accountants will help you to mitigate and avoid tax.

## Your tax allowances and exemptions

Successful tax planning requires common sense and expert advice, in equal measures. So, before you change anything, check that the particular use of an allowance or exemption has a genuine benefit. In some cases the cost of setting up and maintaining the arrangement can outweigh any tax savings. Unless you are very experienced, do consult a qualified accountant. All transactions must comply with current tax law and be carefully documented.

cool
advice

Before you change anything, check that the particular use of an allowance or exemption has a genuine benefit.

There are three main personal allowances and exemptions. A full set of figures is provided in Table 18.1, but briefly, for the 2002–2003 tax year, each member of your family has:

- The income tax annual personal allowance of £4615.

- The capital gains tax annual exemption of £7700.

- The inheritance tax annual exemption for gifts of £3000.

**TABLE 18.1** ■ Your main tax allowances and exemptions for 2002–2003

| Income tax allowances | £ |
|---|---|
| Personal allowance under 65 | 4615 |
| Personal allowance 65–74* | 6100 |
| Married couples 65–74** | 5465 |
| Personal allowance 75+* | 6370 |
| Married couples allowance 75+** | 5535 |
| **Income tax rates** | |
| Starting rate 10% | 0–1920 |
| Basic rate 22%*** | 1921–29,900 |
| Higher rate 40% | Over 29,900 |
| **Annual CGT exemption** | |
| Inheritance tax 40% | |

Notes: *The age allowance is reduced by £1 to every £2 you earn until you reach the basic personal allowance rate.
** Relief restricted to 10%.
***20% on interest and 10% dividends.

## Income tax and personal allowances

Your personal allowance is the amount you can receive before paying income tax. The source is irrelevant – it can be earned income or investment income.

Most families are not tax efficient because their combined wealth – both in terms of earned income and assets – tends to be concentrated in the hands of the main breadwinner. He or she, therefore, is also responsible for paying most of the tax, usually at the top rate.

One of the best ways to save on income tax is to share income to make use of the non-working or lower earning spouse's allowance. The most common redistribution techniques are to give income-generating assets to your spouse and, where you run your own business, to pay your spouse a salary. This can lead to an overall annual saving of more than £6000. However, do remember that if you pay your spouse a salary you need to be able to justify the income to the Revenue and provide evidence that you actually pay it.

It is also possible to give income-producing assets to children who can make use of their own allowances and, where necessary, their lower and basic rates of taxation. However, you may need to set up a trust so that the income is not classed as your own. As a rule, if the annual income from your gift is over £100, you, as the parents, will be taxed on the entire amount. You can set up a 'bare trust' to hold the assets and avoid paying the tax, but make sure the costs do not outweigh the benefits. Under this arrangement parents are the registered owners who hold the assets in trust as nominees for the children. The income is accumulated until the children are 18. Where the gift is from another family member – doting grandparents, for example – the income generated is classed as the children's own and can be offset against the personal allowance.

> How can you trust a man who wears both a belt and suspenders. The man can't even trust his own pants.
> Frank, C'era una Volta il West (1969)

Finally on this point, do remember that if you give a gift of assets this has to be unconditional, otherwise the Revenue will see through the arrangement and continue to tax you on the asset's value. Think carefully before you give your favourite shares to your spouse or children.

## Capital gains tax (CGT)

The annual exemption of £7700 for the 2002–2003 tax year, is the amount of capital gains you can make before you pay capital gains tax (CGT) at your top rate of income tax. You incur a CGT liability when you make a 'chargeable gain' – that is, when you sell an asset and its value has increased since the time of purchase. Remember, CGT is not charged on the asset itself but on its gain in value. The gain is

> Ambition knows no father.
> The Ten Commandments (1956)

the difference between the original price and the selling price after making an adjustment for inflation, known as the 'indexation allowance'. This allowance applies up to April 1998, after which 'taper relief' applies. Taper relief reduces the rate of CGT according to how long you have held the asset.

As gifts between spouses are exempt from CGT the tax efficient couple should consider sharing assets to make use of both exemptions. Until the March 1998 Budget you could 'bed and breakfast' your shares. Here you would sell them to realise the capital gain and make use of the annual allowance. Then you would buy the same number of shares the following day. In the absence of bed and breakfast it is wise to seek professional advice. One option might be to 'bed and spouse', where your spouse repurchases the shares after you sell.

## CGT and your shares

In practice most investors manage to avoid CGT without making any special arrangements, simply because their liability regularly falls within the annual CGT exemption. Even if you have a very large portfolio and are an active investor, you may still be able to avoid or reduce your liability but this will require some careful planning.

 **c o o l advice** Consider giving income-generating assets to your lower-earning spouse and, where you run your own business, to pay your spouse a salary.

Investors who receive 'windfall' shares when a life assurance society or building society converts from a mutual to Plc status (demutualisation) should bear in mind that the proceeds of any sales will be classed as a pure capital gain unless they are held in a tax-exempt investment such as an individual savings account (ISA).

## Reduce your inheritance tax bill

When you die your estate will be liable to inheritance tax (IHT) on anything over £250,000 (for the 2002–2003 tax year). This is a tax on your wealth at death and is deducted from your estate before it can be passed on to your heirs. There is no IHT liability on the assets you leave to your spouse, but once he or she dies, then the value of the estate in excess of the exemption is taxable.

There are several ways to mitigate your inheritance tax bill. Each year you can give away up to £3000 free of CGT. If you didn't use last year's exemption you can add it to this year's, giving a total gift of £12,000 per couple.

In practice there is nothing to stop you giving away any amount in excess of this exemption, but if you die within seven years the tax assessment is based on when you made the gift and the date of death. A sliding scale of tax rates is used so the longer the period between the two dates, the lower the liability. This arrangement, known as a 'potentially exempt transfer' (PET), may be abolished in a future budget along with other IHT avoidance measures.

One option worth considering, if you anticipate a large IHT liability, is to take out a life assurance policy which will cover the costs when you die. Joint life, second death 'whole of life' policies are often used for these purposes. This should be written in trust for the successors (the children, for example) to make sure the policy does not form part of your taxable estate on death.

> Dear Dad, I am not dead. Stop. Hope you are the same. Stop. Thinking of selling my golf clubs? Stop. Spending my insurance money? Stop!
>
> Captain 'Hawkeye' Pierce, MASH

There are several other useful IHT exemptions. For example, if your children get married you can give them each £5000, while other relatives can give up to £2500 free of any IHT liability. You can also make unlimited gifts to charities.

One underused exemption is modest gifts from income. These are gifts

> **cool advice** In practice most investors manage to avoid CGT without making any special arrangements, simply because their liability regularly falls within the annual CGT exemption.

that are 'normal or habitual' and leave sufficient income for the donor to maintain his or her standard of living. A good example of this might be where you pay the premiums on a life policy for your son or daughter.

## Further information

Expert advice is essential on complicated tax matters. See page 45 for
contact details for accountants who also act as financial advisers.

The Inland Revenue site is very helpful: **www.inlandrevenue.gov.uk**

# A man of property

**Bates Motel ... twelve rooms, twelve vacancies.**

Norman Bates, *Psycho* (1960)

Well, bye Pete. Later, Pete. Listen, don't forget to write, Pete. And remember, the door's always open to ya, Pete. You can come home to the pad and all your friends. But write first 'cos we're renting your room!

Micky, *The Monkees* (1966)

# Letting: The caretaker

After reading this chapter you will

*see people as an excellent source of income*

*move your granny into a nursing home and rent out her house*

*give up socialism altogether*

**THE VOLATILITY OF WORLD MARKETS** has encouraged many investors to look at property. This is a very different asset class from equities and can generate a healthy income that can be used to supplement a pension in retirement. Property should also benefit from capital growth, but do bear in mind that this is a long-term investment. Do not go into property as a way of making a fast buck.

The simplest way to invest in property is via collective funds but it is also possible to build up a portfolio of directly held properties or just to retain your home for letting purposes when you move house. Some 2 million households rent through the private sector in the UK. According to the letting agents there is a national shortage of rental property in every area from the executive home to the studio flat.

An increasing number of people are making the decision to keep their house or flat when they move on. Older people may have an ideal family house that they could rent out profitably when they move into a smaller property in retirement.

If you think your home is a desirable property for short-term lets you may well be able to cover your mortgage and other costs *and* make a profit. This has proved particularly true of property in the South East where the demand for rented accommodation is high.

 **Property provides a source of income and capital growth.**

The alternative is to go and buy somewhere with the sole intention of renting it out. If you have capital to invest and you are comfortable with the idea of taking on another mortgage, then you might do well out of a 'buy to let' scheme. The average gross return on rental income in Britain today is about 8–10 per cent. The gross return is the amount you receive before deducting the costs of letting (including the mortgage where applicable) and the management fees. Capital appreciation is likely to match if not exceed retail prices inflation for the foreseeable future.

Bear in mind though these figures assume the property is let continuously. If you do not choose your property with care it may stand empty for several months at a time, which will put a serious dent in your return.

## Financial health warning

If you buy residential property directly, rather than through a pooled fund such as an authorised unit trust, you are not covered by the Financial Services Act, even if you purchase through an independent adviser who is regulated by the Financial Services Authority. This means that you have no protection if you are given bad advice or if the properties in which you invest turn out to be poor quality. Caveat emptor!

# Taxation

Taxation is discussed in Chapter 18. As far as investment property is concerned, net rental income (that is after expenses) is subject to income tax at your marginal rate (22 per cent or 40 per cent in 2002–2003). Expenses include the loan interest. Furthermore a wear and tear allowance of 10 per cent of the rent, less water rates, is available where the property is furnished.

**cool advice**    **If you buy residential property directly, rather than through a pooled fund such as an authorised unit trust, you are not protected by the Financial Services Act.**

Any growth in the value of the property between purchase and sale is subject to capital gains tax (CGT), although the actual amount will depend on the length of time you have held the property as an investment.

# Buy to let

About 50 per cent of rentals are arranged through letting and managing agents, most but not all of which are members of recognised professional organisations. Buy to let is the initiative launched by the Association of Residential Letting Agents (ARLA) and supported by eight major mortgage lenders: Alliance & Leicester, Capital Home Loans, Clydesdale Bank, First Active, Halifax Mortgage Services, Mortgage Express, NatWest Mortgage Services and Paragon Mortgages. Its aim is to stimulate the rented property market by encouraging private investors to take advantage of low interest rates and the medium- to long-term potential for capital growth in property.

## The loan

Historically, investors in property who wanted to raise a loan found that lenders imposed a hefty surcharge on retail mortgage rates and would not take the rental income into consideration when calculating the maximum loan. Now many lenders – including those in the buy to let scheme – offer rates comparable to those extended to owner-occupiers and take the rental income into account when assessing the maximum loan that you can service.

> A woman's place is in the home ... making money.
>
> Patty, *Hot Millions* (1968)

Loans can be arranged for a single property or a mini-property investment portfolio of up to five houses and flats. Loans of between £15,000 and £1 million per investor are available for periods of between 5 and 45 years. Typically the loan will cover up to 80 per cent of the valuation.

Methods of servicing the loan are flexible in most cases and mirror terms available to owner-occupiers. There are even loans which allow for overpayment and use the surplus to provide a repayment holiday or to cover future periods when you may be short of cash if the property is temporarily empty.

## Which type of property?

ARLA's advice is to keep your choice of buy to let property simple: 'The common denominators sought by potential tenants are location, amenities and facilities.' Don't make the mistake of buying somewhere quaint because you could see *yourself* being very happy there. 'Ignore personal tastes and avoid property with potential maintenance problems such as a lot of woodwork or a large garden. These features will add nothing to the rental value but cost a lot to keep up,' ARLA warns.

> Can two divorced men share an apartment without driving each other crazy?
>
> Narrator, *The Odd Couple* (1970)

Before you buy it is wise to seek the advice of a letting agent who will be able to give you the lowdown on whether it will rent out easily. You need to find out about local demand – whether it's for four-bedroom houses or flats, how many bathrooms are required per number of bedrooms, whether gardens and patios add to rental value or just to your maintenance costs.

In addition, mortgage lenders may have their own stipulations. For example, they may not like properties with more than one kitchen and four or five bedrooms in case they are converted to bedsits.

Transport is a key issue. In some areas you can expect tenants to be commuters and so you need to consider how far away is the nearest bus route,

British Rail station or tube station. Alternatively, can people park outside the flat or house?

This list is by no means comprehensive but it should give you some idea what is involved with selecting the right type of property. Rentals tend to be short term – typically six months to three years. A good agent will vet tenants carefully and make sure there is the minimum amount of time between lets.

## The letting agent

If you are a landlord, the agent will act as your guard dog, helping to protect an expensive asset by selecting reliable tenants and looking after the property in your absence. In return the agent will deduct a percentage of the rent for his or her services. This will vary depending on the size and type of property and whether you want the agent to look after the maintenance as well. Typically you could expect an ARLA agent to charge 10 per cent of the rent for finding the tenant and to cover the inventory and paperwork. If you want a full management agreement, where the agent stands in loco parentis as it were, you can expect to pay an additional 5–7 per cent. Remember, these fees are tax deductible.

| cool advice | **If you do not choose your property with care it may stand empty for several months at a time, which will put a serious dent in your return.** |

After a tenant's offer has been accepted the agent is responsible for taking up references and making credit checks before preparing to change the utility accounts and drawing up the tenancy agreement. The agent will also need to make an inventory of all the furnishings and fittings and will write up a condition report so that any damages can be assessed and a suitable deduction made from the tenant's deposit where necessary. Both the tenant and landlord should be present when these are compiled and should sign each other's copies.

Most lets, unless for very high rentals, are arranged under an assured shorthold tenancy. This covers tenancies from six months upwards but usually there would be a cap at 12 months with an option to renew. This will list all the dos and don'ts and set out any rules, for example, on children and pets.

## Further information

The ARLA hotline is open from Monday to Friday 9 am to 5.30 pm. Telephone 01923 896555 for details of the nearest ARLA agent, the mortgage lenders on the buy to let panel and the recognised buy to let mortgage brokers for your region.

If you are interested in home reversion property (see Chapter 20), contact Home & Capital Trust 01234 340511 and PIFC on 01234 244016.

**Unfortunately, there is only one thing standing between me and that property – the rightful owners.**

Hedley Lamarr, *Blazing Saddles* (1974)

# Keep that room with a view

After reading this chapter you will

*persuade your parents to sell out and give you your inheritance now*

*put your old folks on a strict regime so they'll live longer*

*realise just how morbid you've become*

**A HOME INCOME PLAN (HIP)** might be something you want to consider for yourself later on but right now this is more likely to be a solution for your elderly parents. These plans offer elderly people who are 'house rich, cash poor' the opportunity to tap into the equity in their homes and use this to generate an extra income.

> It's a fine thing when you come home to your home and your home is gone.
>
> Nicholas Collini, *The Long Long Trailer* (1954)

HIPs are particularly attractive because you don't have to sell up and move. You can take the money as a regular income or as a lump sum, depending on the scheme rules. The plans sold in the late 1980s led many pensioners to make unwise investments and they were banned in 1990. But with increased longevity, cuts in state welfare and low interest rates, asset rich, cash poor pensioners are once again turning for financial assistance to a second generation of much more respectable equity release plans.

## Home income plans

Following the bad publicity of the earlier plans, several providers joined together in 1991 to form SHIP, the Safe Home Income Plans Company. The SHIP secretariat is based at the independent adviser and HIP specialist Hinton & Wild. The website, listed below, provides contact details for all the companies but it is wise to seek expert independent advice before you proceed.

The code of practice offered by members of SHIP includes the following important features:

■ You have complete security of tenure and are guaranteed the right to live in the property for life, no matter what happens to interest rates and the stock market.

■ You have freedom to move house without jeopardising your financial situation.

■ You will be guaranteed a cash sum or fixed regular income; your money will not be sunk into uncertain investments.

## How equity release schemes work

There are two basic types of safe equity release scheme – those where you negotiate a fixed rate loan against the property and those which involve the sale of part or all of your property. The company will take the proceeds of the sale or loan out of your estate when you die and the house is sold.

**cool advice**   Mortgage annuities have been much less popular since the 1999 budget, which abolished interest tax relief at source.

Mortgage annuities are still available but have been much less popular since the 1999 budget, which abolished tax relief on mortgages. Nevertheless depending on your age and circumstances this might still be an option worth considering. A mortgage annuity allows you to remortgage part of the value of your house – usually up to £40,000 to £50,000. The lump sum is used to buy a 'purchased life annuity' from the lender, which in return guarantees an income for life. This pays the fixed rate of interest on the mortgage and what's left is yours to spend how you wish. Until the 1999 Budget the mortgage interest for HIPs was net of MIRAS at the concessionary rate of 23 per cent but only loans taken out before April 1999 continue to qualify. This move has made the 'reversion' plans more suitable in most cases.

# Reversion plans

Under a reversion plan you sell, rather than mortgage, part or all of your house but continue to live there rent free. As a rough guide, you can expect to receive up to 50 per cent of the value of your house (or the portion sold) as the price takes into account the fact that the company will not be able to take the proceeds of the sale until you die.

There are two types of reversion plan. With a 'reversion annuity' the purchase price is used to buy an annuity, which provides an income for life in the same way as the mortgage annuity described above. The income is higher because there is no mortgage interest to pay but because you have *sold* rather than mortgaged, you will not gain from any rise in house prices on that portion of your property.

Under the 'cash option', again you sell part or all of your home in return for a lump sum which is tax free, provided the house is your main residence. You continue to live there, rent free, until you die. You can, if you wish, use the money to buy an annuity but this is not obligatory.

## What proportion of my house can I sell?

This is up to you and will depend on how much income you need. You should balance your income needs with any desire you have to pass on the value of your house to your heirs. Of course, if you end up in a nursing home, then almost certainly you would be expected to use any remaining proceeds of the house to pay towards fees.

The minimum sale is usually between 40 per cent and 50 per cent of the value of the property and with some companies you can sell up to 100 per cent.

## Qualifying conditions

You must have cleared your mortgage and have full ownership of your home. Also, the property must be in good condition, otherwise the company concerned may have trouble selling it in the future.

Advisers suggest that equity release is only really worth considering if you are over 70. The annuity income is based on the yields available on gilts and corporate bonds, which are comparatively low at present. It is also based on your life expectancy so the longer the insurance company expects you to live, the lower the income it will pay.

> **Clusiot** You're Louis Degas. I'm Clusiot. How come you ended up in a place like this?
> **Degas** Favouritism.
>
> *Papillon* (1973)

Equity release is a big step and can affect other aspects of your financial position. For example, you should consider how the additional income would affect your tax position and the possible loss of means-tested social security benefits. In particular, care is needed if you receive income support or council tax benefits as these may be reduced or lost altogether. Clearly, the home income plan benefits must more than compensate for this loss.

You should also check how an equity release scheme would affect your inheritance tax position and you may wish to discuss your plans with your family since it will reduce your estate. Moreover, before entering into an agreement ask what would happen if you have to move into sheltered accommodation or a nursing home later in retirement.

Finally, do consider all the costs involved – for example, the survey, legal fees and administrative charges. Some plan providers make a contribution but the amounts vary.

---

❄ **cool advice**    The minimum age for reversion plans is 65 to 70. The minimum sale is usually between 40 per cent and 50 per cent of the value of the property and with most companies you can sell up to 100 per cent.

## Further information

Independent Financial Adviser Promotion (IFAP) offers a free fact sheet. Call 0800 085 3250 or go to **www.unbiased.co.uk**

Safe Home Income Plans: 01242 539494 or **www.ship-ltd.org**

# The long goodbye

**KAOS Agent** Look, I'm a sportsman. I'll let you choose the way you want to die.
**Max** All right, how about old age?

*Get Smart* (1965)

Now you go home and write 'I am sorry for what I did to Frosty' a hundred zillion times. And then maybe – just maybe mind you – you'll find something in your stocking tomorrow morning.

Santa Claus, *Frosty the Snowman* (1969)

# State pensions: Big Brother

After reading this chapter you will

*wonder whatever happened to the welfare state*

*invest in your private pension with renewed vigour*

*realise why you can't get to the Post Office counter on Mondays – it's pension day!*

**THE GOVERNMENT'S NEW STAKEHOLDER** schemes should extend low-cost private provision to those not already in a company scheme. However, despite the low level of the state pension, for many people it still forms an important element of their overall retirement income. It is helpful, therefore, to understand how your state pension is earned and how it relates to your private schemes and plans.

## State pension forecasts

The calculation of the pension is ridiculously complicated. If you feel there must be more to life than wading through a morass of documents, ask your local Department for Work and Pensions (DWP) for a pension forecast (form

BR19). This should provide a fairly intelligible explanation of your entitlement. You can get a pension forecast provided you have more than four months to go to pensionable age. If you just want to find out what your additional pension will be, ask for leaflet NP38. This type of forecast should help you decide whether or not to contract out of the additional pension scheme, for example, if you want to take out a personal pension plan. Each forecast takes between three and six weeks to process, longer if you are widowed or divorced where the assessment will be more complicated.

## How the state pension works

The pension has two elements: a basic flat rate pension, known as the old age pension; and a pension which is linked to the level of your earnings, known as the 'additional pension' or State Earnings Related Pension Scheme (SERPS). From April 2002 a new State Second Pension replaces SERPS but you retain any SERPS rights built up to that date. Eligibility to both state pensions is built up through the compulsory payment of National Insurance (NI) contributions on part of your earnings.

> ❄ cool advice   The calculation of the state pension is ridiculously complicated. If you feel there must be more to life than wading through a morass of documents, ask your local Department for Work and Pensions for a pension forecast.

The maximum single person's basic state pension for the 2001–2002 tax year is £75.50 per week, while the maximum additional or SERPS pension is just over £130 per week. State pensions rise each year in line with retail prices, are taxed as earned income and should be included in the end of year tax return.

The official pension age – 65 for men and 60 for women – is the minimum age at which men and women can claim a state pension in the UK. By the year 2020 the UK will have a common pension age of 65 for both men and women. This move to equal pension ages will result in a rather complex phasing period. Basically, women born after April 1955 will have to wait until age 65 to claim. Older women should check with the Department of Social Security to find out their proposed retirement date. The phasing period will last ten years between 2010 and 2020.

> I could use my own money, the $25 I got in the bank.
>
> Theodore 'Beaver' Cleaver, *Leave it to Beaver* (1957)

Don't fall into the trap of thinking that you will automatically receive the full rate of pension even if you have worked for 40 years before retiring. The state pension system works relatively smoothly if you are employed from age 16 up to state pension age. However, the career pattern of the vast majority of people involves periods in self-employment, periods spent not working in order to raise a family, periods in and out of company pension schemes, and a whole host of other variables.

# National insurance and the state pension

State pensions come under the general heading of 'social security benefits', which also include benefits paid to people who are sick, disabled, out of work, or on a low income. Most of these benefits are paid for out of the National Insurance Fund, which is built up from National Insurance (NI) contributions levied on earnings and paid by employers, employees and the self-employed. Purists might disagree, but essentially NI contributions can be regarded as another form of direct taxation.

NI for employees is levied on what are known as 'band earnings', that is earnings between lower and upper limits (known as the lower earnings limit or LEL and the upper earnings limit or UEL). These are £89 and £585 per week for the 2002–2003 tax year. The contributions are deducted automatically from an employee's pay packet while the self-employed pay a flat rate contribution each month to the Department for Work and Pensions and an earnings-related supplement which is assessed annually through the tax return.

## The married woman's stamp

Women's state pensions are particularly complicated due to a two-tier NI contribution system which still allows some older women (those who were married or widowed before 5 April 1977) to pay a reduced rate, known as the married woman's stamp. The married woman's stamp was originally popular because it meant a much lower deduction from the weekly or monthly pay cheque. But if you pay this rate you do not build up a right to a state pension in your own name. Instead you have to claim through your spouse's NI contribution record and claim a Category B state pension, which is worth about 60 per cent of the full rate.

# The basic pension

To get the full weekly rate of the basic pension, worth £75.50 in 2002–2003, you must have 'qualifying years' for about 90 per cent of your working life – broadly speaking that is years in which you paid the full rate of NI contribution for the complete period. In some cases you will be treated as though you had received qualifying earnings if you are eligible for certain benefits, for example, Home Responsibilities Protection, invalid care allowance, unemployment benefit and sickness benefit, among others.

> Running a farm, working like a mule every day with no guarantee anything will ever come of it. This is bravery.
>
> O'Reilly, *The Magnificent Seven* (1960)

To get the minimum basic pension payable (25 per cent of the full rate) you normally need a minimum of ten qualifying years.

It is not possible to claim the state pension before you reach official pension age but it is possible to defer claiming for up to five years and earn increments.

## Married couple's pension

The combination of the single person's pension and the spouse's pension (Category B – £45.20 in 2002–2003) form what is generally known as the married couple's state pension, which is worth £120.70 for the 2002–2003 tax year.

## Minimum Income Guarantee

The government offers a range of benefits to provide extra support to very low income pensioners. In particular the Minimum Income Guarantee (MIG), paid through Income Support, tops up the basic pension to £98.15 for a single person and £149.80 for a married couple if you qualify.

## The basic pension and your company scheme

'Integrated' company schemes are very common. Under this system, the level of pension promised by the company scheme takes into account the basic state pension. Effectively this means that the employer does not provide any pension for earnings up to the lower earnings limit (£89 per week in 2002–2003) or a multiple of this. Low earners and those who do not qualify for a state pension in their own right are particularly affected by this and if there is sufficient family wealth the spouse should consider paying a contribution to a Stakeholder scheme for the lower earning partner (see Chapter 24).

# Additional pension (SERPS)

If you retire before April 2002 you will not be affected by the replacement of SERPS with the State Second Pension (see below). Until that date the second tier of the state pension is provided through the 'additional pension' or State Earnings Related Pension Scheme (SERPS). This pension, worth a maximum of just over £130 in 2002–2003, is paid at the same time as the basic pension, that is, at age 65 for men and between age 60 to 65 for women depending on when you retire.

If you are an employee and you were not contracted out of SERPS, either through a company pension scheme or an appropriate personal pension plan, automatically you would have been a member and paid for the pension through your NI contributions.

 **Don't fall into the trap of thinking that you will automatically receive the full rate of pension even if you have worked for 40 years before retiring.**

The value of the pension depends on the level of your earnings and the contribution period. It will also depend on when you reach pension age because the government has reduced SERPS for those who retire after 5 April

1999. Combined with the planned phased increase in women's pension age from 60 to 65 which kicks off in 2010, this makes the calculation of the additional pension an extremely complicated exercise.

## How SERPS is calculated

Broadly, your SERPS pension will be worth 25 per cent of your NI band earnings averaged over the period 1978–9 and 6 April 1999. For benefits built up after this date but before April 2002, the formula is reduced over a ten-year period from 25 per cent to 20 per cent of band earnings averaged over your entire working life.

 **By the year 2020 the UK will have a common pension age of 65 for both men and women.**

If you are a member of a company pension scheme which is contracted out of SERPS or if you have an 'appropriate' personal pension, your additional pension is replaced by the private scheme or plan.

## 'Inherited' SERPS

From 6 October 2002 a new rule comes into force that will reduce the maximum amount of SERPS pension that a widow or widower may inherit on the death of their husband or wife. This cut from 100 per cent to 50 per cent does not affect anyone who was widowed before this date or whose husband/wife reached retirement age before this date.

# The State Second Pension (SSP)

The SSP is intended to offer a more generous benefit for low earners, certain carers of invalids and the elderly, and people with a long-term disability. This kicks off as an earnings related benefit but in due course will convert to a flat rate benefit.

Although it is not yet compulsory, most people will be expected to opt out of the new state second pension and have a private scheme or plan.

Although it is not yet compulsory, all earners who do not fall into the above categories will be expected to opt out of the SSP and use the rebate of NI contributions to start a private pension scheme or plan.

## Appeals

Given the complexity of the state pension system it is not surprising that from time to time the DWP makes a mistake in the calculation of benefits. If you claim a social security benefit – whether it is your pension or some other form of payment – and you are unhappy about the decision made by the adjudication officer or adjudicating medical authority, you can request a review or make an appeal. However, first you should the DWP leaflet 'A Guide to Reviews and Appeals' to make sure you understand the rules.

## Further information

The Department for Work and Pensions publishes several guides to national insurance and social security benefits that are available, free of charge, from local DWP offices, post offices, libraries and Citizens' Advice Bureaux (**www.nacab.org.uk**). You can also write for free copies:
DWP
Freepost BS5555/1
Bristol BS99 1BL
Tel: 0845 7313233
**www.pensionguide.gov.uk**

**You're gonna have to answer to the Coca-Cola company.**

Colonel 'Bat' Guano, *Dr Strangelove* (1964)

# 22

# Gold watch blues

After reading this chapter you will

*love your company pension scheme even though you don't understand it*

*treat actuaries with more respect*

*realise that when your employer replaces your scheme with 'something simpler' you are going to lose out*

**FOR MOST EMPLOYEES** membership of the company pension scheme represents the most important benefit after the salary itself. But don't assume just because there is a company scheme that it is automatically going to see you right in retirement. Scheme benefits vary considerably and you may need to top up your pension if your employer is less than generous.

> Don't forget that most men would rather protect the possibility of becoming rich than face the reality of being poor.
>
> John Dickinson, *1776* (1972)

Company schemes are very tax efficient. The employer's contributions are tax deductible, the employee's contributions are paid free of basic and higher rate tax, the pension fund builds up virtually free of tax and a significant chunk of the final benefits can be taken as tax-free cash at retirement. The pension, whether drawn from a company scheme or from a life office in the form of an annuity, is subject to your top rate of income tax.

 **Under a final salary scheme the employer bears the investment risk and backs the pension guarantees. This is good.**

There are two main types of occupational schemes: 'final salary', also known as 'defined benefit', and 'money purchase', also known as 'defined contribution'. With a final salary scheme the employer bears the investment risk and backs the pension guarantees. With a money purchase scheme the investment risk falls fairly and squarely on your shoulders as the scheme member and there are no guarantees. No prizes for guessing why an increasing number of employers are switching from a final salary to money purchase scheme.

## Stakeholder schemes

These new schemes, introduced in April 2001, are discussed in more detail in Chapter 24. Stakeholders represent a low-cost private pension scheme for employees who do not have access to a more traditional company scheme. If you earn less than £30,000 you can pay into both a company and stakeholder scheme.

## Final salary schemes

Final salary schemes (also known as 'defined benefit' schemes) are still the most prevalent among employers in the UK and base the pension calculation on the number of years of service and your salary at or near retirement. A typical scheme guarantees to provide a pension that builds up at the rate of one-sixtieth of your final salary for each year of service up to an Inland Revenue maximum of forty-sixtieths – that is, two-thirds final salary at retirement (restricted for some higher earners – see below).

## How much can you contribute?

Employees can contribute up to 15 per cent of gross pay to an occupational scheme although the most common rate is about 5 per cent. 'Pay' in this context is defined as basic salary plus, in some cases, benefits such as overtime, bonuses and the taxable value of fringe benefits. If overtime or sales commission form a significant proportion of your gross earnings and this is not taken into account in your pensionable pay, you could consider top up provision through additional voluntary contributions (see below and Chapter 23).

> I am putting myself to the fullest possible use, which is all I think that any conscious entity can ever hope to do.
>
> Hal, *2001: A Space Odyssey* (1968)

The pension itself may be based on your average salary during the last three years before retirement or possibly your average salary during the period of scheme membership. A minority of schemes base it on the period of maximum earnings, which is ideal if you are in a job where earnings peak mid-career rather than towards the end of your working life.

## Topping up your company pension

By law every scheme, with a few minor exceptions, must provide an additional voluntary contribution (AVCs) scheme, which allows members to top up their company scheme benefits. From April 2001 a member of a company scheme who earns less than £30,000 can also pay in to a stakeholder scheme (see Chapter 24). However, you can use any investment to supplement your pension and many people prefer the more flexible individual savings account (ISA) because there are no restrictions on when you take the money and there is no obligation to buy an annuity. These options are discussed in Chapter 23.

## Transfers

This is one of the most complex pension issues. If you change jobs after two years' membership in a scheme you cannot claim a refund of contributions but instead have three main options.

- You can leave your pension where it is. This is known as a preserved or 'deferred' pension since your right to a pension from that company scheme is put off or deferred until you reach pension age. By law the value of a deferred pension must increase by retail prices (RPI) up to a cap of 5 per cent. This is known as limited price indexation or LPI.

- You can transfer the benefits to the new company scheme. This has the advantage of keeping all your benefits under one roof, but for various reasons you may not receive the same number of 'years' in the new scheme as you had built up in the old scheme.

Despite the vagaries of deferred pensions and inter-company pension transfers, usually these two are the best options.

- The other alternative is to transfer your benefits to an individual investment product – either a personal pension or a 'buy-out' bond. This transaction will incur costs and the plans do not offer the guarantees associated with a final salary company scheme pension. Transfer options should always be considered with the help of an independent pensions adviser.

## Integration

About 50 per cent of company schemes reduce the pension by 'integrating' with the basic state pension. The idea behind this is to provide a maximum two-thirds final salary pension including the state benefit. Of course it also cuts company pension costs. Where a scheme is integrated, no pension is paid for the first slice of salary up to the NI lower earnings limit (see page 239). No employee or employer pension contributions are levied on this amount either.

## Contracting out of SERPS or SSP

Most final salary schemes are contracted out of the State Second Pension (and, previously, SERPS). As a result the employer and employees pay a reduced rate of National Insurance contribution with the balance invested in the company pension fund. Where the scheme is not contracted out the employee would receive the SERPS pension and the company pension on top of this.

## Tax-free cash

The maximum tax-free cash you can take from your company pension scheme is one and a half times your final salary after 40 years service. This is limited in the case of some higher earners (see below). If you take the tax-free cash – and almost everyone does – your pension will be reduced (apart from in the public sector where the pension is automatically adjusted to allow for the tax-free cash).

## Pension increases

Company schemes typically increase pensions by 3–5 per cent each year. However, you need to check which increases are guaranteed and which are 'discretionary' (a voluntary payment on the part of the trustees when the fund has a surplus). Public sector pensions automatically increase in line with the full RPI.

## Family protection benefits

Most final salary schemes provide other important family protection benefits in addition to the pension itself, for example, death in service benefits worth up to four times annual salary, widow's and dependent children's pensions and similar death in retirement benefits. Disability pensions and private medical insurance are also common features of the overall benefits package. However, if you are not married to your partner check whether he or she is still entitled to the benefits.

**cool advice** Under a money purchase scheme the investment risk falls fairly and squarely on your shoulders as the scheme member and there are no guarantees. This is not so good but still worth having.

## Contributions and benefits for higher earners

The Inland Revenue restricts the pensions of certain high earners. In particular, some employees are subject to a cap of £97,200, for the 2002–2003 tax year, on which contributions and the final pension can be based. The cap applies to members of final salary schemes set up after the 1989 budget and members who joined any final salary scheme after 1 June 1989. For these employees the maximum contributions for the 2002–2003 tax year are limited to £14,580

(15 per cent of £97,200), while the maximum pension will be £64,800 (two-thirds of the cap).

## 'Unapproved' company schemes

There are two main types of pension to cater for earnings above the cap. 'Funded unapproved retirement benefit schemes' (FURBS) are company schemes that are recognised by the Revenue but are 'unapproved' for tax purposes. Under a FURBS, the employer sets aside contributions to build up a pension fund for the employee's earnings in excess of the cap. FURBS usually operate on a money purchase basis. The FURBS member will still remain in the main company scheme and receive benefits in the usual way up to the level of the cap.

If you have a FURBS you will be taxed on the employer's contributions, which are classed as a benefit in kind, rather like membership of the company's private medical scheme. However, the employer can treat these contributions as a trading expense for corporation tax purposes. The FURBS fund is subject to income and capital gains tax.

Where the fund is used to buy an annuity, the income is subject to tax. However, the entire benefit can be taken as a tax-free lump sum on retirement – a far more attractive option and the most common choice. The death in service lump sum benefits can be paid under discretionary trust and therefore should be free of inheritance tax.

> You *do* wear it on your head! I just *love* finding new places to wear diamonds.
>
> Lorelei Lee, *Gentlemen Prefer Blondes* (1953)

An alternative option under Inland Revenue rules is the unfunded unapproved retirement benefit scheme. In these arrangements your employer does not pay any contributions and there is no fund earmarked for the employee. Instead the pension benefits are paid out of company funds when the employee retires. When this happens the employer receives an allowance against corporation tax.

With this arrangement there is no tax liability until you receive the benefits, but when that happens all lump sums and pensions are taxed as earned income. Where the employer decides to buy an annuity for the employee, the purchase price will be taxed as well as the resulting regular income. Death benefits, as with the FURBS, should be free of inheritance tax if paid under a discretionary trust.

## How does your company scheme rate?

If you want to check how your company pension scheme rates consult your scheme booklet and compare the benefits listed with our ideal scheme.

■ **Retirement pension:** paid from age 65 (age 60 would be a real bonus), based on service and final earnings.

■ **Accrual rate:** (that is the rate at which the pension builds up), one-sixtieth of final pay for each year of service.

■ **Pensionable earnings:** all earnings (apart from overtime or similar bonuses paid only during earlier years of employment).

■ **Final pay calculation:** the higher of either total earnings in the year prior to retirement or average annual earnings over any three-year period ending within ten years of retirement, uprated in line with the retail price index.

■ **Pensionable service:** total service including maternity leave and certain temporary absences.

■ **Lump sum on retirement:** Revenue maximum (that is the maximum amount of pension that can be converted to tax-free cash – normally one and a half times final remuneration after 40 years, possibly limited by the earnings cap).

■ **Pension increases:** linked to the Retail Price Index.

■ **Ill-health pension:** equivalent to the amount the employee would have received had he or she remained in service until normal retirement age, at his or her current rate of pay.

■ **Death in service benefits:** this should include a dependent adult's pension of four-ninths the member's total earnings at death plus pensions for dependent children. Also a lump sum of four times annual earnings.

▶

- **Death in retirement benefits:** this should include a pension worth two-thirds of the member's pension to be paid to a nominated adult dependant plus a pension for any dependent children under age 18.

- **Scheme leaver benefits:** the whole of the preserved pension should be increased in line with RPI up to retirement.

*Source:* Based on Union Pension Services *Pension Scheme Profiles*

## Money purchase company schemes

With a money purchase (defined contribution) scheme you bear the investment risk and there is no guaranteed pension linked to salary. Personal pensions, group personal pensions (GPPs), stakeholder schemes and contracted in money purchase schemes (CIMPS) all fall into this more risky category. The contribution and benefit rules vary depending on whether you belong to a scheme based on personal pension legislation – for example, a group personal pension or stakeholder scheme – or on occupational scheme rules, such as a contracted in money purchase scheme.

 **cool advice**    If you are not married to your partner check whether he or she is still entitled to the dependant's pension.

Under all these money purchase schemes your contributions are invested to build up a fund that is used at retirement to provide a tax-free lump sum and to buy an annuity, which pays an income for life. Annuity 'rates' – that is the level of income each £1000 of your fund will buy – depend largely on long dated gilt yields and these are also volatile. It is possible to defer the annuity purchase and to draw an income directly from your fund, keeping the rest fully invested. 'Drawdown' is complicated and requires a substantial fund size and expert advice in equal measure.

Despite these variations in rules, the way your pension builds up under a contracted out money purchase scheme (COMP) and a group personal pension is virtually identical. This is particularly important point for COMPS/CIMPS members where, rather confusingly, the maximum contribution and benefits are expressed as a proportion of your earnings.

The most important point to bear in mind with money purchase is that the level of income which your fund buys is not guaranteed but will depend on several factors, including:

- how much you and your employer contribute
- the investment performance of the fund
- the level of charges deducted from your fund by the pension company
- annuity 'rates' – that is the level of income your fund will buy at the time you retire.

Clearly it is important to ensure your contribution is adequate. Leading pension consultants suggest a 15–20 per cent contribution rate is appropriate in the current economic climate where investment returns are falling and the cost of buying an annuity is rising. Your employer may contribute to your pension and if this is the case you should almost certainly stick with the scheme. Employers rarely pay in to employees' individual plans.

Your employer should give you an idea of what your pension fund will produce in the way of retirement income. If this looks too low you might consider paying more into your scheme or spreading the investment risk by building up other savings (see Section 4).

## Contributions

Some money purchase schemes – particularly those operated by larger employers – follow the same maximum contribution and benefit rules as final salary schemes (see CIMPS below). However, most small to medium sized employers set up group personal pensions (GPPs). Under a GPP, your individual personal pension plan can be used to contract out of SERPS and to invest additional regular or single premiums to boost the pension provided by the NI rebate.

Personal pension contribution limits start at 17.5 per cent of 'net relevant earnings' (equivalent in this context to pensionable pay) for employees up to age 35, and rising in stages to 40 per cent for employees age 61 and over. Employer contributions must be included in these limits but there is no obligation for employers to pay anything other than the redirected NI contributions.

## CIMPS

Contracted in money purchase schemes (CIMPS) are Inland Revenue approved occupational pensions and as such will follow the same contribution and benefit limits as final salary schemes. The maximum employee contribution is 15 per cent of salary (restricted for higher earners). However, although your maximum pension is calculated as a proportion of your salary, the pension will actually depend on the size of your fund at retirement and annuity rates.

There is a version that contracts employees out of the State Second Pension (SSP) (previously the state earnings related pension scheme, SERPS) and in return receives a rebate of employee and employer national insurance (NI) contributions. The rebate terms are not particularly attractive for contracted out money purchase schemes (COMPS) so most schemes have changed this feature and are now 'contracted *in* money purchase schemes (CIMPS) but you can still contract out on an individual basis through a special type of personal pension. Seek advice on this subject.

CIMPS are regarded as more complicated than GPPs but have several distinct advantages for employees. As a type of occupational scheme CIMPS tend to be fairer than GPPs as the employer is likely to bear the administration charges, leaving the employee only to pay for the investment management. It may also be possible to take a larger proportion of the CIMPS fund as tax-free cash than is possible with a personal pension where the lump sum is restricted to a maximum of 25 per cent of your fund.

---

cool advice   Senior executives often belong to a fast stream version of the main company pension scheme that builds up the pension more quickly and provides better benefits all round.

---

However, it is important to note that the quality of CIMPS varies considerably. Some of the earlier insurance company packages sold to smaller employers in the late 1980s and early 1990s may still incorporate high charges, poor investment management and exit penalties, so you should check this point before you join and find out if the provider intends to reduce these charges and change the terms. Several insurance companies – Standard Life and Norwich Union, for example – have reduced charges on all their personal pension products to bring them in to line with their low cost stakeholder scheme.

Standard Life's charges on individual plans and GPPS, for example, are between 0.6–0.825 per cent.

## How does your company money purchase scheme rate?

Use the following checklist to find out if your employer's money purchase scheme is well designed. Ideally it should:

- *Aim* (but it cannot guarantee) to match the pension and risk benefits equivalent to your old final salary scheme.
- *Invest* minimum employer and employee total contributions of between 15–20 per cent of annual salary, depending on age (the older you are the more you need to pay in).
- *Delegate* the investment management to a major institutional fund manager which has a proven track record in the pensions market.
- *Incur* modest administration and investment charges which are shown to be among the most competitive for group schemes.
- *Impose* no financial penalties if you leave the scheme when you change jobs, you reduce contributions, or you want to retire early.

If you don't want to make the investment decisions, your scheme should also offer a 'working life strategy'. This is a managed fund that provides you with the long-term growth potential of equities in the early years but protects your capital as you approach retirement by automatically phasing a switch from equities into cash and bonds.

Some employers are introducing money purchase schemes and asking members to switch from the old final salary scheme. If you are offered a choice between staying in your employer's old final salary scheme and joining the new money purchase scheme you need practical advice from someone who fully understands how both schemes work. In particular check that there are no material changes to the level of life assurance offered – typically three times your annual salary.

## Family protection benefits

Death and disability benefits under money purchase schemes can be minimal so it is important to check what your employer provides here. If you are not happy with the level of cover offered, top up your family protection insurance through additional life assurance and disability or income replacement insurance. Private medical cover could also be considered.

## Flexibility and portability

Flexibility is supposed to be one of the main attractions of money purchase pensions since the employee has an easily identifiable and apparently portable pot of money. The important point to check here is what happens to your pot if you leave the scheme when you change jobs.

# Special schemes for executives

Senior executives often belong to a fast stream version of the main company pension scheme that builds up the pension more quickly and provides better benefits all round. But executives and directors can also be provided for through an entirely separate insurance arrangement known as an executive pension plan or EPP. EPPs, although providing a pension linked to final salary, are occupational money purchase schemes designed for individuals or small groups of senior executives and directors.

In the past EPPs have been popular but today most advisers reckon that personal pensions, and particularly self-invested personal pensions (see Chapter 24), offer a package that is just as good and far simpler. Nevertheless, there are still some people for whom the EPP offers greater flexibility on contributions and possibly better and/or more flexible benefits, particularly as you can use an EPP in conjunction with the main company scheme (this is not possible with a personal pension).

So, for example, you could use an EPP to take contributions based on overtime and bonuses and then take the benefits from the plan as part of your early retirement income. You could start to draw benefits from your main company scheme at a later date. However, unlike SIPPs (Chapter 24) and the small business schemes discussed in the next chapter, you cannot usually separate the administration and investment under an EPP and this inflexibility could cost you dear in terms of sales commission payments to advisers and the life office charges.

# Special schemes for small family companies

Small self-administered schemes (SASS) come from the same stable as executive pension plans. These schemes are suitable for up to 12 members. Membership is usually restricted to the directors of the company because the fund can be used to invest in the business – for example, to buy new premises. All investments must be at arm's length – so, in the case of a property purchase, the company would have to pay the scheme a commercial rate of rent. These schemes are complicated and require expert advice.

# Pensions and divorce

For most married couples the chief breadwinner's company pension is the most valuable asset after the family home. Over one-third of marriages in the UK end in divorce but until recently there was no legal obligation to split the main breadwinner's (usually the husband's) pension fairly. Today, however, the court will be able to demand an immediate split of the funds so the lower-earning spouse can invest his or her share of the pension in a personal pension fund.

This whole areas is very complex and you should seek professional advice on the calculation of your pension rights, particularly if you or your spouse has built up a substantial pension.

# Further information

The National Association of Pension Funds (NAPF) publishes a series of leaflets on company schemes and related issues. Many of these will be available free of charge from your pensions manager, but if not write to the association for a guide to its publications:
NAPF
NIOC House
4 Victoria Street
London SW1H 0NX
Tel: 020 7808 1300
www.napf.co.uk
The Department for Work and Pensions is at www.dwp.gov.uk

Well, hardest substance found in nature, they cut glass, suggest marriage, I suppose they've replaced the dog as the girl's best friend. That's about it.

James Bond, *Diamonds are Forever* (1971)

# Give your pension a shot in the arm

After reading this chapter you will

*read the small print of your company AVC scheme very carefully indeed*

*buy an actuary a pint and ask him to explain how AVCs work*

*wonder if pork belly futures are less risky than a with profits AVC*

**TO GET A FULL COMPANY PENSION** – limited to two-thirds of your final salary – normally it is necessary to work for 40 years for the same employer. This is because most company pensions build up at the rate of one-sixtieth of final salary for each year of service and the maximum is forty-sixtieths or two-thirds (restricted in the case of some higher earners).

 Despite the wide range of pension options, it is important to understand that your retirement income can be derived from other, more flexible sources as well as pension arrangements.

Today very few employees follow this career pattern. Most change jobs a few times and spend at least some time out of employment to raise a family, in further education, due to unemployment, self-employment, and so on. This can have a serious impact on your pension, but it is possible to fill in the gaps in a tax-efficient way.

The investments specifically designed for this job are called 'additional voluntary contribution' (AVC) schemes. These are run by employers. There is also an individual version known as a 'free standing' AVC, but these are rarely recommended due to the higher costs.

> You could have robbed banks, sold dope or stole your grandmother's pension checks and none of us would have minded. But shaving points off a football game, man that's un-American.
>
> Caretaker, *The Longest Yard* (1974)

Since April 2001 it has been possible for company pension scheme members who earn less than £30,000 to pay up to £3600 (£2808 after basic rate tax relief) into a stakeholder scheme or personal pension. This has the advantage of generating a tax-free lump sum as well as an income through the purchase of an annuity. You can even pay into the company AVC scheme on top of this – if you can afford it or if you have a higher earning spouse prepared to fund the stakeholder contribution.

Despite this choice of pension options, it is important to understand that there are restrictions regarding the way you can take benefits from any pension arrangement. In practice your retirement income can be derived from several sources other than pension arrangements. For example, you might earmark the proceeds of an individual savings account (ISA) or a company share option scheme. You might also release part of the equity in your home by moving down. With the increase in life expectancy many people are working part time into retirement.

## Tax treatment of top-up pensions

### AVCs

Additional voluntary contributions are Inland Revenue approved pension arrangements and almost as tax efficient as company schemes. This means:

- full tax relief on contributions
- the fund grows virtually tax-free
- in certain cases a tax-free cash lump sum at retirement but only where you joined the scheme before April 1988.

As with the main scheme, the income from the annuity purchased with your fund is taxable. Generally you would take AVC benefits at retirement from the company main scheme although there is some flexibility in the timing.

## Stakeholder scheme/personal pensions

These schemes are discussed in the next chapter. Briefly, the above tax efficiencies apply and you can also take up to 25 per cent of the fund as a tax-free lump sum. Under personal pension rules you can draw the benefits any time between age 50 and 75. You can also continue contributions for five further years after you stop work.

## Your employer's AVC scheme

This is a company top-up scheme set up by the employer or the trustees of the main company pension scheme. In most cases the investment and administration of the AVC scheme is subcontracted to a third party. The majority of AVC schemes are run by the life offices and, in the case of deposit-style accounts, by the building societies. There are also a few unit trust and investment trust companies in the market.

> **cool advice** The choice of AVC provider is usually left to the trustees of the main pension scheme. Research from actuarial consultants indicates that they don't always take this role very seriously.

The choice of provider is usually left to the trustees of the main pension scheme and research from actuarial consultants indicates that they do not always take this particular role very seriously. This is unfortunate because the difference in results between the best and worst company can knock about 20 per cent off the value of your fund. Having said that, AVC scheme charges are tumbling in response to competition from stakeholder schemes and some providers have removed the unfair penalties that used to apply to AVC scheme members if they stopped payments or retired early.

It is still important to check how flexible your contributions can be. Ideally you should be able to pay what you like, when you like, within Revenue limits of course. But some life offices are likely to lock you into regular monthly contributions and if you stop or reduce payments you might be penalised.

# How do they work?

Most AVCs operate on a 'money purchase' basis. This means that although the main scheme may provide a pension linked to salary, the AVC scheme is likely to invest the contributions to build up a fund which, at retirement, is used to buy an annuity from a life office. This annuity provides a guaranteed income for life but the value of the annuity is dependent on the investment returns achieved by the AVC fund and has no link to the value of your final salary (see Chapter 22.)

Some AVC schemes – mainly those in the public sector – offer 'added years'. This means that contributions help increase your main pension, which, in the public sector, is likely to be inflation linked.

## Stakeholder v AVC

Some employees might be better off using a stakeholder scheme as the top-up rather than the AVC scheme. In particular the stakeholder scheme is guaranteed to be low cost and have flexible terms. It also provides a tax-free lump sum.

> Well, look at me. I'm old, lacking in vigour, my mind's in a turmoil. I no longer know if I'm coming, have gone or even been. I'm falling to pieces; I no longer even have any clothes sense.
>
> The Doctor, *Doctor Who* (1963)

To be eligible for concurrent membership of a stakeholder and company scheme you must earn less than £30,000. You do not qualify if you are a controlling director in the year of making the contribution or at any time during the past five years. A controlling director is someone who alone, or with a family associate such as a spouse, controls at least 20 per cent of the ordinary share capital of the company.

The £30,000 earnings limit is more flexible than it seems. Benefits in kind are excluded, as are contributions to an occupational pension scheme, Give As You Earn charitable donations, Save As You Earn (SAYE) and Approved

Employee Share Ownership Plans. This means that your total remuneration before these deductions could exceed the £30,000 limit by a significant amount.

Possibly of greater significance, under the concurrency rules an individual's earnings need be within the £30,000 threshold only for one tax year within each five-year period. So, where you have control over your remuneration – for example, in a family business – you will be able to make concurrent contributions by ensuring that you keep to the £30,000 limit for one year in five.

## Contribution limits

If you are eligible to pay into a stakeholder/personal pension then you can pay £3600 per annum on top of the main scheme and AVC contributions.

As for AVCs, under the Revenue rules you can pay a total of 15 per cent of your earnings into the main scheme and AVC combined. Since most employees pay about 5 per cent, this leaves up to 10 per cent for the top-up scheme. If you are lucky enough to belong to a 'non-contributory' scheme, where the employer is the only one paying contributions, you can in theory invest the full 15 per cent of earnings into your AVC.

> **c o o l advice** Ideally you should be able to pay what you like, when you like to your AVC scheme but some life offices may penalise you if you stop or reduce payments.

Some employees will be caught by the 'earnings cap', which limits total pension contributions to 15 per cent of £97,200 (for the 2002–2003 tax year). The earnings cap affects employees who joined a new occupational scheme set up after 14 March 1989 and for new members who joined an existing scheme after 1 June 1989.

Finally on this point, if you accidentally exceed the benefit limits, the AVC provider can refund excess contributions, but a tax deduction must be paid to the Revenue.

# How you take the proceeds

## Stakeholder/personal pension

Here you can take the proceeds of your fund at any time between age 50 and 75. You can take up to 25 per cent of the fund as tax-free cash and the rest is used to buy an annuity from an insurance company. This pays the regular income in retirement. You can also take a regular income directly from the fund but 'drawdown' is an expensive arrangement and only suitable for large funds (at least £100,000 where you also have a company pension and a minimum of £250,000 if this is your main pension). An alternative might be an investment-linked annuity. These options are discussed in Chapter 25.

## AVCs

The rules here are unnecessarily complicated due to the introduction of various restrictions over the years. It all depends on when you started paying contributions.

- Where AVC contributions began before April 8 1987, the whole fund can be taken in cash provided the total cash taken from AVC and main scheme combined is within Revenue limits.

- From 17 March 1987 the Revenue restricted the level of salary on which the tax-free cash calculation was based. The ceiling was £100,000 so that the maximum cash taken from AVC and main scheme pension combined was £150,000 (one and a half times the £100,000 salary limit).

- Where contributions to the AVC scheme started on or after 8 April 1987, the whole of the fund must be taken in the form of pension, although its value is taken into consideration when the tax-free cash from the main scheme is calculated.

- Since FSAVCs were only introduced in 1987, there is no tax-free cash option.

## Individual savings accounts to boost retirement income

As mentioned in the introduction to this chapter, in theory you could use any savings plan as a source of retirement income. The most obvious is an ISA (see Chapter 13 for full details).

 **Some employees might be better off using a stakeholder scheme as the top-up rather than the AVC scheme.**

The way the tax breaks apply to ISAs is different from AVCs but broadly equal. Both AVC and ISA funds grow virtually tax free. However, AVCs qualify for full tax relief on contributions but most of the benefits must be used to buy an annuity to provide a taxable income. With an ISA there is no tax relief on contributions but the fund can be withdrawn tax free and does not have to be used to buy an annuity. Moreover, you have free access to the ISA fund whenever you like.

ISAs may prove particularly attractive to those caught by the earnings cap and whose pension contributions are therefore limited.

## Further information

Your company pension trustees should automatically provide you with details of the AVC scheme. However, if you are keen to improve your retirement income, it is a good idea to consider more flexible investments as well as pension. An independent financial adviser will be able to explain the alternatives. See Chapter 4.

**A poor girl without a dowry can't be so particular. You want hair, marry a donkey.**

Golde, *Fiddler on the Roof* (1971)

# Pensions:
# This time its personal

After reading this chapter you will

*wonder why the government expects you to put your money with the very companies that constantly screw up*

*realise, that when it comes to personal pensions, fair terms and flexibility are recent discoveries*

*remember the good old days when parents died young and left you a fortune*

**OVER THE PAST COUPLE OF YEARS** there has been a welcome rationalisation in the personal pension market so that you can expect good value for money from the stakeholder scheme or personal pension you choose. However, the general trend to reduced charges and improved terms is not universal so do check these points carefully.

## Tax efficiency

Like company pension schemes, personal plans are a very tax efficient way of saving for retirement:

■ Contributions qualify for full tax relief.

■ The pension fund grows virtually tax-free.

■ Up to 25 per cent of the pension fund at retirement can be taken as tax-free cash (this does not apply to the fund built up from NI contribution rebates).

The rest of the fund must be used to purchase an annuity although it is possible to defer the annuity purchase and draw an income directly from the fund (see Chapter 25).

## Stakeholder schemes

In April 2001 the government introduced stakeholder schemes to encourage those who do not have access to a more traditional company pension scheme to save for their retirement. These new schemes follow the same rules as personal pensions, but to qualify for stakeholder status they must offer fair terms, low costs and penalty-free entry and exit.

> **cool advice** Some providers have reduced their personal pension charges in response to competition from stakeholder schemes and one of these might offer a broader investment choice than is available under a stakeholder.

The new schemes are a type of personal pension and you can contribute up to £3600 a year (£2808 after basic rate tax relief) even if you have no earned income. At retirement you can take up to 25 per cent of the fund as tax-free cash while the remainder is used to buy a regular income in the form of an annuity. Other retirement investment options are available for those with a substantial fund (see Chapter 25).

Stakeholder schemes are mainly available through employers that do not provide a more traditional occupational pension scheme but they are also available direct from many financial institutions. Clearly if you do not have a pension then the stakeholder scheme provided by your company is likely to offer good value for money, particularly where the employer is prepared to make a contribution on your behalf.

If you do not have a pension arrangement then your basic choice is between the stakeholder scheme nominated by your employer and a personal pension. The differences between the two are not as great as you may think.

> That is all. I want comfort and security.
>
> Colonel Stok, *Funeral in Berlin* (1966)

As mentioned above, stakeholder regulations ensure that these schemes guarantee modest charges (a maximum annual charge of 1 per cent of your fund) and penalty-free entry and exit terms, among other features. They do not claim to be the cheapest, nor do they guarantee good performance. Personal pension charges on many plans have fallen in response to competition from stakeholder schemes and many of these offer a broader investment choice than is available under a stakeholder.

Where you want something more dynamic or need broader diversification, you could look at multi-manager personal pensions. The number of funds on offer through these plans varies as does the cost, so do seek independent advice. If cost is an issue, several investment trusts offer personal pensions and these are likely to be cheaper than stakeholder schemes over the long term. Foreign & Colonial, JP Morgan Fleming and Edinburgh Fund Managers only provide links to their own funds. Govett Investments pension plan also offers access to a range of general and specialist investment trusts, while Alliance Trust offers a self-invested personal pension (see below).

# Contributions to stakeholders and personal pensions

The much-quoted £3600 annual contribution is not an absolute maximum – it is only relevant where you do not have any earnings or insufficient earnings on which to base your contribution. This figure includes tax relief at the basic rate so, for example, if you paid £2808, the Inland Revenue would make this up to £3600 by way of tax relief. The tax relief is credited even if you do not pay tax – which is why this is such a good deal for non-earners.

If you want to pay more than this you will need the earnings to justify the contribution. For personal pensions and stakeholders, the maximum annual payment varies according to age, starting at 17.5 per cent for those aged 35 and under, rising to 40 per cent for those aged 61 and over.

Table 24.1 shows the percentages of annual earnings that you can pay into a personal pension/stakeholder. If your employer contributes, this must be included in the overall maximum. There is a cap on the level of earnings on which you can base your contributions and this is £97,200 for the 2002–2003 tax year.

**TABLE 24.1** Annual contribution limits for personal pensions

| Age | % net relevant earnings |
| --- | --- |
| Up to 35 | 17.5 |
| 36–45 | 20 |
| 46–50 | 25 |
| 51–55 | 30 |
| 56–60 | 35 |
| 61–74 | 40 |

Note: All personal pension contributions (but not the emerging pension itself) are subject to the earnings cap, which limits the amount of salary that can be used for pension purposes to £97,200 for the 2002–2003 tax year.

If you would like to improve your pension prospects, the simplest way is to increase your contribution to your stakeholder scheme. This is deducted from your salary by your employer through the payroll system and forwarded to the provider. You pay your contributions net of the basic rate of tax. The pension provider reclaims this tax from the Inland Revenue and credits it to your fund. You are responsible for claiming any higher rate relief to which you are entitled through your annual tax return, or alternatively you can contact your inspector of taxes and ask to have your PAYE (pay as you earn) code amended.

Due to the costs involved it is not worth setting up a separate pension plan for a small additional contribution. Moreover some stakeholder schemes wisely reduce the annual charge as your fund size grows as an incentive for you to concentrate all your contributions in the one scheme.

However, for more substantial contributions it may be worth considering a separate personal pension in order to gain access to a wider range of funds and external investment managers. In this case it will be up to you or your financial adviser to select the company and arrange to make monthly payments through a direct debit arrangement. As with the stakeholder scheme, the personal pension provider will be able to reclaim the basic rate tax relief and add this to your fund. You will still be able to reclaim any higher rate relief through your tax return.

## Contracting out of the state scheme

Personal pensions and stakeholder schemes can be used to contract out of the State Second Pension (previously the State Earnings Related Pension Scheme) on an individual basis and in return receive a rebate of National Insurance (NI) contributions to invest in your individual plan or stakeholder scheme. Employees who are not contracted out automatically are in the SSP. The self-employed do not pay into the SSP and this point is not applicable.

If you are not sure whether you should contract out, seek independent advice.

# How to get best value

With the help of a good independent financial adviser you should be able to narrow down your choice of pension companies by considering the following:

- *The financial strength of the provider*: it is important to be confident that your pension company can survive. This very competitive market is in the throes of merger mania.
- *The performance track record*: with the emphasis on consistency over the long term and stability of staff.
- *The level of charges deducted throughout the investment period*: this is a maximum of 1 per cent per annum for stakeholder schemes.
- *The flexibility of the contract*: for example, there should be no penalties for reducing and stopping contributions, transferring the fund and early retirement. This feature is guaranteed with stakeholder schemes.

## What can you buy with your fund?

The fund built up from the NI rebates is known as 'protected rights' – a daft name because the fund's value is not protected or guaranteed in any way – what you get depends on how well it is invested.

There are certain restrictions on what you can do with the fund at retirement. It cannot be used to provide tax-free cash and the pension must be taken at the same age as the state pension, currently 65 for men and 60 for women (rising to 65 between 2010 and 2020). The annuity purchased with the fund must provide for a spouse's pension worth 50 per cent of the personal pension plan holder's and the annuity payments must increase, typically by 3 per cent per annum. There are no restrictions on the annuity you purchase with your main plan.

---

**cool advice**  Make sure that you are paying in a sensible amount each year. Experts suggest we should pay about 15–20 per cent of salary (including the employer's contribution, if applicable).

---

You can run more than one personal pension plan provided total contributions fall within the limits shown in Table 24.1 but do consider the impact of start up charges. You can only have one plan for the annual rebate if you contract out of the SSP. However, you can review this on an annual basis – the only requirement is not to split the rebate for any given tax year.

Make sure that you are paying in a sensible amount each year. Experts suggest we should pay about 15–20 per cent of salary (including the employer's contribution if applicable). This is higher than in the past due to falling investment returns and the fact that we are living longer. Don't forget – employers can contribute to an individual employee's plan, although there is no legal requirement for them to do so.

## High earners

All high earners with personal pensions are restricted by the 'earnings cap', introduced in the 1989 budget, which limits the amount of salary that can be taken into consideration for contributions. For the 2002–2003 tax year the cap is £97,200, which means that the maximum contribution is the relevant percentage of this figure (see Table 24.1 on page 268).

# Life assurance

It is also possible to use up to 5 per cent of the contribution limit to pay for life assurance, which effectively gives you tax relief on the premiums. Life assurance rates vary considerably so do shop around. If your pension provider's terms are expensive it might be cheaper to buy it elsewhere.

# Retirement annuities

Many people still have a retirement annuity plan – the predecessor to the personal pension. After July 1988 sales of these contracts stopped but existing policyholders can continue to contribute to their plans.

The contribution and benefit rules for retirement annuities differ slightly. Retirement annuity contribution limits are lower in terms of percentages than for personal pensions but the total salary on which these contributions are based is not subject to the earnings cap. The limits are shown in Table 24.2.

**TABLE 24.2** Contribution limits for retirement annuity plans

| Age | % net relevant earnings |
| --- | --- |
| Up to age 50 | 17.5 |
| 51–55 | 20 |
| 56–60 | 22.5 |
| 61–74 | 27.5 |

*Note:* The earnings cap does not apply. It may be possible under these plans to pay a larger contribution by using tax relief left over from previous years.

Depending on your age at retirement and the prevailing annuity rates when you retire, it may be possible to take more than 25 per cent of the retirement annuity fund as tax-free cash since the calculation is not a straight percentage of the fund. The other main difference between the two arrangements is that you cannot contract out of the SSP with one of these older contracts – you must use a personal pension.

Finally, it is possible to contribute to both a personal pension and retirement annuity at the same time but you should seek advice on how to keep within the Revenue's maximum contribution rules.

## Who sells stakeholders and personal pensions?

To find a list of the stakeholder providers see further information at the end of this chapter. The market for stakeholders and personal pensions is dominated by the life offices but an increasing number of unit trust and investment trust groups also offer plans and these are certainly worth considering. Most banks and building societies tend to sell the plans run by their own life office or have an arrangement with a separate life office to sell exclusively that company's plans. As in the ISAs market, some of the big retail operations, like M&S and Virgin, also sell pensions.

## Investment options

You can base your pension on a variety of different fund structures – unit-linked funds, life office funds, unit trust and investment trust, for example. You might also consider a with profits fund. These are discussed below and also in Chapter 12. Bear in mind that the taxation of these funds is different where they are used as a pension investment.

But before you get bogged down with the different options, remember that the main consideration is the underlying asset mix. Advisers tend to recommend that younger people should invest virtually 100 per cent in equities because this offers the best long-term growth prospects, although you may decide that a mix of equities and bonds is preferable in the current investment climate. As you get older and closer to retirement you need to switch gradually into safer assets such as bonds and gilts and by the time you are within a few years of retirement (or, more accurately, the time you intend to purchase your annuity) you should probably be entirely in cash (deposits) and gilts.

Having said that, if you intend to transfer to an 'income drawdown' plan at retirement, which allows you to keep your fund fully invested, you may prefer to maintain a high exposure to equities. This option is discussed in Chapter 25.

# Which fund?

Most stakeholder schemes and personal pensions offer a choice of collective funds similar to those discussed in Chapter 12. The choice will vary but there should be at least one fund for each major asset class, plus a 'lifestyle' option that makes the asset allocation decisions for you (see below). Ideally you should seek independent advice to make sure the pension funds you choose dovetail with other investments.

Try to diversify within your equity holding. You might choose a global equity fund or split the contributions so that 60 per cent go into the UK equity fund and 40 per cent into the overseas equity fund.

As you get older and closer to retirement you need to switch gradually into safer assets such as bonds and gilts. By the time you retire and want to buy your annuity, a good benchmark is to aim to be 75 per cent in an 'annuity matching' fund, which would consist of gilts and bonds, and 25 per cent in cash. This enables you to calculate with some accuracy the value of your cash and annuity at retirement. It also avoids any unpleasant surprises at the eleventh hour. If you stay in equities your fund could fall sharply just before retirement and you will not have time to make good your losses through your earnings.

> That's a bargain all right, but a bargain ain't a bargain unless it's something you need.
>
> Jesse Buford, *A Big Hand for the Little Lady* (1966)

A good stakeholder or group personal pension scheme will recognise that some employees don't have the time or inclination to make asset allocation decisions. This is why they offer a 'lifestyle' programme, which keeps you in equities until a few years before retirement and then gradually switches you into gilts, bonds and cash.

Experts agree that the lifestyle structure is the best default programme for investors who do not want to make their own decisions or who might otherwise put too much into cash and bonds at an early age. However, it does have its drawbacks. For example, you may feel that to start switching out of real assets (that is, assets that grow in value with the economy) ten years before retirement is too soon. Arguably the effect of compound interest on regular contribution plans is at its greatest during this last decade of investment. For this reason some schemes delay the switch out of equities until five years before your retirement date.

Moreover, standard lifestyle programmes do not cope well with those who retire early who may find themselves 100 per cent in equities at the wrong time. In contrast, members who intend to transfer to an 'income drawdown' plan at retirement, which allows you to keep your fund fully invested while drawing a regular income, may need to maintain a high equity exposure and should not automatically switch to gilts.

## Summary of pension investment choice

A good stakeholder scheme or personal plan will offer at least the following basic funds, which should be run by a competitive asset manager and allow you to switch when you need to change your asset allocation:

- **Equities** – possibly a global equity fund or a choice between UK and overseas equities. There may also be a passive UK equity fund which offers a lower risk profile than a more aggressive actively managed fund, assuming the FTSE All-Share is your benchmark.

- **Bonds and gilts** to enable you to match the assets that back annuities as you draw closer to retirement. This might be called a pension or annuity-matching fund.

- **Cash** to enable you to allocate part of your fund to generate the tax-free cash lump sum (typically 25 per cent of your total fund).

- **Lifestyle**, which selects the asset mix for you typically starting with 100 per cent in equities until you are 5–10 years away from retirement when you gradually switch into cash and gilts/bonds.

# Unit-linked funds

Unit-linked plans are sold by life offices. Under this arrangement your contributions buy units in a fund and the value of these units fluctuates in line with the market value of the underlying assets. Funds range from low-risk deposit, index linked and gilt, to medium-risk UK and international equity funds, to higher-risk emerging markets funds. Companies make much of their often huge fund range but in practice most people go for the managed fund, which invests in a range of the provider's other main funds and in this way offers a balanced spread of investments. Some companies offer investment links to top institutional managers. This is an excellent feature, but in non-stakeholder plans make sure the charges do not outweigh the potentially higher returns.

## Unit trust

Unit trust plans offer a similar investment choice to unit-linked plans and again the value of your units will fluctuate in line with the performance of the under-lying assets (see Chapter 12). The choice of unit trust personal pensions was limited to about half a dozen at the time of writing, but more companies are expected to launch plans over the next few years. Low-cost index-tracking funds generally offer access to a wide spread of equities at low cost but don't assume this is a low-risk option. If markets fall so will your tracker fund.

## Investment trust

Over the past few years a handful of investment trust personal pensions have been launched. An investment trust is not a trust as such but is a British com-pany, listed on the UK stock exchange, which invests in the shares of other companies in the UK and overseas. It has a fixed number of shares and most prices are published daily in the *Financial Times*.

The investment trust's share price is affected by the value of the company's underlying assets – as is the case with unit-linked and unit trust funds. How-ever, it is also affected by the supply and demand for shares. This means that the share price does not necessarily reflect the actual value of the underlying assets. If the share price is lower than the value of the underlying assets the difference is known as the discount. If it is higher, the difference is known as the premium. Buying at a discount is a good thing. Buying at a premium is generally considered to be a bad thing. Investment trusts can also borrow money to invest – an activity known as gearing.

As a broad rule of thumb, investment trusts offer additional opportunities for active investors but they are also potentially more volatile. Charges tend to be lower than for unit trusts (with the exception of index trackers), particularly on some of the larger older investment trusts.

## With profits

Until recently these worthy but complicated funds formed the backbone of the individual pensions market because they provided a reasonable degree of security together with good potential for long-term capital growth. However, over the past few years these funds have been criticised for lack of clarity and for the managers' apparently heavy-handed use of the market value adjuster (MVA – see below) to make arbitrary deductions if policyholders pull out at a time when markets are falling or the company is undergoing a difficult period. Most people assume 'with profits' refers to the smoothing mechanism that allows the fund manager to hold back profit in the good years to maintain a decent return when market conditions are poor.

Certainly this mechanism is used by with profits funds but the concept implies a great deal more. In most cases, with profits policyholders also share in the profits and losses from the company's other lines of business – term assurance and annuities, for example. When a proprietary company suffers a loss, this is borne by the shareholders as well as the with profits policyholders. But for mutuals the with profit policyholders are the owners of the business and ultimately benefit from the profits – but also suffer the losses.

This means that when you invest in a with profits policy you are investing in the skill of the investment manager but you are also likely to be buying in to the company's fortunes – for good or for bad. Until recently being a member of a mutual was seen as a win-win situation and many have bene-fited from the windfalls that have followed demutualisation. After the Equi-table Life debacle, policyholders may appreciate that there can be a significant downside to mutual membership.

> ❄ **cool advice**  If you want to make substantial contributions and maximum investment flexibility you might consider a low-cost, self-invested personal pension.

Arguably investors have also misunderstood the MVA, which is an impor-tant feature of with profits policies. With profit guarantees only apply if you stay put, and even then the smoothing mechanism will not fully insulate you from movements in the financial markets. Equitable Life's use of the MVA in 2001 brought home to investors the potentially high-risk nature of this 'low-risk' investment. The MVA allows a company to penalise investors if they want to get out at a time when markets are falling or the company is in trouble. In Equitable's case both factors applied.

Companies justify the MVA by pointing out that when policyholders start leaving in droves the company is forced to sell investments for less than they are worth, often at a time of falling markets. So basically, the fund suffers as a result and the MVA aims to share this suffering between those who leave and those who stay put.

Of course Equitable was not the only with profits company to impose the MVA. During the volatile markets of the past few years virtually every company in the popular with profits bond market has penalised leavers by imposing an exit penalty of up to 12 per cent of the fund value.

## Self-invested personal pensions (SIPPs)

Self-invested personal pensions follows the same basic rules as standard personal pensions, but in addition allow you to exercise much greater control over your investments. The appeal of the SIPP lies in the product's ability to 'unbundle' the two key features of modern pension plans, namely the administration and the investment. What generally happens is that you buy a basic plan from a company that will handle the administration and either tackle the investment yourself or appoint an investment manager (a stockbroker, for example) to construct and run the portfolio for you. If you are unhappy with the performance, you can change the manager without having to upset the underlying administration arrangements.

> The Constitution guarantees citizens the right to private property. To a car. To a home. To a dacha. To money. Money, comrades. Nobody outlawed money yet!
>
> Shop salesman, *Beregis Avtomobilya* (1967)

SIPPs can also be used by partnerships and professional practices, which cannot use a company sponsored small self-administered schemes. Instead you can use a SIPP with virtually the same effect and if you pool with other partners you can achieve beneficial economies of scale.

## Investment choice

The choice of investments is very wide and includes the following:

- stocks and shares (e.g. equities, gilts, debentures) quoted on the UK stock exchange and including securities on the Alternative Investment Market
- stocks and shares traded on a recognised overseas exchange
- unit trusts and investment trusts
- insurance company managed funds and unit-linked funds
- deposit accounts
- commercial property.

A SIPP fund cannot purchase a firm's existing business premises from the partnership but it can buy new offices into which the partnership can move, provided the property is leased back on a commercial basis. You can also use your SIPP fund to borrow on the strength of its assets to help with property purchase. However, the SIPP cannot lend part of the pension fund back to you, the investor.

## Low-cost online SIPPS

An increasing number of SIPP providers run a low-cost online version. Before selecting a SIPP it is important to consider how frequently you intend to trade and to check the annual charge (if applicable) in conjunction with dealing costs as these vary considerably. You should also consider the set-up costs and the range of services offered. Those who require advice are likely to need a standard SIPP from an investment manager, but even here charges are coming down.

# Group personal pensions

Before the introduction of stakeholder schemes, many employers set up a group personal pension (GPP) as a relatively low-cost way to offer a company pension scheme. Like stakeholder schemes, these are a combination of individual plans but where the employer usually deducts contributions from the payroll and in some cases pays towards the administration costs and makes a contribution on the behalf of employees.

If your employer offers a group personal pension do check the charges and terms to see if they are competitive with stakeholder schemes.

# Pensions for children and spouses

The new tax regime for personal pensions introduced in April 2001 offers attractive tax-planning opportunities for the wealthier investor because it breaks the traditional link between earnings and pension contributions. For the first time investors can contribute to pension schemes and plans on behalf of other people.

There are three main tax-planning opportunities here. You can pay up to £3600 (£2808 after tax relief) on behalf of:

- a child
- a non-earning spouse/partner
- a spouse/partner who is in a company scheme but earns less than £30,000.

In each case you should consider your long-term investment requirements to decide whether a stakeholder, a multi-manager personal pension or a self-invested personal pension is appropriate. There are no exit charges on a stakeholder scheme so you can always move to a more flexible plan once the fund has built up.

Advisers report considerable interest in children's pensions, but before you jump on the stakeholder bandwagon for tiny tots, bear in mind that pension tax breaks do not come unfettered. If your chief concern is saving for school or college fees, for example, or providing a deposit on a house, then a stakeholder will not do because the money is locked away until your offspring is at least 50 (under the present rules).

As far as spouse/partner's pensions are concerned, it is not just the non-earner who can benefit from your contributions. The new 'concurrency' rules allow an employee who earns less than £30,000 and is a member of an occupational pension scheme to pay up to 15 per cent of salary (that is, up to £4500) into the main scheme and AVC scheme combined and in addition to pay up to £3600 into a personal pension or stakeholder scheme.

As you get older and closer to retirement you need to switch gradually into safer assets such as bonds and gilts.

This provides an excellent opportunity for the higher earner to fund the spouse or partner's stakeholder pension. If you do this over the long term your partner could end up virtually doubling total contributions and be on target for a retirement income worth far more than the two-thirds of final salary maximum pension allowed from the traditional occupational scheme.

## Further information

For a full list of stakeholder providers go to www.opra.gov.uk

Information on low-cost personal pensions and Sipps is available from the following:

Alliance Trust www.alliancetrusts.com

Bestinvest www.bestinvest.co.uk

Charles Schwab www.schwabb-europe.com

Edinburgh Fund Managers www.edfd.com

Foreign & Colonial www.fandc.co.uk

Govett Investments www.govett.co.uk

JP Morgan Fleming Life www.jpmorgan.com

Killik & Co www.killik.co.uk

Sippdeal www.sippdeal.co.uk

Suffolk Life www.suffolklife.co.uk

In this world it is the wealthy who are criminals. Some day their wealth will be ours.

Perchik, *Fiddler on the Roof* (1971)

25

# You pays your money and you makes your choice

After reading this chapter you will

*buy an annuity, stop smoking and get to the gym*

*understand the real reason why your adviser might wan to manage your pension fund*

*still not know what to do*

**IF YOU ARE COMING UP TO RETIREMENT**, one of your greatest fears might be that you will outlive your income and capital or that there will be nothing left to pass on to your children when you die. Alternatively, you might be concerned that an overly frugal income combined with an unexpectedly early death will leave an excessive amount to your heirs at the expense of your own lifestyle. No investment strategy can entirely remove these threats but the risks can be insured – at a price.

 Conventional annuities are the only products that guarantee a lifetime income no matter how long you live or what happens to investment markets.

Of the major assets at your disposal your pension fund is likely to require the most detailed analysis due to the complex Inland Revenue rules, the number of annuity providers (about 40 but only a dozen serious players), the wide range of options and far-reaching consequences of your decisions. How well you deploy this asset may dictate your financial welfare in retirement and your family's inheritance.

Annuities represent one of the biggest and most controversial financial markets for retired investors, who hand £6 billion to annuity providers each year, most of which is used to secure an income stream that is guaranteed for life – irrespective of investment returns and longevity. This guarantee represents the insurance element of the contract and is not available through any pure investment or savings product.

> They are all farmers. Farmers talk of nothing but fertilizer and women. I've never shared their enthusiasm for fertilizer. As for women, I became indifferent when I was 83
>
> Old Man, *The Magnificent Seven* (1960)

Annuities are bond-based insurance contracts. It is important to understand that like any insurance product, risk is pooled and therefore there are 'winners' and 'losers' among the members in that pool. The risk is that you do not know how long you will live and therefore you might outlive your capital and income if you do not 'annuitise'. The pooling mechanism uses the funds of those who die early to subsidise the income of those who live longer than average. Those blessed with longevity are the 'winners' and benefit from what is known as the mortality cross-subsidy.

A strong insurance element is present in the state schemes and in traditional company pension schemes. The *primary* purpose of a salary-linked company pension, for example, is to guarantee an income stream that is based on your length of membership and salary.

In recent years the income or yield on annuities has fallen, which has led investors to believe that they offer poor value for money. Arguably, this view may represent a misunderstanding of how the annuity works. In this chapter we summarise your annuity and investment options if you contribute to a 'money purchase' (defined contribution) pension arrangement.

# Retirement income options for investors for money purchase pensions

Money purchase arrangements fall into two categories. The first is based broadly on personal pension legislation and includes:

■ personal pensions

■ retirement annuities

■ stakeholder schemes

The second includes certain occupational schemes:

■ occupational money purchase schemes

■ executive pension plans (EPPs)

■ small self-administered schemes (SSASs)

■ additional voluntary contributions (AVCs) and 'free standing AVCs (FSAVCs).

The distinction between personal pension and occupational rules is important because it affects the timing as well as the way you can take benefits. For example, you can take the benefits from a personal pension any time from age 50 onwards – although annuity rates tend to be very low indeed for younger investors. Investors with occupational pension schemes usually have to wait until the scheme pension age and if they want to take benefits earlier there could be a penalty, so do check this point.

Under personal pension rules there is no limit on the income you secure with your fund, whereas occupational scheme rules limit the maximum benefits and these will be based on your length of service and salary at or near retirement. This is fairer than it might appear because the combined employee–employer personal pension contributions are more strictly controlled than those for occupational schemes, where employers can pay substantial sums on your behalf if they wish.

In most cases the Inland Revenue rules allow you to take part of your pension fund as tax-free cash – for example, up to 25 per cent of your personal pension fund. The major exception here is AVCs started after April 1987 and all FSAVCs.

For the risk averse who will rely solely on their pension fund for a retirement income, the most prudent option is to buy an annuity. In terms of a guaranteed income for life, an annuity is a hard act to beat. This is because the mortality cross-subsidy, mentioned above increases the annual income you might otherwise achieve if you invested your fund in gilts and bonds and lived off the yield and withdrew a proportion of the capital each year. This might be worth an additional 7.5 per cent at age 80 and almost 15 per cent at age 85.

The cross-subsidy is an important feature of all annuities irrespective of the underlying investments. For this reason it is very difficult to compare an annuity, with its combination of insurance and investment features, with the returns from a pure investment – for example, a bond or equity fund – or even with 'income drawdown', which allows you to defer the annuity purchase (until age 75) and instead draw an income direct from your fund.

 **The difference between the best and worst annuity rates at any given time can be as much as 20 per cent.**

Of course for those with large funds or other sources of income in retirement it is worth considering a more flexible arrangement. However, if you opt for anything other than a conventional annuity you run the risk of capital loss, which in turn could reduce your income. You also increase your costs.

It is important to remember that, provided your fund is large enough, you can divide it between different arrangements. In this way you could, for example, secure a basic income that is guaranteed for life through a conventional annuity, while at the same time keeping part of your fund in an arrangement that invests in the stockmarkets, in the hope of increasing your income during retirement and/or passing on capital to your dependants.

## Your choices at retirement

To summarise, at retirement your options fall into five broad categories:

1   If you have other sources of income you may be able to defer the annuity purchase and leave your fund in the pension plan or scheme until age 75 at the latest. (In the case of certain occupational money purchase schemes this option would only apply if you retired late.) Hopefully it will

continue to grow in this virtually tax-free environment but you will not be able to draw on it or take your tax-free cash. The fund value might fall if you invest in assets other than fixed interest.

2 The traditional choice at retirement is to buy a conventional annuity from an insurance company. Unless you pay for a guarantee, once you hand over your money it is gone for good. Rates of income have fallen in recent years due to lower gilt yields and the increase in life expectancy. However, contrary to popular opinion, annuities can represent good value and there is a wide range of options to enable you to meet your requirements. Those in poor health may be able to secure a higher than average income.

3 A handful of insurance companies offer 'investment-linked' annuities where you can invest in a choice of funds. Your income is determined partly by the mortality cross-subsidy (as with the conventional annuity) and partly by the performance of the underlying investments. For some people this might be a sensible option for all or part of their fund.

4 Flexible annuities provide a link to a range of stockmarket funds and allow you to vary your income and the amount you pass on to you dependants on your death. This new breed of annuity offers many advantages to the more sophisticated investor with a substantial fund.

5 You can transfer your fund to a 'drawdown' plan that allows you to draw an income directly from your fund, which you keep invested in accordance with your objectives. This is not an annuity so there is no mortality cross-subsidy to enhance your income. However, drawdown offers greater flexibility for inheritance provision than, say, the flexible annuity.

Whichever option you choose, you should seek independent financial advice from a firm that is able to offer expertise in pensions, annuities, investment and taxation.

## Why leave the fund where it is?

If you are moving into semi-retirement and likely to draw a reduced salary for several years, or perhaps you have other sources of income – for example, from a business – you may decide to leave your pension fund where it is, *provided* you are happy with the charges and performance. This has three distinct advantages:

1 It is simple.

2 There are no annuity purchase costs at this stage.

3 If you have a personal pension plan and you die, the entire fund passes on to your dependants free of inheritance tax, although it could also be used to buy an annuity – for your spouse, for example. Death benefits under company scheme rules vary.

You don't have to stick with the same pension provider and those in occupational pension schemes may be required to transfer to a personal pension if the scheme rules do not allow you to defer taking your benefits. Even if you are already in a personal pension or similar plan you should review charges and performance. Those with a large fund who would like a more flexible investment choice might consider transferring to a self-invested personal pension (SIPP), which allows you to invest directly in equities and bonds as well as in a wide range of collective funds. You can stay in a SIPP or personal pension until age 75 when you must convert to an annuity. Bear in mind that all transfers carry a cost either on exit from the old scheme or entrance to the new arrangement – in some cases both.

As soon as you need to draw an income or take the tax-free cash, you must 'vest' part or all of your fund – that is, take it out of the personal plan or SIPP and switch to one of the other options outlined above.

## Conventional annuities: more flexible than you think

The controversy that surrounds annuities is largely due to the perception that they offer poor value for money. In recent years the income from annuities – based on bond yields – has fallen. But this has not happened in a vacuum. Over the long term there has tended to be an inverse correlation between equity returns and the yields on gilts. In theory, therefore, your fund size should rise to compensate for the drop in the amount of income an annuity will secure for each £1000 of your capital.

However, retail and institutional investor behaviour affects this relationship. Bond yields will fall if demand rises significantly and pushes up bond prices. Demand for bonds will rise when investors switch to this asset class as a safe haven. Maturing occupational pension funds also weight their asset allocation more heavily towards bonds in order to pay the guaranteed pensions. The combined impact of these two developments could change the long-term relationship between equity returns and bond yields. In this situation bond yields and equity returns can fall simultaneously.

## How does the annuity work?

What makes annuities so complicated is the fact that they combine investment with insurance and it is the insurance element that provides the rock solid guarantee of the lifetime income. This means you cannot compare the 'return' from an annuity with the return from, say, an equity or gilt fund because the pure investment route offers no lifetime guarantee. When you look at annuities it is helpful to keep in mind these two elements and examine how they interact.

To calculate its 'rate' the insurance company assumes it will return your capital, with interest, over the number of years it expects you to live. On top of this it adds a rate of interest. This is broadly equal to half the yield on bonds at the time of purchase. The reason it is only half is that your capital effectively runs down over the payment period.

On top of this there is a cross-subsidy from the pool of lives within the annuity fund. Those who die early effectively subsidise those who live longer than average. Those who live an average number of years effectively 'break even'. To summarise, the annuity income guaranteed by the insurance company in return for your lump sum investment is based on:

- a return of capital spread over your expected lifetime (based on mortality tables)
- the yield on long-dated gilts and bonds (and occasionally, property) – the assets insurance companies buy to generate the guaranteed income
- a cross-subsidy between the annuitants who die early and those who live longer than expected

Women live longer than men on average and so the income they can secure will generally be less than that for a man of the same age. Those in poor health may be able to secure a higher than average income if their life expectancy is reduced (see below).

**TABLE 25.1** How long will you live?

| Current age | Life expectancy (yrs) | |
|---|---|---|
| | Male | Female |
| 55 | 29 | 32 |
| 60 | 24 | 27 |
| 65 | 19 | 22 |
| 70 | 15 | 18 |
| 75 | 11 | 14 |

*Source:* Continuous Mortality Investigation Bureau

Even if you want a conventional annuity with no frills, those with a personal pension or similar plan – for example, a retirement annuity or stakeholder scheme – are under no obligation to buy from the original pension company. The 'open market option' allows you to take the proceeds of your pension fund away from the plan provider and to buy your annuity from a more competitive company.

Do seek expert independent advice for this exercise. The top names in personal pensions are quite different from the top names in annuities and rates change frequently. The difference between the best and worst annuity rates at any given time can be as much as 25 per cent and even among the top ten companies there could be as much as a 10 per cent difference. Your adviser will also weigh up any penalties or loyalty bonuses that affect your pension fund if you move it away from your original company. These may negate the better terms available elsewhere.

The situation is different for members of occupational money purchase schemes. Here the trustees usually buy the annuity on your behalf and pay the income to you. Check that the trustees shop around for the best rates using an annuity specialist or their independent consultant. The scheme should be able to negotiate the best rate for you. In most cases it would only add to the costs if you took a transfer out and bought direct from an insurance company.

Those who use their pension scheme or plan to opt out of the earnings-related state pension must use the fund built up from the rebates of national insurance in a specific way. The rules vary depending on when you were contracted out but generally these funds must buy a spouse's pension and must increase each year – usually at 3 per cent.

## Important options

When you look at annuity rates the benchmark figures relate to the level annuity – that is, an income that remains static throughout the payment period and is payable to a single male. There are several useful features sold as optional extras in addition to the basic annuity. You may consider that some of these are essential but your choice will depend on your personal circumstances and financial goals in retirement. Any options you choose will reduce the annuity rate so consider your priorities carefully. Once you hand over your money you cannot change your mind about the choice of insurance company or the special features selected.

If you need a conventional annuity you should consider these options very carefully with the help of your independent financial adviser. Those who are concerned about passing on their wealth cannot leave a lump sum for a dependant but can secure a lifetime income. An alternative for those who purchase their annuity later in retirement is to buy a ten-year guarantee so that the income continues for up to a decade if they die soon after buying the annuity.

## The impact of your options on initial income

- **Guarantee period:** most annuities are guaranteed for five years, which means that if you die after two years the remaining payments over the following three years are paid to your estate. The maximum guarantee is for ten years. *Reduction in initial income for five-year guarantee: 1 per cent age 60; 5 per cent age 75.*

- **Joint life annuity:** this pays your spouse, partner or other dependent person a pension if you die. The individual's health and life expectancy will affect the price. *Reduction in initial income for a 50 per cent dependent's pension: 12 per cent (assuming male annuitant 60 with spouse 57).*

- **Escalating annuities:** here the income rises in line with full retail price inflation or at a fixed rate each year – for example, 3 per cent if you stop work in your sixties you could be drawing the annuity income for 20 years or more, so some form of inflation proofing is essential unless you have other sources of income to draw on later. *Reduction in initial income for a 3 per cent annual increase or link to retail prices: 30 per cent at age 60.*

*Source:* Figures provided by Watson Wyatt

# Higher income for those in poor health

Annuity rates are based on average life expectancy so if you are in poor health you will be at a disadvantage. Fortunately, several companies, including Britannic, GE Life, Prudential, PAFS, Sun Life and Scottish Widows, offer 'impaired life' annuities, which pay a higher than average income – in some cases double or treble the standard rate – because they assume you will have a lower than average life expectancy.

This is particularly good news for those with a very serious condition who need the maximum income possible to allow them to enjoy a better quality of life for their remaining years. But even those with a less serious condition might be able to increase their income by a significant amount if they are individually underwritten. Typical conditions which qualify for an 'impaired life' annuity include:

- heart attack, heart surgery, angina
- life-threatening cancers
- major organ diseases – for example, liver or kidney
- other life-threatening illnesses – for example, Parkinson's disease
- strokes.

To qualify you would have to complete a detailed questionnaire and in some cases the insurance company would also require a medical report from your doctor.

The options available under a standard annuity are also available but where you want to provide a pension for your spouse, for example, his or her life expectancy will affect the rate you secure, so it may be better to use another source of capital for this purpose, if you have one.

# Investment-linked and flexible annuities

If you are coming up to retirement and have a large money purchase pension fund you might consider a more flexible alternative to a bond-based conventional annuity, which provides a guaranteed income for life but offers limited scope for inheritance planning and no potential for investment growth.

Do bear in mind though that flexibility in the choice of investments and/or the amount you leave for your dependants carries a cost both in terms of your adviser's fees and the risk to your capital. Independent advice from a firm with expertise in annuities, investment and taxation is essential.

One way to reduce the impact of charges and investment risk is to divide your fund between different arrangements. For example, you could use half of your fund to buy a conventional annuity to secure a basic guaranteed income and with the other half you could invest in the stock-markets in the hope of increasing your income during retirement or passing on a larger pro-portion of the fund to your dependants when you die.

> Young men make wars and the virtues of wars are the virtues of young men: courage and hope for the future. Then old men make the peace, and the vices of peace are the vices of old men: mistrust and caution.
>
> Prince Feisal, *Lawrence of Arabia* (1962)

Clearly individual circumstances vary but as a general guideline experts recommend that you should not consider alternatives to the conventional annuity unless you have substantial funds or other sources of income. For 'substantial' read an absolute minimum of £100,000, where you have other sources of income, and at least £250,000 if this is your main source. Some put the figure as high as £500,000. Given the uncertainty over these figures, a more appropriate exercise is to consider how much guaranteed income you need to support your basic expenditure and decide how much of this must be generated by your pension fund. Once you have set aside enough to cover the essentials you can take a risk with the remainder if you wish.

Conventional annuities offer a fixed income or one that rises at a predetermined rate each year. The income is based on bond and gilt yields, among other factors, and therefore effectively locks you into the yields available at the time of purchase, no matter how long the retirement. The benchmark 'rate' of income you are likely to see in tables is the 'level' annuity, which is the flat rate for a single male. Any options – such as a partner's pension or annual increases – will reduce this rate.

A traditional annuity is more accurately described as a non-profit policy because policyholders get a guaranteed level of income irrespective of whether the insurace company makes a profit or loss. Investment-linked annuities enable you to benefit from investment profits – but equally you share the downside risks. As with any approved pension arrangement your fund continues to grow virtually tax free.

This type of product is still an annuity so your fund reverts to the insurance company when you die unless you buy a pension for your partner or a 'guarantee' that the income will be paid for at least five or possibly ten years from the date of purchase.

The big advantage of 'annuitising' your fund, however, is that you benefit from the cross-subsidy between different 'lives'. This means that the capital released from those who die early subsidises the incomes of those who live an average or longer than average number of years. According to Watson Wyatt this cross-subsidy might add anything from 1 per cent to your annual income at age 65, to 10 per cent by the time you are in your early 80s and this is irrespective of the type of fund in which you invest. Some investment-linked annuities allow you to convert to a conventional annuity at any age up to 85, although you cannot move to a different provider at this point.

## How your income is calculated

The income for the first year is broadly based on what you might expect from a standard annuity but can be varied between a minimum, which assumes there will be no investment growth and an upper limit, which assumes the maximum investment growth permitted by the provider. The maximum is likely to be the same or slightly higher than what you could expect from a conventional annuity. You can vary this level of income by assuming a certain rate of return over the course of the year – typically between zero and 5 per cent. If the actual investment return is more than you expected you can increase your income for the following year if you wish – or just allow your fund to build up so it can provide a higher income later. If the actual return is lower, then your income will fall. As a rule of thumb experts suggest that where the fund has an equity content of at least 50 per cent it is probably reasonable to assume a return above bonds of 1–2 per cent over the long term.

## Choice of fund links

The main structure used for investment-linked annuities is the with profits fund. It is possible to buy a unit-linked annuity but these are rare. If you go in for a unit-linked fund your income will rise and fall directly in line with the underlying assets. The most common choice is the managed fund, which invests predominantly in equities but also in gilts, bonds and cash.

The with profits fund invests in a similar range of assets as a managed fund although the asset allocation will be more conservative – for example, 65 per cent in equities, 25 per cent in fixed interest and 10 per cent in property. The smoothing mechanism holds back some of the profit in good years in order to maintain a reasonable return in the lean years. This helps to reduce volatility.

> **cool advice** Advisers recommend that you should not consider an investment-based annuity or 'drawdown' plan unless you have substantial funds.

With profits funds have been the subject of criticism in recent years due to their lack of transparency and the problems that policyholders with Equitable Life have experienced. However, some advisers believe that their use as a retirement investment vehicle is appropriate. So with profit annuities may be an ideal choice for those who want to benefit from investment growth but at the same time want to avoid volatility. This product is available from Prudential, Britannic, Norwich Union, Standard Life, Legal & General and Scottish Widows. Equitable Life's product is closed to new business.

## Investment choice

The standard investment-linked annuity usually offers a choice of funds run by the provider. However, the latest products also offer access to a range of external managers and clearly this is an important feature. If you retire at age 60 you could live another 25 years or more and it is unlikely that any one company is going to provide first-class investment management throughout this period.

The investment choice for the Prudential Flexible Lifetime Annuity, for example, offers fund links to M&G (owned by Prudential), Perpetual, Phillips and Drew, Schroder and Merrill Lynch. It also offers three risk-rated investment options based on Prudential and M&G funds. You can make switches between the funds as your investment objectives change. Every three years your investment choice and income level is reviewed, although a monthly check is also carried out to ensure you are not depleting your fund too much.

But investment choice is not the only important new feature. The new generation of annuities offered by Prudential, Canada Life and London & Colonial,
gives you much more control over the level of income you draw and the death
benefits. The upper limit for the income is about the same as you would get
from a conventional annuity, but if you want to conserve your fund you can
take as little as 50 per cent of this figure.

The death benefits issue is important. Under a conventional annuity you
can buy a guarantee so that if you die the insurance company continues to pay
the income to your dependents. This is possible because the income is based
on gilts and so the yield is known and the cost
of the guarantee can be assessed.

> We all dream of being a
> child again, even the worst
> of us. Perhaps the worst
> most of all
>
> Don Jose , *The Wild Bunch* (1969)

With an investment-linked annuity the
income cannot be assessed precisely because
the returns will vary. However, a flexible annuity product like the Prudential Flexible Lifetime
Annuity adopts a different approach by allow-
ing you to identify the proportion of the fund that you want to pass on, in the
form of income, to dependants. Like the conventional annuity guarantee, this
'ringfenced' fund can run for up to ten years and can account for up to 80 per
cent of your total fund. The ringfenced fund, which can be transferred to the
main annuitised fund at any time, does not benefit from the mortality cross-
subsidy but is still invested and provides part of your income. After ten years
any ringfenced fund is automatically converted to the main annuitised fund.

London & Colonial's new Open Annuity is even more flexible when it comes
to death benefits but there is no mortality cross-subsidy and therefore this
arrangement is more akin to income drawdown. However, the chief advantage
of this product over drawdown is that you don't have to convert your fund to
a more conventional annuity by age 75. According to annuity experts, this is an
expensive and high-risk product for the retirement market and only suitable for
very wealthy investors who are keen to use their pension fund for inheritance
planning rather than to generate a reliable lifetime income.

## Conclusion and warning

While it is cheering to see a range of innovative products coming onto the
annuity market to provide investors with greater flexibility, the number of companies involved remains very small at present. This is expected to grow rapidly

over the next few years and the increased competition will help reduce charges.

Professional advice from a firm with expertise in pensions, insurance and investment management is essential so it is vital to check the credentials of your adviser before proceeding. While the purchase of a conventional annuity is a one-off transaction, any other arrangement requires ongoing advice to ensure the fund is well managed and the income levels are appropriate both for your needs and the capacity of your fund.

# Drawdown and phased retirement

The latest investment-linked annuities offer a welcome increase in the choice of investment and flexibility for those want maximum flexibility you might consider phased retirement, income drawdown, or a combination of the two.

The main disadvantage of income drawdown and the Open Annuity from London & Colonial is that you don't benefit from the cross-subsidy between different 'lives', as you do when you buy a conventional annuity. With an annuity – even the investment linked or flexible variety – the capital released from those who die early subsidises the incomes of those who live an average or longer than average number of years.

## Summary of phased retirement rules

- The pension fund is divided into segments. Each year you withdraw however many you need to provide tax-free cash (usually 25 per cent of each segment) and to buy a conventional or invested annuity to provide a lifetime income.

- If you die before age 75 the death benefits will be in two parts:
  - The full fund in the pension plan will go tax-free to your beneficiaries (different rules apply if you transferred from an occupational scheme).
  - The balance of any guaranteed or spouse's pension on the annuities you have arranged each year.

Under phased retirement you build up your required annual income by withdrawing only part of your pension fund, leaving the remaining fund invested in the original plan. Like any Inland Revenue approved pension arrangement, your investments continue to grow virtually tax free. The chunk withdrawn is used to provide an element of tax-free cash and the rest is used to buy an annuity. This pattern is repeated each year.

Phased retirement is not suitable for investors who want to use their tax-free lump sum for a capital project because the cash forms an important part of your annual income. However, if you don't need the tax-free cash at retirement, phased retirement is particularly attractive for those who are keen to pass on as much capital as possible to their heirs. When you transfer your fund into an annuity you cannot arrange to leave a lump sum as death benefits – only income and even this is limited to a period of ten years from the date you buy the annuity. With phased retirement the fund that remains in the original personal pension can be passed on as tax-free cash to your beneficiaries on death and is not subject to inheritance tax.

Under income drawdown plans you can take your tax-free cash and then draw your taxable income direct from your fund. The income level is flexible although it must fall between a minimum and maximum set by the Inland Revenue, based broadly on the annuity rate you would otherwse have secured with your fund at retirement. If you die your fund goes to your dependants, not the insurace company, so there are important tax and financial planning benefits as well. By age 75 at the latest you must convert your fund to an annuity.

> **cool advice** While with profits funds have been the subject of criticism in recent years, their use as a retirement investment vehicle is still considered appropriate.

The main risk with phased retirement and drawdown – as with investment-linked annuities – is the lack of any guarantee that your income will remain steady. There is little point in investing the bulk of your capital in cash and gilt funds, as these are very unlikely to generate sufficient capital growth to cover the cost of the arrangement.

If you decide to go for drawdown the most flexible route is the 'self-invested' plan, which allows you to run the fund yourself or appoint an invest-

## Summary of income drawdown plan rules

If you have a personal pension or similar plan, at retirement you can take part of the fund (typically one-quarter) as tax-free cash and use the rest to buy an annuity. If you choose to defer the annuity purchase using an income drawdown plan, the following rules apply:

- You can buy the plan from age 50 but must convert the fund to an annuity by age 75.
- You cannot make further pension contributions to the plan once it is in operation.
- During the deferment period investment income and capital gains continue to roll up virtually tax free
- The income you draw must fall between a minimum and maximum set by the Inland Revenue and based on the annuity rate you could have purchased at retirement.
- Your plan must be reviewed every three years to ensure the income level you are drawing is still appropriate. If the fund has fallen too much you must convert to an annuity immediately.
- If you die before age 75 there are three options:
  - Your spouse can use the fund to buy an annuity.
  - Your spouse can continue to draw an income but must convert the fund to an annuity by the time you would have reached 75.
  - The fund can be taken as cash (less a 35 per cent tax charge)

ment manager to do the job for you. Under this type of plan y6ou can invest in a very wide range of funds and asset classes including collective funds (investment trusts, unit trusts and insurance company funds), direct equities, bonds and commercial property.

Phased drawdown combines the two arrangements. Here you draw your income from the fund directly but make use of the tax-free cash in the same way as for phased retirement. As you do not purchase any annuities this has the benefit of increasing the death benefits but at the expense of the guaranteed income from the annuities.

The hallmark of food investment planning is to know in advance when to get out. Under income withdrawal, by age 75 at the latest you must buy your annuity and it is unwise to leave this until the last minute. If you intend to buy a conventional annuity then you should start to move your fund out of equities and into safer asset classes well before the date of conversion. However, there is nothing to stop you transferring to an investment-linked or flexible annuity at age 75, which will allow you to keep your fund invested in a range of assets rather than locked into the gilt yields that datermine the bulk of the income available under a conventional annuity.

## Further information

Expert advice on tax, pensions and investment is essential, particularly with more complicated annuity options and drawdown arrangements. See Chapter 4 for how to find a good adviser.

### Useful annuity websites

The Annuity Bureau: 020 7902 2300 (**www.annuitybureau.co.uk**)
Annuity Direct: 020 7684 5000 (**www.annuitydirect.co.uk**)
William Burrows Annuities: 020 7430 0734 (**www.askannuity.com**)

**I'm drinking some wine, eating some cheese, and catching some rays, you know ...**

Oddball, *Kelly's Heroes* (1970)

# Retiring in the sun

After reading this chapter you will

reconsider Bognor Regis as a desirable location

start a time-share scam

become a tax exile just like Mick and Phil – only poorer

**GLOBAL WARMING HAS HAD A GLOOMY IMPACT** on traditional British weather. Summers are wet and windy and, well, so are the winters. The prospect of retiring in the sun is very appealing. The choice of location may seem paramount, but if you want a financially healthy retirement the most important task is to arrange for all your pensions and other sources of income to be paid abroad without double tax penalties.

> **cool advice** Annual cost of living increases for the state pension are only paid if you live in a European Union country or a country with which Britain has a social security agreement that provides for uprating.

Expert advice on pension and inheritance tax planning is essential for would-be expats but there are several important steps you can take in advance to reduce the administrative headache as well as your professional adviser's fees.

Today's flexible career patterns tend to result in a bewildering variety of retirement benefits but essentially there are three main sources of pension:

- state schemes
- company schemes
- private individual plans.

# State pensions

Chapter 21 deals with the UK state pensions in detail. Briefly, the pension, which builds up through payment of National Insurance contributions, is made up of two elements – a basic flat rate benefit and an earnings-related supplement, which from April 2002 is known as the State Second Pension. The SSP replaced SERPS (state earnings related pension scheme) but your SERPS benefits built up to that date remain intact.

> I'm a retired investor living on a pension. I went to Israel because I wanted to live there as a Jew in the twilight of my years.
>
> Hyman Roth, *The Godfather Part II* (1974)

The pension is paid at age 65 for men and between age 60 and 65 for women depending on when you retire. (The female state pension age is due to be raised in line with the male pension age and there is a transition period between 2010 and 2020 to achieve this.)

## Cost of living increases

The Department for Work and Pensions confirmed that the state retirement pensions and widows' benefits can be claimed from anywhere in the world. However, annual cost of living increases are only paid if you live in a European Union country or a country with which Britain has a social security agreement that provides for uprating (see box).

## Countries where your state pension qualifies for the annual increase

| | | |
|---|---|---|
| Austria | Irish Republic | Spain |
| Barbados | Israel | Sweden |
| Belgium | Italy | Switzerland |
| Bermuda | Jamaica | Turkey |
| Cyprus | Jersey | USA |
| Denmark | Luxembourg | Yugoslavia |
| Finland | Malta | (including the |
| France | Mauritius | newly |
| Germany | Netherlands | independent |
| Gibraltar | Norway | former |
| Guernsey | Philippines | republics) |
| Iceland | Portugal | |

*Source:* Department for Work and Pensions

This means that if you retire to Australia, Canada, New Zealand or any country not mentioned in the list your state pension will be frozen either at the time you leave the UK or, for those already abroad when they reach state retirement age, at the time of the first payment.

> **c o o l**
> **advice** Most pension statements that explain your future benefits assume retirement is within the UK, so it is essential to check how retiring abroad will affect your tax position.

Clearly, the loss of the annual cost of living increases will rapidly erode the value of the pension over a 15- to 20-year retirement and extra income from other sources will be required to compensate. As a rough guide to the impact of inflation, £100 in your pocket today would be worth £64 in 15 years' time assuming 3 per cent annual inflation, and just £48 assuming an annual inflation rate of 5 per cent.

The only good news is that if you return to live in the UK, your state pension will be paid at the full current rate. UK expats on a temporary visit home can also claim the full rate but only for the period spent in this country.

## Payment abroad

If you go abroad for short periods, the DWP makes special arrangements to pay your pension. No action is necessary where the period is less than three months and in this case your pension payments can be collected on your return. For periods between three and six months you can arrange for your bank or building society to transfer payments to a bank overseas. For periods over six months the DWP will, on request, pay a sterling cheque to an overseas bank. Alternatively you can collect the lump sum on your return.

> I move around a lot, not because I'm looking for anything really, but 'cause I'm getting away from things that get bad if I stay.
>
> Bobby, *Five Easy Pieces* (1970)

For over 12 months, a more permanent arrangement is made to pay your pension by automated credit transfer to your overseas bank. However, if you wish, you can leave the pension for up to a maximum of two years and collect the lump sum on your return.

# Company and private pensions

Company and private individual pensions can also be paid abroad. If you want to check the value of your pension you should contact the pensions manager of the company scheme, or the financial institution – often an insurance company – in the case of a personal pension, for example.

Bear in mind that most statements that explain your future pension rights assume retirement is within the UK, so it is essential to check how retiring abroad will affect your tax position. For example, the tax-free cash lump sum that is an important feature of UK private pensions is not recognised in North America and if you receive the benefit there it may be taxed along with the pension.

Also, remember that your pension will be subject to currency fluctuations. If the local currency in your retirement country rises against the pound, then the value of your UK pension will reduce in real terms.

## Pensions from previous employment

Many people change jobs several times before reaching retirement so it will be necessary to contact previous employers to check the value of any benefits you left in the former employers' schemes. These benefits are known as 'deferred' pensions. Where a company has been taken over or become insolvent and it is difficult to track down the trustees, the Pensions Register will trace your benefits free of charge.

## Foreign pensions

If your career included overseas employment with foreign state and company pension entitlements, the tracing problems could be multiplied tenfold. To add to the complications, foreign pensions may fall due at a different retirement age from the rest of your UK pensions.

> ❄ cool advice    Where the country has a double taxation agreement with the UK, the Inland Revenue will allow pensions to be paid gross – but first you will need a declaration from the foreign tax authorities stating that they are taxing you on your worldwide income.

As a general rule, whether state or company pensions, outside of the UK it is up to you to keep track of your benefit rights and to make the claims. There is no central source of information about foreign state pensions so you may have to contact each authority, although where there is a social security agreement with the UK, the Department of Work and Pensions will help.

# Dealing with the tax man

Once you have checked your sources of pension it is time to examine how they will be taxed. Most of the tax details need to be sorted out at the time of retirement, but it is useful to know in advance how the system works and where the pitfalls lie.

Expert advice is essential here and clearly the adviser must be conversant with the tax and pensions rules in the country of retirement. The object of the exercise is to pay tax on pensions and investment income just once – usually in your country of retirement.

Where the country you choose has a double taxation agreement with the UK (there are over 80 of these agreements in operation), the Inland Revenue will allow pensions to be paid gross. But first you will need a declaration from the foreign tax authorities stating that they are taxing you on your worldwide income.

> We did it, man. We did it. We did it. We're rich, man. We're retirin' in Florida now mister.
>
> Billy, *Easy Rider* (1969)

This declaration should be sent immediately to your UK tax office. If there is a delay your pensions will be taxed twice – once in the UK, at the basic rate of income tax, and once again in your country of retirement. However, if there is a delay in sending the form, the Inland Revenue confirmed that the withholding tax could be reclaimed when it receives the declaration from the foreign tax authority.

## Tax havens not so heavenly

Finally, don't fall into the trap of thinking that if you move to a no-tax environment you will escape with your pensions tax free. If you are lucky enough to retire to the Caymans or Bermuda, for example, you will find that there is no double tax treaty with the UK in operation. If there is no local equivalent of the Inland Revenue, you will not be able to get the declaration that you are being taxed on your worldwide income. As a result the Revenue will impose the withholding tax on all your pensions paid from the UK.

## Further information

Ask at your local Department for Work and Pensions for leaflet NI 106 'Pensioners or Widows Going Abroad' and NI 38 'Social Security Abroad'. To get an idea of the value of your future state pension, ask the DWP for the pension forecast form BR19. Visit the website at **www.dwp.gov.uk**

# Surfing for information

**THERE ARE MANY GUIDES** to the internet itself and to the rapidly growing number of financial services now available.

## What's available?

Today, most large companies, financial institutions, stock exchanges, government departments, regulators and financial trade organisations have their own website so you can read all the latest news and trawl through the offers in the comfort of your own home. Whether you want to investigate a company's trading history or buy shares and collective funds at bargain rates, the internet can help.

## Wealth warning

What you must remember though is that the internet is like a high street. Indeed it has even been referred to as a galactic car boot sale, a description that conveys very well the potential dangers for the unsuspecting investor.

Bear in mind that although many of the companies that sell services or goods are themselves regulated, the internet itself is not. Like the car boot sale, all the vendors display their wares in the most attractive way possible, but you are given no advice to help you spot the genuine bargains and information. The websites are totally indiscriminate. The financial companies that offer value for money and well-regulated services jostle for space with the rip-off merchants and plain fraudsters.

So, use the internet with caution and check out any service very thoroughly before using it. Before you buy anything check the company's address and its regulatory status. The Financial Services Authority has a register of all firms authorised by the Financial Services Act in the UK. If a firm is not authorised in the UK and you lose your money there is virtually no hope of getting it back and if the company goes bust, you won't get a penny from the Financial Ombudsman Scheme.

Watch out in particular for the 'copycat' sites which fraudulent companies set up and incorporate legitimate companies' web pages. The FSA urged internet users to take a close look at the website address. It may be very similar to one used by a well-known company but, for example, it might have an unusual overseas location or contain additional, misleading letters.

The internet makes it easy to buy goods and services from organisations in other countries without knowing that they are based abroad. A website with an address which includes .co.uk or just .uk doesn't necessarily mean it is based in the UK. If in doubt, the FSA recommends that you look up the firm's number in the phone book and call in person to double-check their site address. Don't rely on any phone number given on the site – the chances are that this will be false too.

The Consumers Association also recommends that you print out relevant web pages, including terms and conditions, so that you have a permanent record in case of future disputes.

## Internet services

This section does not set out to provide a complete guide to internet services and trading but merely offers some tips on where to start.

An excellent guide to financial information and dealing on the internet is Stephen Eckett's *Investing Online* (Prentice Hall, price £39.99, including a financial internet directory).

One of the best guides to online services is *e-cash* by Marianne Curphey (£10, also published by Prentice Hall). This includes a run-down on the main online trading and information services. Marianne runs The Guardian Unlimited Money site at **www.guardian.co.uk**.

Also useful for the dedicated online trader is *The UK Guide to Online Brokers* by Michael Scott (Scott IT, 2000). There is an online version of the book at **www.investment-gateway.com**

Many websites have share price charts, details of volume – that is how many people are trading a specific share at the time and a portfolio tool that allows you to see how your shares are performing. There will be a time delay for most information, although this is usually just a matter of 15 minutes. Real-time prices for shares usually hold for 30 seconds while you decide whether or not to buy.

Once you have registered, have opened an account and submitted a password you can get access to the secure part of the site. The services are broadly similar, but sites do try to differentiate themselves from the competition by including special features, so it is worth visiting a few to see which suits you best.

## Online brokers

If you are after an online stockbroker go to the APCIMS website which will help you search the register of members for this type of service. APCIMS is at www.apcims.co.uk

Several other services list online brokers and these include:
www.iii.co.uk
www.investorschronicle.co.uk
www.ftyourmoney.com

## Information sites

The following information sites (some of which also offer dealing services) might be of interest but are not in any way intended as a recommendation:
BBC finance **www.bbc.co.uk/finance**
Charles Schwab **www.schwab-worldwide.com**
DLJdirect **www.dljdirect.co.uk**
E*Trade **www.etrade.co.uk**
The *Financial Times* **www.ft.com** and its personal finance site
Hemmington Scott **www.hemscott.net**

Market Eye www.marketeye.co.uk
UK-invest www.ukinvest.co.uk

## Stockmarket news

Bloomberg www.bloomberg.co.uk
Financial Times www.ft.com
Yahoo! Finance www.yahoo.co.uk/finance

## Portfolio construction

Useful information sites, which in certain cases provide information on how to
construct a portfolio, include:
Interactive Investor www.iii.co.uk
Investors Chronicle www.investorschronicle.com
Motley Fool UK www.fool.co.uk
UK Invest www.ukinvest.co.uk

## Fund prices and information

For collective funds www.iii.co.uk lists total expense ratios (TERs) which add up
all the charges, fees and costs incurred by managers to give you a more complete picture of the total cost than you will find in marketing literature. For
information about funds and their performance try:
Micropal www.micropal.com
Standard and Poor's www.funds-sp.com
Trustnet www.trustnet.co.uk
A useful site for collective funds that includes details on the movement of star
fund managers is www.bestinvest.co.uk

## Fund supermarkets

These are largely designed for individual savings accounts as they allow you to
mix and match funds from different managers within a single ISA. Some offer
a limited selection of funds. Also, do bear in mind that investment trusts are
not well represented on these sites. ISAs are discussed in Chapter 12:
Egg www.egg.com

Fundnetwork **www.fidelity.co.uk**
Fundsdirect **www.fundsdirect.co.uk**
Interactive Investor **www.iii.co.uk**
Tqonline **www.tqonline.co.uk**

# Where there's a will there's a relative

**FOR MOST PEOPLE, MAKING A WILL** is a simple and cheap exercise and represents a small price to pay for your own peace of mind and for the ease and comfort of your family. Yet only one in three adults bother.

If you meet your maker without a valid will you die intestate. This means you don't get to choose your beneficiaries – the government does it for you. The laws of intestacy will decide which of your dependants receives your money, while your friends and favourite charities will receive nothing. In particular, if you have young children you will not have the chance to make careful arrangements for their inheritance of capital (this would happen automatically at age 18 under the intestacy rules), and you will not have appointed the executors, the trustees and the children's guardians who will oversee their upbringing.

Remember also that there are certain events which render it essential to rewrite your will – in particular if you marry or remarry. As a general guide, even if there are no major changes relating to marriage or children, it is worth checking your will is up to date every five years.

Making a will does not involve a huge amount of work, unless your finances are very complicated. Most solicitors do the legwork for you and simply ask you to complete a short form that provides the information they need to draw up a draft.

# Avoid common mistakes

When making a will, there are several common mistakes that can be easily avoided. For example, you should make sure you dispose of all of your estate because if you do not then this could result in partial intestacy. You should also make provision for the fact that one of your main beneficiaries may die before you. Above all else, consider the legal rights of your dependants. If you do not make suitable provision they may be unable to claim their right to a sensible provision under the law. Remember in this context that 'children' refers to legitimate, illegitimate and adopted children, although it does not usually include stepchildren.

You should also include any gifts to charities or specific gifts of assets to specific beneficiaries (for example, your jewellery to your daughter/grand-daughter). The powers of the trustees should also be set out here.

Don't forget – you can use your will to make some important arrange-ments about your own wishes. For example, if you have a strong preference for burial or cremation, and know where you wish to be buried/your ashes to be scattered, this is the place to make your wishes known.

You should also discuss any specific role with an appointed executor or trustee before you put it in writing. These responsibilities can be onerous or may conflict with some other role which the individual already performs. Where you have young children the appointment of willing and responsible guardians is essential, particularly where only one parent is alive.

Finally, if you own any property overseas you should draw up a will under the terms of that country, with care to ensure consistency with your UK will.

# Executors and trustees

The executor is responsible for collecting your estate and distributing it in accordance with the law. This can include paying any outstanding taxes and dealing with other financial affairs. The executor takes over from the date of your death but is not officially appointed until the will is 'proved' and the appointment is confirmed by a grant of probate.

Most people appoint as an executor a spouse or close relative plus a pro-fessional – for example, your solicitor or accountant. Where the will includes a trust, it is helpful if the executor and the trustees are the same people.

# What happens if you don't make a will?

To summarise, the main disadvantages of dying intestate are as follows:

■ Your estate may not be distributed in accordance with your wishes.

■ The appointed administrators may not be people whom you personally would have chosen – or even liked.

■ It may take longer for the estate to be distributed, whereas when a will has been made an executor can take up his duties immediately after death occurs.

■ The costs may be greater, leaving less to pass on to your beneficiaries.

■ Children will receive capital automatically at age 18, whereas you may have preferred this to take place later at a less 'giddy' age. What's more, the family home, where your widow or widower lives, may have to be sold in order to raise the capital.

■ A testamentary guardian is not appointed for young children.

■ Trusts may arise under an intestacy that give rise to complications, including statutory restrictions on the trustees' power to invest and advance capital.

# Distribution of an estate under the laws of intestacy

The following details refer to the law in England and Wales. The laws that apply in Northern Ireland and in Scotland differ. 'Issue' refers to children (including illegitimate and adopted), grandchildren and so on. It does not include stepchildren. If the deceased dies leaving:

■ *a spouse but no issue, parent, brother, sister, nephew or niece*: the spouse takes everything.

■ *a spouse and issue*: the spouse takes £125,000, personal 'chattels' (car, furniture, pictures, clothing, jewellery etc) plus a life interest – that is the income only – in half of the residue. The children take half the residue on reaching age 18 or marrying before that age. In addition, on the death of the deceased's spouse, the children take the half residue in which the spouse had a lifetime interest.

■ *a spouse, no issue, but parent(s), brother(s), sister(s), nephew(s) or niece(s)*: the spouse takes £200,000, plus personal chattels, plus half the residue. The other half goes to whoever is living in order of preference: parents, but if none, brothers and sisters (nephews and nieces step into their parents' shoes if the parents are dead).

■ *no spouse*: Everything goes to, in order (depending on who is still alive): issue, but if none, parents, but if none, brothers and sisters (nephews and nieces step into their parents' shoes). The pecking order then moves on to half brothers and sisters or failing them, their children, but if none, grandparents, but if none, uncles and aunts (cousins step into their parents' shoes), but if none, half uncles and aunts (failing that, their children). If all of these relatives have died then the estate goes to the Crown.

Where part of the residuary estate includes a dwelling-house in which the surviving spouse lived at the date of death, the spouse has the right to have the house as part of the absolute interest or towards the capital value of the life interest, where relevant.

## Source material

This chapter is based on Section 14 of *Kelly's Financial Planning for the Individual* by Simon Philip, published by Gee Publishing. Sections reproduced are by kind permission of the author.

# I hate to complain but …

**MAKING A COMPLAINT** about a financial product used to be a complicated process. In the past there were hordes of ombudsmen, each covering different products and, what's worse, different elements of what looked like a simple package of insurances and investments to pay for a mortgage, a pension, or school fees. Fortunately things got a lot easier in December 2001 when most of these organisations merged under one roof at the Financial Ombudsman Service (FOS).

So, if a company authorised by the Financial Services Authority (FSA) sells you an investment product that is inappropriate for your needs you may be able to claim for compensation.

## What's covered?

Not everything sold as an investment has to be authorised. Most regulated investments are 'non-tangible' assets like shares, gilts, bonds and collective funds. When you buy physical or 'tangible' assets directly rather than through a collective fund – gold coins and fine wines, for example – you are not covered by the Act. This means the FOS cannot investigate your case and you are not entitled to compensation if things go wrong. There may be another scheme that covers the asset you purchased and you should check this point before you buy.

Insurance companies are covered by the FOS but, rather oddly, insurance brokers were not (at the time of writing), although the scheme expects to include them in due course. You may come across insurance brokers if you are looking for a mortgage or car insurance, for example. At present most insurance brokers belong to the General Insurance Standards Council (GISC). This is a reputable organisation but membership is voluntary, so make sure any broker you use is a member. Mortgage brokers should adhere to the new mortgage code, but again this is voluntary so check before you buy.

Another gap in coverage is store cards and this is a controversial service that the FOS hopes to tackle in due course. Frankly, you should think twice before you opt for a store card or consumer credit. All a store needs to offer these services is a licence from the Office of Fair Trading (OFT) and they can get away with charging you 30 per cent interest on outstanding balances whereas with a credit card you might pay 19 per cent.

## Pensions are complicated

The regulation of pensions is complicated and different aspects fall under the aegis of different regulators. If your complaint relates to an occupational scheme you may need to go to a different authority. As a rule of thumb, the FOS covers anything you were sold, like a personal pension. If you have a problem regarding your rights or benefits under a company scheme then you should approach the Pensions Advisory Service, which is an independent and voluntary organisation that provides free help to members of the public. You can find an adviser through your local Citizens Advice Bureau. The service may also be able to help you with a general enquiry about your state pension but it cannot give specific advice. For this you would need to go to the Department for Work and Pensions, which has its own appeals system.

## What makes a valid complaint?

As a general rule it is the sales process that is at fault. For example, let's suppose you tell an adviser or insurance company representative that you want a mortgage payment method that guarantees your debt will be clear after a given number of years. If the individual proceeds to sell you an investment product like an endowment that cannot possibly provide such a guarantee, then you have a valid complaint. This happened in 2001 when representatives of Winterthur Life missold endowment mortgages due to a glitch in their software program. The program allowed them to recommended these investments even though it was quite clear from the client records that a repayment was the most suitable arrangement.

However, just because you feel wronged doesn't mean you will get a sympathetic hearing from the FOS and it is important to consider your part in the sales process before you complain. Let's suppose that you invest in a collective fund and you tell the adviser or company representative that you are prepared to accept a high level of risk in the hope of achieving a high return. In this case you cannot complain if the value of your investment plummets when the aggressive investment strategy does not pay off. Provided the company can prove that it explained the risks clearly – and it will ask you to sign a declaration to this effect when you agree to the sale – then your complaint is unlikely to be upheld.

## How to complain

Your first step is to contact the company that sold you the product. Write to the person who you dealt with and send a copy to the company's compliance officer. If you do not get a satisfactory response write to the most senior person in the organisation. Only if this fails should you contact the ombudsman. In effect you have to reach a deadlock with the company concerned before the ombudsman will step in.

It is always best to write or, even better, type a formal letter. The FSA recommends a clear procedure for making a complaint and you will get a result more quickly if you follow it carefully. Keep copies of all your correspondence and do not send original policy documents in case they get 'lost'. Mark your letter 'complaint' and make sure the policy number is included as well as any relevant dates. Generally you should avoid using the phone during the complaints procedure but if you have to make a call, keep notes of the date, the person you speak to and any relevant points made in the discussion. Then write a follow-up letter to confirm what was said. For full details of how to make a complaint get a copy of the FSA's guide, which is available on the website (see below).

If the company is no longer trading, call the FSA Consumer Helpline for advice (see below). Where the company was regulated by the FSA at the time of the sale then you may be entitled to recompense from the FSA Compensation Scheme, which acts as a last resort in such cases.

## Should you take the case to court?

If the FOS rejects your case you still have the right to go to court, although clearly you should consider the ombudsman's reasons very carefully before committing to what could be an expensive process.

## Further information

The FSA Consumer Helpline is 0845 606 1234.

The address of the FOS is:

Financial Ombudsman Service

South Quay Plaza

183 Marsh Wall

London E14 9SR

Tel 020 7216 0016

Website www.financial-ombudsman.org.uk

To check that an adviser is regulated, contact the FSA central register, phone 020 7929 3652; website www.fsa.gov.uk

The consumer help section of the FSA website (www.fsa.gov.uk/consumer) includes a wealth of information on how to choose a firm of advisers and explains your rights when you buy different investment products. In particular you will find the FSA guide to making a complaint very useful. You can either order this or simply download the pages to your printer.

The address of OPAS is:

Pensions Advisory Service

11 Belgrave Road

London SW1V 1RB

Tel: 020 7233 8080

Website: www.opas.org.uk

The Pensions Ombudsman is at the same address as OPAS and can be contacted on 020 7834 9144. However, you are advised to approach OPAS in the first instance.

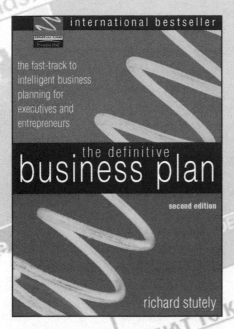

international bestseller

the fast-track to
intelligent business
planning for
executives and
entrepreneurs

the definitive
business plan

second edition

richard stutely

# THE DEFINITIVE
# BUSINESS PLAN
## 2e
**Richard Stutely**

**ISBN 0 273 65921 9**

A good business plan is the difference between success and
not even getting the chance to try.

This international bestseller is the ultimate guide to
business planning.

Whether the goal is raising start-up or development finance
for a new business, requesting venture funding from a
corporate parent or directing operational management,
*The Definitive Business Plan* will help you deliver the
information that the decision-makers are really looking for.

# momentum – it's a talent thing
# momentum – a publishing philosophy that revolves around one thing: YOU.

In print and online, it's the force behind your personal development, your talent, your skills, your career, your effectiveness, your work and your life.

It is time to make things happen in your life – visit www.yourmomentum.com for information, stimulation, ideas and answers…

The momentum series will give you the right stuff for a brighter future, just try one of these titles – they speak for themselves:

## CHANGE ACTIVIST
### make big things happen fast
Carmel McConnell

## FLOAT YOU
### how to capitalize on your talent
Carmel McConnell & Mick Cope

## LEAD YOURSELF
### be where others will follow
Mick Cope

## THE BIG DIFFERENCE
### life works when you choose it
Nicola Phillips

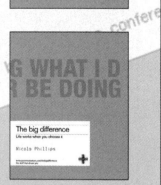

Find out more about momentum and try the ideas out for yourself at
# www.momentum.com